# SMASHED

Copyright © 2025 Todd Ley

All rights reserved. No part of this publication may be reproduced, distributed, or transmitted in any form or by any means, including photocopying, recording, or other electronic or mechanical methods, without the prior written permission of the publisher, except in the case of brief quotations embodied in critical reviews and certain other non-commercial uses permitted by copyright law.

Ley, Todd (author)
*Smashed: Tennis prodigies, parents and parasites*
ISBN 9780645899764 (paperback)
ISBN 9780645899740 (ebook)

Unsportsmanlike Publishing

Cover design by Anomaly

Typesetting by Green Hill Publishing

greenhill
https://greenhillpublishing.com.au/
Typeset Calluna Regular 11/16

# SMASHED

Tennis prodigies, parents and parasites

# TODD LEY

'I'm not crazy about reality,
but it's still the only place to get a decent meal'

– Groucho Marx

# Preface

I'VE BEEN ADVISED to give readers a warm welcome and build their trust in this initial part of the book. I'm supposed to write about who it's for and what impact it's going to have on them and their lives. But expectations are silly things, and I really don't like giving people advice, despite making a living from telling people what to do as a tennis coach. So, instead of starting by slanging out empty hope and promises, let me state a few things and tell you who I'm absolutely not interested in being. That ought to build some trust.

Vengeance, dissatisfaction and a lingering sense of injustice have compelled me to write a highly self-referential version of the gentleman's game. Within the realms of elite sport, the content of this book is not uncommon, but will be considered wildly controversial regardless, and I must emphatically state I have no interest in entering public debates, offering the industry any solutions, or trying to change people's minds about any of the matters. I see no value in trying to awake people who would like to remain asleep. I do not wish to become a spokesperson, motivational speaker, or mental health advocate of any kind. I'm not a philanthropist or courageous activist, nor am I Mr Moral rectitude who thinks he is holier-than-thou. I don't want to be branded into a particular type of self-image that doesn't resemble my own flawed humanity, and I do not want to feel obligated to march in people's pep rallies.

I implore you to filter what I've written through your own experiences, to glean from it what you will. Take what you like, leave the rest.

# Contents

| | |
|---|---|
| An introduction | 1 |
| **Part 1  Identity** | **5** |
| How many ways are there to f*#+ up a brilliant career? | 5 |
| Coming to terms with a wonderland that is not what it seems | 6 |
| Feeding the beast within on the road to perdition | 8 |
| Fast forward a few years | 13 |
| Finding a voice | 15 |
| Young man counselled to maintain the myth of his identity | 17 |
| Learning to live with the fraudulent me | 21 |
| Dazzled by the bright lights of promise—too much, too young! | 24 |
| Grooming children with a promise unnatural | 26 |
| Looking for love but rewarded with mocking laughter | 32 |
| Be careful what you wish for… | 34 |
| Public service announcement to tennis parents who are parading their children all over social media | 35 |
| Don't give your heart to a ramblin' man | 36 |
| **Part 2  Misconceptions** | **43** |
| There's nothing more dangerous than a tennis parent with a plan | 43 |
| Your talented tennis child is not a racehorse | 45 |
| School sucked but it was a holiday from my life | 47 |
| My bubble had well and truly burst by 17 | 48 |
| Comparisons corrupt the decision-making process | 51 |
| Tennis academies—machines that exploit the dreams of tennis parents and their kids | 53 |
| Abandoned at 12 in the compound of dreams and nightmares | 56 |
| Hook, line and sinker | 62 |
| How do you learn to be mentally tough? | 63 |
| Never mind the body, what about the spirit? | 66 |

| | | |
|---|---|---|
| | Simple disciplinary measures at home set the stage for future success | 68 |
| | Being strong is easy, so how easy is it to be weak? | 73 |
| | Misconceptions—a side note | 76 |
| | Caught in the crossfire | 77 |
| **Part 3** | **Delusion** | **85** |
| | To be wrong is human, to be delusional is fatal | 85 |
| | Is your child the best tennis player who never plays? | 86 |
| | The dreaded dinner to dish the dirt on Dimitri's dream | 91 |
| | The problem with desiring sexy technique | 95 |
| | A permanent pitstop | 98 |
| | The long buck! | 103 |
| | Weaving the camouflage that hides delusion | 104 |
| | Praying for formidable problems | 109 |
| **Part 4** | **Roles and boundaries** | **113** |
| | Jockeying for position | 113 |
| | Time to give the devil his due | 118 |
| | Cheers—I did my best coaching in the pub | 120 |
| | Romantic relationships: not encouraged but not surprising | 128 |
| | Looking for love in all the wrong places— avoiding Stockholm syndrome | 129 |
| | The problem with a parent picking up the balls | 135 |
| | Confronting the offer that's too good to refuse | 138 |
| | Great coaches, shocking mentors | 145 |
| | Sinking into the dark side of normality | 146 |
| | Hanging in with the hangers-on | 152 |
| **Part 5** | **Culture** | **155** |
| | When it comes to assessing talent, you can't see what's invisible | 155 |
| | Myself versus my self-image | 159 |
| | Learning to play on the dark side of the court | 165 |
| | Character assassination | 167 |
| | The intergenerational difference in culture | 172 |
| | Some questions you should NEVER ask your Mum | 173 |
| | Say hello to Hollywood! | 175 |
| | Squeezing into the impossibly tiny, tall poppy box | 180 |
| | Time to square the ledger with Langman | 181 |

|  |  | |
|---|---|---|
| | Ladies and gentlemen, the trainer has been called to the court | 187 |
| **Part 6** | **Complexes** | **189** |
| | Finding the formula for unconditional love—or something like it | 189 |
| | A hole in my soul—a dull ache you couldn't touch but couldn't ignore | 192 |
| | Taking a risk on intimacy to get close to the truth | 202 |
| | Pretending to know but not having a clue when it came to intimacy | 205 |
| | Wild coupling is the reward for years of denial | 211 |
| | When it comes to love, the first cut is the deepest | 212 |
| | Lackey Langman supersedes Messiah Max | 218 |
| **Part 7** | **Burnout** | **223** |
| | It's a long way to the top if you want to be No. 1 | 223 |
| | Not everyone is treated in the same way | 226 |
| | Big boy with a giant appeal | 226 |
| | Turning a teen into a princess then publicly dethroning her | 228 |
| | Arranged friendships and evolving into who you are paid to be | 230 |
| | Welcoming the day the deal turns sour | 233 |
| | Please don't talk about losing while I'm eating | 234 |
| | The psychology behind injury (when you're not there to win) | 241 |
| | Is a lie really a lie if you believe it's the truth? | 243 |
| | The academy that taught Max his final lesson | 248 |
| | Mourning what was never there | 253 |
| | Trophy coaches | 255 |
| | Hovering at the edge of the pit of despair | 258 |
| Conclusion | | 263 |
| Epilogue | | 267 |

# An introduction

IF YOU'VE BEEN to a decent circus, you've experienced being hypnotised by total chaos. You've been entranced by acrobats defying death on invisible wires suspended high in the air infused with the lingering smell of mouth-watering popcorn. You've seen clowns being violently ejected from cannons and sailing past daredevils walking tightropes as exotic animals pace beneath, desperate to engorge themselves on acrobat flesh, hoping for someone to fall. Whatever they're selling, you're buying.

As a spectator, you leave the circus awestruck by the show, you tell your friends about it and wait desperately for a ticket to the next extravaganza. But what you don't see is the circus in the early hours of the next morning, when underpaid handlers wrangle the malnourished animals into tiny cages while an alcoholic acrobat washes down Ritalin tablets with the remnants of the vodka bottle that finally knocked him out at 5am. The freaks and geeks squabble over peanuts until they all rejoin the caravan, which lurches inexorably onwards towards the next destination, reeking of shit and piss. That's a lot like the tennis world, and I've been in those cages and caravans.

I was the number one 12-year-old tennis player in the world, coached by my father, Max, the self-proclaimed 'Serve Doctor', who couldn't serve himself. Of the thousands upon thousands of children around the world who sweated and slogged on a tennis court, I was the best. On Australian television, I was proclaimed a future World Number One. When my story was aired, I was inundated with offers, not all of them appropriate for a 12-year-old boy to hear. But they did reinforce one thing for certain: I was special.

I became the youngest person ever to be signed by IMG, a sports management company that promised to further polish my already glittering career. I lived for four years in IMG's headquarters in Florida, under the guidance of the masterminds who forged legends—demi-gods like Agassi, Courier and Kournikova, players who performed impossible highwire acts on court and walked away with hundreds of millions of dollars and the adoration of every mortal human on the planet. And there I was, poised at the start of my very own yellow brick road. All I had to do was step from golden brick to golden brick, and into my destined place in sports history. But at the age of 17, I gave it all away.

During the time I was supposed to be winning Grand Slams, tennis-torture—that unique cocktail of guilt, shame, and remorse—was literally killing me. I endured the worst morning after the circus could deliver. There are no severance packages or compensation schemes for the loss of a childhood, unless you count the list of neuroses and complexes I developed in the pursuit of excellence. I was faced with the excruciating job of trying to fit back into 'normal society', which seemed mellow-paced, mediocre and mundane; but it was simultaneously far beyond my abilities to undertake. I could serve, but real life did not feature in my skill set.

Unstimulated by the available prospects, my only viable vocation seemed to be tennis coaching. I begrudgingly accepted the work and was plagued by a savage discontent over the better part of the next 14 years, battling addictions, mental health issues, and suicidality, until I plummeted into the rooms of a 12-step program. I was dazed and confused about where I was and what was going on, but ever so slowly I began to make sense of my distorted and deranged existence. The program of recovery stipulated in order to progress, I had to uncover the origins of my neurotic behaviour. I didn't want to go back through hell—to dive into the psyche of the sporting freak and his puppet master, the tennis parent—without a souvenir to commemorate the journey. So, I decided to write this book.

Initially, I was fearful writing it would emotionally destroy me and disrupt my early sobriety. Luckily, I still wasn't completely sold on recovery and there was no more convenient way of falling off the wagon than to write a pain-inducing memoir. What I didn't expect was it would become my new addiction. I wanted to taste what I had been avoiding and inhale what I was afraid of. I wanted to purge and shiver, convulse, and cry, wither and howl, until it sent me to either the madhouse or the grave. Unfortunately, my tumultuous childhood had so finely engineered my disassociation skills it was almost as if I were writing in the third person, as if these events had never happened to me.

As I travelled limpidly through my haunted inner realm, I couldn't help but be objectively astounded at the danger, dysfunction and disingenuity of the world I grew up in. It wasn't long before I discovered what was making me the sickest: my compliance in maintaining the circus. I was a fraud, only delivering fractions of the truth when it came to speaking about my sporting experience. I was exactly like people I detested, so I thought—people who had withheld vital truths about the tennis world from me and my family years before.

Despite what the gurus and aficionados will have you believe, no one truly knows how a great tennis player, or indeed any other sporting, stage, or screen star, is concocted. The recipe is too intricate and too situation-specific, and the last thing the world needs is another sanitised self-help book for people to get unrealistically lost in. So, this is the opposite, something more like a self-destruct book. Part exposé, part sports memoir, part analysis, with the occasional therapeutic concession to good old-fashioned bitching. Not everything you read in here is a fact, and names have been changed and characters combined, but you can bet your hundred-million-dollar tennis fortune it's the truth. What I've written doesn't necessarily sit well with me, but I know it needs to be written regardless.

Just a warning: this book contains references to domestic violence, addiction, and psychological abuse.

# PART 1

# Identity

### How many ways are there to f*#+ up a brilliant career?

There are many ways to fuck up a tennis career and even more ways to screw up a child's life, and some of them coincide. The rigorous demands of tennis as an elite sport unquestionably require the candle is lit early in a player's life. But while the early start is essential, the decision to go all in at an early age means lines can be crossed and boundaries battered.

In my pursuit of a tennis career, I was left voiceless and isolated. I had been crippled with expectations and was unable to cope emotionally due to a lack of guidance and poor parenting. Paradoxically, no one was to blame because everyone involved tried their best.

We hear a lot about the success stories in tennis, where well-adjusted players have made it through the combative world of professional tennis; but we never hear from the player who burns out and is left damaged and defeated. In this telling, I draw on my own experiences, to analyse the impact tennis has had on my life and the damage similar experiences could have on any other child in the tennis sphere. I explore challenges I have endured while striving for the top of the tennis world, and detail some of the psychological impediments that prevented me from developing a healthy identity long after my dog days in tennis were over.

## Coming to terms with a wonderland that is not what it seems

Tennis is a so-called 'elitist' sport, overpopulated with people who behave like plebs. The sport romantically swindles the public into believing it's facade when underneath the surface is a mixed bag of obsessive, pretentious, and near pathological people who all bring their brand of crazy to a highly regarded sport. Once initiated into the underworld of the tennis, a strange brew of neuroticism, snobbery, and intensity seeps into the blood and bones of everyone involved. This hostile environment tends to set off the 'me-against-the-world' victim mentality, which is a widely shared mindset among fanatical tennis parents. Narcissism and paranoia often surface, and the parent can imagine every competing player, coach and parent is the enemy, and they are all out to ruin their child's career.

The scared tennis parent wreaks psychological havoc on their child by manifesting a world of fear. Because the parent sees this new world as competitive and threatening to their grandiose dreams, they inevitably pass their fear on to their child, who sucks up the energy around them like second-hand smoke. This happens progressively to both the tennis parent and the child, and they often start to withdraw from people, places and things threatening their tennis dream. The irony is that as the child withdraws from the challenges, they are less and less likely to succeed in professional tennis.

The tennis parent relishes the idea of one day becoming the perceived mastermind of their child's success and the beneficiary of that much-dreamed-of blank cheque. But if they are to have total control over their protégé, the tennis parent's voice must be the only one the child hears. Any reasoning outside this could ruin the tennis parent's indoctrination, so they insidiously start to pull the child away from outside influences. The next progression is to also break away from any family engagements. Fear arises exposure to 'normal people' may make the child want to conform to the typical way of life, which would sabotage the Grand Slam plans. But the parent also does not want the child to be around the broader tennis world, as those people are enemies whom they must go to war against. Isolation inevitably becomes the new norm.

It is in isolation the tennis parent feels they have the best chance of doing their finest work in conditioning the player for success. They preach their philosophy without a thought to the potential negative effects or repercussions such extreme views may have on a young mind. This behaviour can warp a child's sense of reality and leave them with a totally twisted outlook on life. My own young adult life was plagued by ideas about the world that were way off. I found myself acting thoughtlessly and hypocritically. I expected the utmost consideration from others while behaving selfishly and believing I was a very thoughtful person. As an individual sport, tennis breeds individualism, which is essentially 'inconsider-atism'—my made-up word to express the link between the progression of a young tennis player and his or her lack of consideration for others.

Time alone, with very little integration into normal society, left me curious yet scared about life in general. As a teen, I slid into using unreliable sources such as social media, pop culture and porn to fill in the knowledge blanks of my limited world. Roles and boundaries often confused me, so to avoid frightening new roles I hadn't experienced in friendships or romantic relationships, it was easier for me to revert to a more transactional relationship; I felt the need to compensate for company by throwing money or gifts/drinks at people in exchange for them hanging out with me. It made me feel more comfortable. However, the story of my own journey into isolation started well before this, perhaps even at around the age of 3.

## Feeding the beast within on the road to perdition

I had an obsessive-compulsive nature from the beginning. I struggled with being around other people, yet when I was alone, I didn't enjoy my own company. I found boredom excruciating, and when something brought joy, I wanted to do it all the time. I knew I needed something I could do autonomously and that was on demand, so hitting the ball off the wall was the perfect activity for someone with my brand of hyper fixation and social proclivity.

When you're a kid, it is one thing to say you want to be a professional tennis player but another for others to take that claim seriously. My father took my declaration in its entirety, as I believe he saw me as someone with similar susceptibilities to society as himself. We were bound by blood as the ultimate outcasts, which worked out perfectly for Dad who always wanted to go offroad without a map. So, when tennis went from my thing to our thing, life got weird, quick.

I was being raised to be radical, but I didn't know that at the time and the insanity seemed, well, normal. Dad could have been a successful cult leader if he had given it a go. He had a mix of madness and genius with a twist of charisma and evil that would impress a young Charles Manson. I remember one afternoon when Dad came home from the Balaklava races with wine-stained teeth and told me it had been medically proven I was a genetic freak. 'Oi, oi!' I agreed. It made total sense to me—I was different. Given how unearthly I felt at large, it had struck an internal chord with me. When you feel like an alien, and then someone comes and tells you you're an alien, it's a relief. Together with the local junior results I was achieving, this was enough evidence for me to believe Dad's propaganda that I was one day going to be Tennis Jesus.

I ventured out further into the tennis stratosphere, and my results soared as I won some of the biggest junior tournaments in the world. Dad started eating breakfast from my winning trophy bowls. Once I started winning tournaments, food served out of regular crockery 'just didn't have that winning taste' he would say. Next level seriousness was served. But the better I was at tennis, and the more I was involved in the tennis world, the more I was cut off from the outside world. Despite getting more attention in a niche environment, I felt more ignored and unnoticed than ever. I wasn't a person with feelings anymore; I had become a commodity. My tennis commitments ruled my family with an iron fist, while one side of the family craved normalcy and the other celebrated the lunacy.

*trophy bowl*

The cart was before the horse, yet I kept on my winning way to becoming the Number 1 junior in the world, beating Del Potro (US

Open champion in 2009) in the final of a 12/U champion of champions in Sun City, South Africa. But behind the scenes I began feeling the overbearing weight of attention. Dad's ceaseless gaze meant I was unnecessarily scrutinised over the most irrelevant things, like how I tied my shoes and over what shoulder I carried my tennis bag. Being watched like a criminal and coddled like a baby made me so chronically self-aware that it felt as if I could watch myself from a birds-eye view. Tennis was taking away from my life more than it was giving, and everything got stripped away. No more family, no more friends, no more school. Dad and I became disgustingly antisocial, a couple of sporting nomads who drifted around the world frequenting tennis courts, airports, and hotel rooms. The isolation left me to my assumptions about the world from afar, with very limited close-up experiences.

*12/U Nationals*

As I moved into my mid-teens, the relationship between my father and me became co-dependent. My mindless obedience shifted to inquisitive scepticism as I became conflicted about having him around all the time. But Dad was the origin of my tennis identity, and when he wasn't there being his usual self, everything felt wrong. On the other hand, when Dad was attached to my hip, I was restricted from exploring outside relationships or experiences, as Dad deemed socialisation to be the ultimate enemy of individual success. So, there was an unhealthy stigma around me mixing with anyone else, and my isolation became my incarceration.

Tennis became a lonely existence. I was left feeling deprived of human connection and forced to hide my desire for a normal life. I associated socialising with misbehaviour and felt guilty and shameful for wanting to interact with other people. The deep and meaningful conversations between Dad and me in the car to and from tennis weren't quite as captivating as they had been when I was little, and I began to push back at the constraints I had been kept under for so long.

Because of the extreme perspectives I was taught as a kid, I didn't have a barometer of what was acceptable and what wasn't. When it came time to re-enter civilisation, I felt like I needed to be de-radicalized to adjust to the flow and social norms of everyday life. Characteristics that were seen as strengths in the sporting world were seen as unusual and egotistical in normal society. For example, the confidence I had been taught in isolation came across as arrogance to a wider audience. The only thing worse than a bad loser is a bad winner, and I tended to rub your nose in it for a while if ever I got something over you. People would either angrily retaliate and my extreme competitiveness would want to bury them even further, or they would sulkily withdraw and not want to play with me in the sand pit anymore.

In my corner of the world, you got top marks for being flamboyant and trash talking; but unbeknownst to me, regular society wanted me to downplay my strengths and be appallingly humble. When it came to tennis and my athletic ability, I did not know how to be modest and I would regularly say things that were regarded as odd or boastful, not knowing my overly confident demeanour was social suicide. My personal experience while growing up had been so unusual that even the smallest things, such as speaking to people beyond small chat or knowing how to behave within a group, were extremely difficult and I felt I had no point of reference, which frustrated me even more. I eventually retreated into isolation to protect myself from the outside world, which was far too sharp for me to process.

## DAMAGE RECEIPT

| Fuck-Up (Cause) | Aftermath (Effect) |
| --- | --- |
| Isolating environment | Overwhelmed by life, extreme loneliness |
| Extreme views taught to a young mind | Warped sense of reality |
| Lack of discernment | Coming across as a fuckwit |
| Social deprivation | Fear of people (social anxiety), lack of connection |
| Family priorities out of order | Hidden resentment within the family structure |

### THANK YOU!

## Fast forward a few years

Tennis really tested the tribe. Resentments festered in my family as we all reluctantly suffered the objectionable demands placed upon us for years. This finally ended in a demolition job, with everyone traumatised in their own special way. The end of my tennis career was treated like a death in the family. Everyone 'won' a prize out of the experience, whether it was PTSD, control issues, anxiety, depression, addiction or, in my case, the jackpot of the whole lot. Finger pointing and intolerance were the new methods of interaction in my family, and we had little or no sympathy for each other's circumstances even though we had somewhat gone through the experience together. Everyone had developed their own issues because of the situation, and it was like the blind critiquing the dress code of the deaf.

## Summary

As the child's tennis career moves from recreational to Priority Number 1, different measures are taken to ensure the child doesn't veer off the professional path. In this realm for the tennis elite, whether a person is deemed insane, or genius is dependent on the results they attain, and very often parents become desensitised to acts of cruelty, that appear to them as good ideas at the time. Wanting something to work so badly jeopardises a person's judgment, and parents commonly don't stop to think about the consequences of what might happen if things don't go to plan. When they are blinded by brilliance, inhumane options are seen as practical procedures, and players end up becoming victims of sporting extremism. Not even in religious passages do I hear of such severe measures as isolating a child from his friends, families, and foes in the name of some greater good. But this is what happens to a lot of junior players, as they are sacrificed to the sport and then condemned for interacting with the outside world. Some may classify that as a professional sporting regime. Me, I lean towards calling it child abuse.

```
━━━━━━━━━━━━━━━━━━━━━━━━━━━━━━━━━━━━━━━
          IT'S TIME TO PAY YOUR BILL.
     WE HOPE YOU HAD A PLEASANT EXPERIENCE!
━━━━━━━━━━━━━━━━━━━━━━━━━━━━━━━━━━━━━━━

     Subtotal:           Fear
     Tip:                Go easy
     Total Costs:        Perpetual anxiety
                         A racing mind
                         Self-consciousness
```

## Finding a voice

A person who is a stranger to themselves is susceptible to outside influence wherein others can manipulate and dictate their life. It's of the utmost importance for a person to become the independent authority over their own existence by forming a solid character to make their own decisions. Most kids receive this basic freedom automatically, but it isn't granted by a lot of tennis parents, who are heavily invested in the creation and outcome of their so-called 'sporting protégé'.

Tennis parents often seem to borrow a page out of a dictator's book; they employ similar types of strategies and approaches to persuade and manipulate the mind of a minor. Obviously, there is a difference between Hitler and a tennis parent, but they both have used brainwashing and fear to encourage a behavioural outcome. In fact, the blank canvas of the young person's mind means no 'washing' of the child's already learned behaviours is necessary. Instead, the simple repetition of a message is enough to indoctrinate, and this is seemingly the best way of getting a child to produce junior results. Many tennis parents leave no stone unturned when it comes to this endeavour and submerge their kids into a plethora of wild ideas and crazy beliefs. The shot clock is ticking down until the player becomes aware of their fragmented reality, but the tennis parent must back their capabilities of getting the child to the WTA or ATP, in a race against time.

Once the player is programmed with the parent's persuasion, fear further instils the lesson, trapping them in this version of reality. When a child is overcoached and frightened of potential consequences, they can begin talking and behaving in a robot-like manner.

Some players even have a specific type of look, almost as if they are trying to listen to you with their sight. If people's eyes are windows to their soul, then the player's gleam speaks a thousand words. In many cases, the stress produced by the pressure can cause children to develop nervous tics, which I've seen worsen in some adolescents who were allowed to remain unhelped or untreated. Children are desperate for the approval of their folks and can very easily convince themselves their parents' desires are actually their own. After all, how many 11-year-olds do you know that know what they want to do when they grow up?

The lack of connection, isolation and loneliness plague the child, and eventually they start to question the mirage. To the untrained eye, this can easily be missed as their tennis potential, trophies and titles take front and centre stage and their psychological wellbeing is often overlooked. The child is praised in a superficial fashion and never truly engages in any authentic manner, and they build a personality on a false and fragile foundation. This takes a heavy toll as the child develops emotionally. Pushing down true feelings and emotions during childhood has been seen to have numerous ramifications throughout the rest of an individual's life. The tennis parent is often unaware of the warning signs, and they continue to mute their child by speaking for them, denying them their own voice. But, like trying to hold a beachball underwater, it is only a matter of time until it comes up.

As the saga continues, the player can start to harvest heavy resentments against their parents for having to be nothing short of flawless for an extended period of time. People-pleasing comes at a poignant price. In just the space of a few years, there can be a radical shift in the player's attitude and behaviour. Strong-arm tactics that prevailed when a player was a child no longer work when they are a teenager; the 'tennis ace' can turn into a 'tennis menace' almost overnight. Unable to voice personal truths in a diplomatic enough fashion, players generally turn their rage inwards, taking their pent-up frustrations out on themselves, while expecting others to properly interpret their cry for help.

A severe sense of injustice grows in the soul of the subservient player, as they feel imprisoned by the family who were supposed to take care of them. The repercussions can be a lifetime of wishful thinking, hoping others will become mind-readers to spare the tennis child the agony of having to find their own voice. The following story tells of my own experience as a young tennis prodigy, unable to find my voice.

## Young man counselled to maintain the myth of his identity

You get some random phone calls after having your face on A Current Affair. In 1999, Mike Munro was broadcasting I was to be next in line for the throne of the ATP Tennis rankings and I was going to be bigger than Lleyton Hewitt, who was the youngest ever Number 1 in the world at that stage. I was too young and naïve to understand the magnitude of the claims I was putting out into the universe when I told the world on prime-time television I was going to make it by the time I was 14 or 15. But that was my version of reality, as I was trained in speech and coached in thought. The short-lived media hype rocketed me into another dimension, and I was on a pink cloud for a moment in time. The 12/U syndrome is a conspiracy theory about players who hit their peak prematurely; it's like the sporting kiss of death. My fate was written in the stars and tennis smooched me on either cheek like an old Italian mobster whose destiny was unavoidable.

I didn't have a mobile at the time and I guess our landline number must have been in the phone book, because the home phone rang hot for months. Prank callers and girls mostly. I was used to the bullies at school, so the prank callers didn't bother me; but the embarrassment of my family knowing girls were calling me was excruciating.

My older sister, Tiffany, got very short with callers from unknown numbers, primarily out of annoyance I think, and maybe a tinge of envy. I was already the golden child, and the extra attention I received likely added insult to injury. One night the phone rang, and I jumped to answer it to save myself any embarrassment or vitriol from my older sibling. It was a man called Bert Sampson who had seen *A Current Affair* and wanted to offer his psychological services to me, pro bono. He asked to speak to my parents and proposed weekly visits to assist in my psychological development.

My parents were perfect dance partners considering they had next to nothing in common. My father was a traumatised yet charismatic character, who was a temperamental 'rageaholic', whilst my mother embodied the paradoxical role of an avoidant caretaker. There would be chaos at night, caused by Dad, then crumpets in the morning made by Mum. This unpredictable landscape meant emotional bombs could explode out of nowhere and smash everything to smithereens, but that didn't mean the house wasn't kept spotless. Mum could move mountains under carpet and her obsessive cleaning all but masked the madness brewing down below. The connotations of her frantic housework spoke clearly, and it said, 'There is nothing to see here, everything's just dandy!'

The lack of communication and transparency surrounding the madness meant my mind had to fill in the blanks, never knowing when it would go from violence to silence. I could somewhat tolerate the craziness but couldn't compute the pretending; yet I knew acting was the fundamental key to my survival. So, I joined the family charade and committed to the role of a 'happy sporting child' I was seemingly assigned.

The thought of expressing my feelings was terrifying because, at the time, I didn't know much about myself apart from what other people had told me to be. I was typecast and I became known to family, friends, and bullies as Tennis Boy, a name that still flies around the place when someone wants to offend me. Since I practically sidestepped out of the womb with a racket attached to my arm, I knew how to handle myself on the court and felt superior in terms of my athletic abilities. But the second I stepped outside the sporting arena, I instantly reverted to feeling like an extra-terrestrial who was posturing as a human being. After the phone call with Bert, my father came to me and said, 'You're going to get a check-up from the neck up!' And it's safe to say I was a little nervous.

So, there we were, speeding along from the 6am on-court morning session, to see a complete stranger to 'talk'. Talk about what? I wondered, as I was getting changed in the passenger seat while being driven to a psychologist's office whilst being lectured on why I needed to eat 15 minutes after training, for the millionth time.

Constant multitasking and overstimulation scrambled my thinking, making it near impossible for me to be an active listener. There was always so much verbal output being sprayed in my direction that I could hear words, but none of them seemed to register. It was all white noise. I had a pre-programmed small-chat game I had borrowed from earthlings which consisted of superficial one-liners such as, 'Good, good, and you?' And I thought maybe, if I could just keep repeating these pleasantries, I would get away unharmed and no one would be able to tell I was just a Martian visiting from outer space.

That morning, it was the blind leading the blind. I was trying to navigate, looking in the street directory for the address as Dad drove around, lost, in the Adelaide foothills like a first day-on-the-job taxi driver. Everything was rushed when I was a kid and there was no sense of flow to life, just urgency and chaos.

My father's erratic ramblings, endless antics, and captivating weirdness made him a problematic ringmaster of our travelling circus. He was disciplined but disorganised, and always found a way to turn simple tasks into epic sagas. We found the joint, but it was a house when I had been expecting an office. It threw me, as I felt more comfortable in offices than in houses. To me it seemed as if offices were neutral territory, whereas houses were a home ground advantage for whoever lived there.

I felt stiff and anxious as I opened the gate and walked down the driveway with Dad, trying not to show how I felt. I knocked on the

This is our next Lleyton

**Advertiser**

Tennis prodigy
# SIGNED UP AT 11

door and an old man answered and warmly invited us inside. Bert had an elderly Grandpa vibe going on where he looked as harmless as his cardigan. As he offered me a yoghurt ice cream and my father a drink, I didn't feel the normal brain static I would usually get around outsiders.

While Bert was absent from the room getting our refreshments, Dad wandered around critiquing the qualifications and memorabilia on the wall. I asked, 'Are you staying?'. But Dad just mumbled back incoherently, 'We are gonna have to get some of your memorabilia in here Todd'. Bert came back with our treats, explained a bit about himself and what he was offering. He asked me a few basic questions and I began to answer, but when I was no further than a few sentences into my reply, my old man jumped in, assuming the role of translator.

The interaction became the two of them talking about me as if I wasn't in the room. I was embarrassed and belittled, and the responses my father gave didn't even slightly align with how I felt. My Dad so badly wanted me to be the person he believed I was, that I wasn't allowed to be myself. It felt if I were to tell the truth, it might collide with the identity that was manufactured for me and destroy Dad's idea of who I was. So, I kept quiet, and that's the way the meetings remained for the next few years between Bert, Max and me.

## Learning to live with the fraudulent me

The weekly visits to the counsellor created an inner conflict and confusion in me, as I was still a stranger to myself. Being silenced stunted my growth and heavily jeopardised my ability to stand up for myself when I had something important to say.

Having his tongue cut out makes a muted man come up with alternative ways of expressing what he cannot say. If you are a child trapped in these circumstances, there are consequences that follow for the rest of your life; so, if you're ready to check out, hang onto your inner voice for when you're brave enough to audit your issues!

## DAMAGE RECEIPT

| Fuck-Up (Cause) | Aftermath (Effect) |
| --- | --- |
| Publicly parading a child | Ruptured identity |
| No open communication among family members | Alienation: inability to connect |
| Overstepping child-parent boundaries | Warped expectations of roles in life |
| Not allowing a child to voice their own thoughts or opinions | Low self-esteem/ invalidated self-worth |

## THANK YOU!

I quickly went from being a quiet, spoken-for child to a rebel with a misguided cause. The lunatic soup gave me a voice and I began behaving in a disorderly fashion while testing the waters on the total opposite end of the social spectrum. I needed to prove to myself that I wasn't just an obedient little bitch boy, and since my psyche couldn't cope with that on its own, I used the help of alcohol, as it was the perfect anaesthetic that put my conscious to sleep, while I ran rampant guilt free. The feeling was liberating, even though somewhere within me I knew I was cutting off my nose to spite my face. But I'd had such a gutful of complying with other people's agendas that I felt morally obligated to a life of chaos and debauchery. I went from being warned about hanging out with the drop kicks, to becoming the head honcho of the drop kicks. But the temporary 'courage from a can' always meant eventually I would have to return to Earth and deal with the real me.

A few years later, when my tennis career was well and truly over and I was ceaselessly tap-dancing on the edge of a cliff face, I received a call from Bert. Someone must have tipped him off about a few of my new lifestyle hobbies and he wanted me to come around and have a chat. Not even the Pope could have got me on the straight and narrow back then, but I had a feeling Bert was going to give it a good go.

My life was swaying between competing chasms and one of the hardest parts was I was completely unable to articulate what was going on in my mind, or how I felt about my past. The words were dulled from years of repression and having my father speak for me. I had never developed my own voice. After living like a monk who was ordered to take a vow of silence, a few years of head-banging and street brawling weirdly helped me restore my balance and find a moderate level of social etiquette. While it's not an option I would advocate, nothing else seemed to be on offer for me at the time. I only made it through by the skin of my teeth, and the werewolf didn't just disappear but got fed just the right amount to stay full and dormant.

## Summary

To me, it seems a lot of juniors who are participating at the elite level of sport aren't really choosing to do it of their own free will but are being externally motivated by their parents. Children are inherently people pleasers, and to a greater extent 'parent pleasers'. That gives the adult a lot of power. And with great power comes great responsibility.

I do think many tennis parents come into the sport with pure intentions, but after a period of time in the dog-eat-dog environment, they generally develop an agenda on what they would like to see happen with their kid. Players end up becoming passengers in their own existence, where they are held hostage by fear. It cannot be overlooked that adults are like gods to young children, and the agonising thought of disappointing his or her own parent is one of the most awful and terrifying feelings the child will avoid at all costs. So, a lot of players really have no option but to mould themselves to the expectations of their own parents, even if it means burying their own voice deep down within themselves.

```
           IT'S TIME TO PAY YOUR BILL.
       WE HOPE YOU HAD A PLEASANT EXPERIENCE!

   Subtotal:           Unhealthy coping mechanisms
   Tip:                Don't do it!
   Total Costs:        Childhood ruined
                       Likely addiction issues, and
                       An overall underdeveloped
                       identity
```

## Dazzled by the bright lights of promise—too much, too young!

Most tennis parents fall victim to The Peacock Syndrome. With the newfound glory of their child's early success, the tennis parent feasts on the accolades. Seeing themselves as an extension of their child, they begin to frolic around the tennis scene, doing victory laps to exert their dominance over their peers with an inflated ego and an exaggerated sense of self. They can even begin to use the plural 'we' when referring to their child. For example, they might be telling people we won, even though the parent didn't play. The handshakes and the ego strokes are almost too much for the tennis parent to handle, as they are aroused by the thought of what potentially awaits at the final destination. The junior circuit is naught but foreplay to the toey tennis parent, and they signed up for the sex.

Ignorantly exposing a child to an extreme world comes at a cost, similar to what's suffered by the mismanaged and mistreated child stars in Hollywood. Even though the two occupations are quite different, the same price is paid for the mismanagement of a child prodigy. Now, not every young tennis player or child actor ends up on skid row, but a common denominator in both fields is parents losing themselves in their child's hype. When a parent prioritises winning more than wellbeing, it confuses the child, sowing seeds of doubt about whether the love they are receiving is unconditional. Instead of fulfilling their duties as parent and protecting their child, the parent's insatiable appetite to climb the tennis ladder becomes more important. Once the adult's desire for glory has superseded their responsibility as a parent, both player and parent are eaten alive by the sporting world, a world full of snakes, sharks, and snobs.

Hollywood is acutely aware of the effect Tinseltown has on child stars. From Aaron Carter to Christian Slater and just about all the Nickelodeon and Disney Channel stars, Hollywood has countless stories of high-profile children self-destructing while in the public eye. Now imagine all the ones we don't see on E! News. It has become so common Hollywood has moved to destigmatise addiction and mental health and now openly acknowledges the impact the industry can have on young actors. But in tennis, the public and even the tennis fraternity are shocked and frankly appalled to see young players showing signs of burnout. 'How dare they say they don't love the sport!' people rail, without ever knowing the specific demands and how many hours athletes have put in since they were barely out of nappies. What's frankly appalling is expecting a normal person to be produced out of these abnormal environments. You'll hardly ever meet anyone in the world of elite tennis who isn't really weird, very difficult, or completely zombified. That's not to say some of them aren't cool and interesting to be around, but they're just not normal people. The sport tries its best to pull a shifty, as it protects its interest while trying to maintain its prestigious heritage as a gentlemanly game, when in reality this kind of insanity has gone on for years. The public and media have a field day with some of the emotionally underdeveloped athletes, who clearly aren't coping with a lifetime of being made a spectacle.

When the penny drops the people around them may have insincere intentions in wanting them to perform, the child tennis star is left with a head full of paranoia and a gut full of tennis. Being unable to trust their closest confidants generally sends the player into a self-destructive spiral, and they can resort to outlandish behaviour and unhealthy coping mechanisms. By this time, for 99.9% of players, it's curtains. Everyone is helplessly left to watch on as the player sabotages the very thing for which they have sacrificed their entire life. Take my own story as an example.

## Grooming children with a promise unnatural

The results of the biggest Under 12 tournaments in the world are analysed more than the Melbourne Cup form guide. Tennis coaches, academies, and management agencies from all over the world set out to groom the winners of these tournaments; and we, as a society, are addicted to watching youngsters attempt pursuits of greatness. There is something unnatural yet fascinating about it that captivates the broader community and awakens something in the tennis parent. Academies are well versed in using smart marketing tools to sell the fantasy to the delusional consumers—tennis parents, like my father, Max.

My father always said, 'It doesn't matter whether you win or lose' but because his deep-seated belief was that I could be winning, it still made losing very hard to swallow. And when he tried to swallow the loses, Max would choke on it, spit it up, and I wouldn't hear the end of it. I think he hated losing more than he loved winning. It didn't matter if it was tic-tac-toe or tennis, wherever there was a contest or competition, Max would enter me and have me jumping for the opponent's jugular.

Dad marvelled over high achievers, and I idolised my father and craved his respect more than anything in the world. He had brief brushes with success in many obscure arenas but was never able to stay on the bull long enough to fully reap the rewards of a risky ride. Some of these were legit hard luck stories and others, I came to find out, were made-up fairy tales. Dad never let the truth get in the way of a good story, like the one about when he owned a racehorse with David Bowie or was going to replace Mel Gibson for the lead role in the movie Gallipoli. One of his biggest claims to fame was teaching his brother Des to screw punt the American Gridiron football and getting him drafted over to the NFL as a punter. But each crazy story had a sad and similar ending: 'I should have done this differently' or 'I should have done that differently'. He 'should've'd' all over himself. I wanted to right his wrongs and I believed I would be the hero to bring glory, once and for all, to the Ley name.

Winning some of the biggest junior tournaments immediately gave me the golden pass into the tennis world. It was an instantaneous transition. We went from a couple of merciless missionaries training on community asphalt courts, to limousines, agents, sponsorship, endorsements, and extensive media publicity. The makers and takers came knocking on our door when I was 11. My parents were wined and dined by management companies, and ultimately signed a pretty shitty 5-year endorsement deal at a time when the AUD was on the decline. Despite being sold out cheaply, I was the youngest-ever athlete to sign with a management company and the news somehow made the front page of the paper. Across the state, my mug was littered across newsagency stands and shopfronts, with a blasé look on my face as if it was just a matter of time until I made it.

Although I arrived on the scene like a bat out of hell, my future was nowhere near guaranteed, despite the papers and tennis fraternity calling me the next Lleyton Hewitt. But there was still a lot of water left to go under the bridge before I was to make a single cent from my sporting talents. People of the tennis world love to get their crystal balls out and predict who's going to make it, and I felt chained to an expectation amplified by an entire community, plenty of whom had never held a racket before. Tennis has a shocking habit of crowning juniors as professional before they have even touched the sides of the tour, and the high expectations are a brilliant recipe for creating under achievers or even abject failures.

My parents' inexperience in the world of tennis, together with the inflated hype the media attention had created, resulted in my tennis life being prioritised over my personal development. I had no idea what I was agreeing to at a young age would have such life-altering implications, as part of wanting to be a tennis star clearly required me to be ostracised from the rest of society. I felt like an unperson with no life outside tennis; I didn't have any interests, hobbies or other passions, and I was barely going to school. I also barely had a life within tennis because socialising with other players was frowned upon and was to be kept to a minimum.

I soon realised the mood of the manor was dependent upon my performance. If I played well and could keep Dad happy, then everyone else in the family could be happy too; but if I didn't do well, then everyone had Mad Max to contend with. At the age of 11, I felt responsible for my family's happiness and safety, and I suffered

*West Adelaide centre half-forward Des Ley, 23, today out-kicked and out-classed 10 interstate rivals to win the Australian final of The Herald $50,000 Superkick final at the MCG.*

Uncle Des

severe guilt and shame when the consequences of my losses spilled over onto other people.

I started to hate the fact the only thing people spoke to me about was my tennis; and in turn, I began to loathe myself for being so congenial about a game causing so much hidden travesty. I found it difficult to distinguish between my true self and my reputation, and I went from revelling in the recognition to fucking hating it. I wanted to be treated normally. When family friends or other people would speak to me, it was as if they had created this false world they thought I must have lived in. I think tennis coverage on TV really affects people's understanding of the sport, and they would glamorise my life. It made me want to kick back at the opinions people held of me, to show everyone what a 'great time' I was having.

In the world of tennis, age doesn't seem to matter, and having unique friendships based on tennis standard rather than age is quite common. Since my standard was ahead of my age, it meant I was mixing with people who were generally 4 to 8 years older than me. Todd Langman, a local desperado seven years my senior became my pre-arranged tennis friend approved by Max himself. Langman passed my father's litmus test, as it was clear he would sever off a limb to get a taste of the tour. Langman looked up to Max like a messiah, while I idolised my sparring partner for his crude demeanour and degenerate taste in music and movies. Pre-teens model their behaviour on what they are exposed to, so since my closest friendships were with a motley crew of wannabes, I morphed into an ill-suited gangster persona, AKA 'Dr Ley' from the eco-friendly streets of downtown Adelaide.

Deprived of a schooling and social life, I missed out on being cool and just felt like a highly neurotic sporting freak. Discovering the genre of Hardcore Rap changed everything, giving me the identity makeover that I couldn't manufacture for myself. Even though our social and cultural circumstances were worlds apart, I could connect with the frustration and anger coming through my headphones, and it felt as if hardcore music was as therapeutic as yoga or meditation. I was trying to soothe the inner rage simmering from years of unspoken injustice, but I just came off looking like a spoilt, middle-class wanker, formerly known as 'Snoop Todd'.

As I was locked away at the IMG Academy at night, I would watch TV shows like Dawson's Creek and The OC, trying to get a taste of what normal life looked like. I began to envy people with a simple life, whom I had been trained to believe were boring and mediocre. I started to compare my father with Sandy Cohen from The OC, who seemed to be the ultimate father, giving his son the right combination of freedom and structure. My own father, on the other hand, taped over his wedding day video with an Australian open quarter final, so we could watch it while he gave me nightly rubdowns with his mystical lotion called, Emu oil. Which was a rather weird smelling ointment Max said could cure cancer.

Starting the pursuit of becoming a professional tennis player at such a young age was beginning to catch up with me and I felt a strong pull to rebel against my sporting identity. I could've been a candidate for having multiple personality disorder, seeing my identity changed minute to minute as I imitated a long litany of outlandish characters. Unfortunately, none of them wanted to hang around with me after the performance was over. My allegiance to being cool corrupted my tennis and I was more concerned with how I was coming across than how I was playing. By this point, the end was near for me.

## DAMAGE RECEIPT

| Fuck-Up (Cause) | Aftermath (effect) |
| --- | --- |
| Not mixing with kids of similar age | Fear of missing out. Left to my own imagination to experience things I didn't experience |
| Narcissistic parenting | Unable to take criticism and a fear of rejection |
| Glorifying success | Hypocritically judge people based of achievements and 'excellence' |
| Constant tennis talk | Resent the sport and rebel in a self-destructive fashion |
| Unfair expectations | Self-esteem issues, inferiority complex |

## Looking for love but rewarded with mocking laughter

Looking back, I can see I was unconventionally trying to show people I was more than just a tennis player. It was a cry for help—attention-seeking behaviour—and an attempt for recognition beyond my sporting abilities. Unfortunately, instead of seeing the subtext of my humiliating personas, everyone laughed and paid me out.

When my tennis accession ended abruptly, I felt as if I had every right to make up for what I'd missed out on when I was younger. I spent a decade (and change) consumed by pills, potions, and powders, and running from reality like a rebel without a clue. Going totally off the rails was a wildly cathartic ride after being controlled for so long. For the first time I was the one who had power over my life, and I wanted to demonstrate my disgust with the past by protesting in an attention-seeking and self-destructive manner.

It was cleansing yet scary to destroy the reputation that I, and others, had spent years creating.

In a way, I feel as if I've been waving my arms around in the air my entire life, desperately wanting someone to help me with the daily dilemma of being myself. The irony of it all is my parents have bent over backwards trying to help me. But the more time we spent in the sporting bubble, the more self-seeking my father became. Human nature prevailed as he became evermore intoxicated by his own selfish desires. This disingenuous assistance was easily guised through the cloak of being a caring parent. Our society admires involved parents as if they're selfless humanitarians, which meant the sincerity of his help never came into question.

Anybody who touches tennis on more than a social level tends to become infected with pettiness, greed, and an insatiable ambition. When a parent is an unremitting presence in their child's sporting career, it's the hallmark sign of a person who is losing themselves to the dark side of the game. Traditionally, the more involved a parent gets in the tennis world, the more emotionally neglected the child becomes. Despite my father being my relentless shadow, I felt about as emotionally abandoned as a teenage orphan, and I spent countless nights feeling bereft of family members who were only a few whiskers away from me. Unfortunately, most tennis parents fall prey to this common theme, as their egotistical and unconscious agenda can easily remain hidden underneath their charitable labour. It's for this specific reason I believe the most selfish thing a tennis parent can do is help their child too much with their sporting career.

## Summary

Once tennis becomes the tribe's main priority, there seems to be no separation between family members, and therefore there is no individual identity. So even though tennis is an individual sport, there is more than just one person playing the game, so to speak. Instead of buying a racehorse, or joining a book club, tennis parents tend to live vicariously through their children, seeing themselves as extensions of what they have created. When parents put on too many hats, mismanagement occurs and the two separate entities create a clear conflict of interest, of which the child becomes aware. Problematic decision making confuses the player, and they start to genuinely question the motives and intentions of their own parents. It is a bewildering inquiry no young child should ever have to ponder.

```
      IT'S TIME TO PAY YOUR BILL.
TENNIS HOPES YOU HAD A PLEASANT EXPERIENCE!

    Subtotal:        Shame
    Tip:             Sane parent
    Total cost:      Family
                     Reputation
                     Dignity
```

## Be careful what you wish for...

When a parent interferes in the evolution of a child's personality to try to turn them into a tennis machine, individuality is lost. A child's innocent nature can easily be manipulated by the intense tennis environment. A sporting detour taken in the early learning years prevents the child from gaining the beneficial insight into themselves that provides the basis for a balanced life once the tennis curtain closes. With carrots dangled for young players on the scene, tennis unhealthily promotes sporting extremism. These appetising incentives will make tennis parents salivate and encourage them to put the pedal to the metal prematurely, in respect to their children.

A new period has now arrived in professional tennis. Players are starting to find their best tennis typically in their late 20s, much later in their careers than in previous decades. Even though this new trend is upon us, tennis parents don't seem to be changing their behaviour. They are in a bigger rush than ever, and fail to realise it's not a sprint, it's a marathon. I have seen no real change taking place in regard to subjecting young players to isolating environments, unrealistic expectations and a lack of freedom to authentically develop a healthy identity.

As a coach, I have posed this question to tennis parents: 'Would you prefer an 18-year-old tennis freak with no life skills, or a well-adjusted 25-year-old who still makes a decent living out of the sport?'

What do you think they say?

## Public service announcement to tennis parents who are parading their children all over social media

We are yet to see the consequences of flooding excessive photographs and videos over the internet of a child who is trying to grow into their own skin. There has never been a generation like this before, where a preconceived identity has already been created for the child, in the way of oversaturated Instagram posts from thoughtless parents. Not satisfied with making an obnoxious profile for their French poodle, tennis parents are taking to X, Facebook, Instagram and every other social media platform you can imagine, to prematurely pump the tyres of their little sporting superstar in hope of making them Instafamous. While I know how hard it can be trying to restrain yourself from letting the world know how good your children are, YOU are creating something for them, which THEY are supposed to be creating from themselves: an identity. If ever they want to step out of the character been created for them over the internet, these photos and videos have already pigeonholed them. Parents are potentially creating an unnecessary coming-out-of-the-closet type of moment for a kid to endure.

## Don't give your heart to a ramblin' man

They say opposites attract. From what I've seen, maybe they can connect momentarily in a whirlwind of romance and magnetic lust, but it is inevitably destined for doom. My parents could second this notion, I reckon, if they ever had a moment of honest reflection.

But I'm not going to hold my breath. They had no business whatsoever entering a relationship of the normal kind, and us kids paid the price for their naivety in a range of different ways. A lot of their relationship is still a mystery to me, including the marriage proposal, where apparently, they conveniently skipped out on paying the bill for a Moet and Lobster late-night dinner. According to my father, Max, the pair of them were kicking on after hours when my mother, Sharon, nonchalantly recommended the two of them should probably get hitched. Whenever I mention this to my mother I am met with an undignified glare and a vow of silence. I don't know if it's true or not, but one thing I know for certain is, making massive life decisions while being under the influence certainly runs in the family.

Sharon took on the suicide mission of attempting to make a man out of the maniac, Max. He was a baffling mix of confidence and self-depreciation, he was intense but humorous, unpredictable yet consistent, and intolerable but great to have around. I guess it's up for debate whether her venture was an act of bravery or sheer madness because Dad was clearly a wild knockabout who was not going to be caged like a Persian housecat. From the outside looking in, it must have seemed like Max's tendency towards risky behaviour was just a scheme to finally get him on easy street. But ultimately Dad just felt more alive when he owned racehorses and rib shops, mixed with undesirables, and sold fertilizer or X-rated calendars from door to door. But alongside Dad's thrill-seeking nature came a ferocious temper, always a light poke away from rearing its ugly head. Having to adapt to a challenging childhood meant it didn't take much for Max's survival instincts to takeover. So, it's not that the warnings signs weren't there for my mother to see; they were undeniable.

Throughout this book, I chop and change the way I speak about my father. Because as a kid, I both idolised and endured him. So, one moment he is a heartless and selfish swine who piggybacked off others to enhance his own agenda, and the next he is a trailblazing entrepreneur who sacrificed his whole life to give me a shot at superstardom. I think it would have been easier for me if he was just a sadistic old bastard because when someone impacts you so deeply with their complex personality, you become quite conflicted. And that's probably how you would best describe me—conflicted. Conflicted about a lot of things.

*Dad's thoughts on intimacy*

I used to always say I don't believe in luck, but you can't choose your parents. That's luck, and it's the biggest lottery of all. Me and my older sister Tiffany lucked out on a couple of parents whose only similarity was they both breathed oxygen on the planet Earth. Not overly paternal, Max instead assumed the role of provider and tried slogging it out in real-world jobs. It was not that he wasn't good at the work or was disinclined to put in the hours, but Dad just always had a problem with people, as he never played well with others. The most minor of incidents could make him clear his desk in the blink of an eye. His pride was always more important than the penny, so Dad was never afraid to march, regardless of the circumstances it may put him and his family under.

It's hard to control a man who's not persuaded by money. I guess some rare individuals can't be tamed or tempted. Max was looking for more out of life, not necessarily financially, but a cause or a mission to chase. The injustice of a missed childhood seethed in his bloodstream and served as endless ammunition when it was pointed at the right target. But when there wasn't an appetising enough goal to pursue, Max's hardships had a way of unravelling at home.

That's not to say our household was all doom and gloom, as Mum constantly put on festive events where they both got on famously. Weirdly enough, the better they got on, the more I knew horror was just around the corner. Fighting became a familiar night cap. The second the cameras stopped rolling, Dad's temper usually flared up and the jovial atmosphere turned unrecognisable. His volatility was generally directed at my mother, while my sister and I helplessly listened on from another room when we weren't actively involved. Mum seemed to internalise a lot of the abuse, and I think Dad manipulated her into feeling responsible for most of his issues and outbursts. Since she felt so guilty about it, suppression became the religion of the household, which poisoned the place with a certain kind of eeriness reminiscent of a Stanley Kubrick film.

Being a growing, sensitive child in-between two warring adults made me develop survival skills to endure the bumpy ride. Whacking tennis balls off the wall turned out to be my adaptation, providing me with some much needed psychological and emotional consistency. The addict in me was hooked from the first hit, I couldn't get enough of it. And neither could my Mum, because my interest conveniently became Dad's interest, which meant she was almost off the hook as he was out of her hair.

My sister Tiffany wasn't impressed with my new hobby, as the sport curtailed our close relationship, and it heavily interrupted her plans of bossing me around all day. She knew way too early I was a people pleaser and had no defence against what she asked me to do. Her neediness came from being deprived of my father's attention. Max was only interested in things that he was interested in, and he found it hard to engage with anything outside these interests, including her hobbies and ventures. So, Tiffany was forced to mould her life around what she thought my father would give her attention for; and when my passion for tennis outshone her efforts, her new hobby became climbing trees, maybe to get the fuck away from everyone. The never-ending sound of the tennis ball thudding against the outside of her bedroom wall was a constant reminder of who the favourite child in the household was.

After graduating from the school of hard knocks, Dad had developed a fantastic knack for telling other people how to live their lives, despite his being in disarray. It was set in stone very early on in my life that I was going to be a professional tennis player, and everyone signed off on it. The perfect shitstorm unfolded for the tennis madness to transpire. Dad needed the rush, Mum needed the out, Tiffany was overlooked, and I was a people pleasing sporting freak.

Incredibly, my tennis talents served as a marriage respirator for my parents' dysfunctional relationship because now, instead of ranting and raving at Mum at home, Dad was ranting and raving at me at the courts. We had traded spots; Mum had served me up like a sacrificial lamb, and my tennis talents gave me a lifetime sentence to spend with 'Mad Max'. Human beings tell themselves all kinds of justifications to avoid the pain of feeling the truth, and I feel conflicted as to whether I blame my mother or not. Depends on which day you ask me, I guess. But if they hadn't made a go of it, I wouldn't have been born. Don't get me wrong. I am glad I'm here and have partially survived it, but if you gave me a choice to do it all over again or not be born at all, you would have to give me a night to sleep on it. Tennis started out as mind-numbing activity to help me survive an unpredictable household, and ironically turned into exactly what I was trying to avoid.

PART 2

# Misconceptions

### There's nothing more dangerous than a tennis parent with a plan

Tennis coaching is an industry that tries its hardest to disguise how difficult it is to make a professional player. Tennis parent talks to tennis parent but neither is informed, and this creates misconceptions. The myths that abound on subjects such as schooling via correspondence, the role of tennis academies and the all-important development of mental toughness, require proper investigation before they are tried at home willy-nilly.

The failure to thoroughly investigate does children a massive disservice, as they are the ones who suffer when the dream dies. The lack of a contingency plan for a child who goes all in is dangerous and a sign of irresponsible parenting. This chapter examines three common hurdles most parents trip over.

When, or if, a tennis parent decides to pull a child out of school to have them play tennis full-time, is one of the biggest decisions they must make. The many factors that influence the tennis parent can cause them to make the decision for the wrong reasons. Gambling with a child's future is extremely costly and tennis has no money-back guarantee if things don't go to plan. Just because a child does correspondence courses, it doesn't mean they are going to make it—a fact many tennis parents seem to miss.

The typical tennis parent is always on the lookout for ways to get an advantage over the competition. Local tournaments provide a measuring stick against which they can compare their kid's ability with the rest of the players around town. Unhealthy comparisons form the basis of irrational plans, as parents are not fully aware of how difficult it is to create a professional player at an international standard, and the attributes the child must possess to have a fighting chance in the long run. When their child is a big fish in a small pond, the short-sighted tennis parent typically becomes overly enthusiastic and is prepared to take ridiculous risks.

School is soon seen as a hindrance and the tennis parent panics when they read Agassi was home schooled—and so is their child's local rival. In fact, the schooling environment can be a useful break from a very demanding and repetitive sporting life, but it is not often viewed that way by tennis enthusiasts. The title 'full-time tennis player' leaves no escape hatch for the child to change their often-coerced career choice, creating extra unhealthy and unnecessary pressure. Most kids can't decide what they want for dinner let alone what they want to do with their future, so juniors come to find the terminology 'full-time tennis player' is simply a decorative expression for being trapped.

The stakes are raised when the parent is forking out hundreds of dollars a week for training and the kid isn't going to school anymore. This can cause the child to be overcome with distress, as they feel the increase to the sporting thermostat and are swamped by expectation. With all the eggs in one basket, tennis' function shifts from enjoyment to employment and is seen as an investment by the tennis parent, who wants a sizeable return in the future. However, the tennis parents' limited perspective of 'more = better' generally ends up with the child resenting the sport and struggling with education requirements, and even being defeated by social situations schooling would have prepared them for.

## Your talented tennis child is not a racehorse

I was approached once by a father who wanted me to collaborate with him to coach his daughter. She was one of the best Under 12 girls in the country, but it was obvious from the get-go her dad wanted it more than she did. He had way more intensity when talking to me about her tennis than she had in her effort on the court. As I watched her train one afternoon in the scorching heat, he casually said, 'I'd prefer her to burnout early than have her go nowhere later on,' as if he was talking about a rundown racehorse he didn't care about. The comment shocked me even though I understood what he meant; and in a weird way it seemed reasonable, but totally unreasonable and cruel at the same time. His assumption correspondence schooling was a way to leapfrog the rest of the pack to the finish line triggered him to pull her out of school. It would have been easier to pull an elephant through a keyhole than to get her to top 100 by her teens, but this is what this tennis parent did instead of backing her into her 20s and letting her have a proper crack. Lengthening the process might have cost him some of his superannuation, but it would have given her a fighting chance. He went full steam ahead and ended up burning her out just before her 16th birthday. He ruined her life, leaving her with huge developmental delays, but he did save himself a few dollars in the long run.

Then there is the type of tennis parent who has the audacity to pull their kid out of school even though they are not playing in any tournaments or competitions. Instead, they prefer to spend an inordinate amount of time on ball feeding and drilling to protect their fantasy from being popped. This type of imaginative tennis parent tends to avoid matches (losses) to keep the pretence their kid is further advanced than they are. I have noticed this becoming more common, with parents seemingly lacking humility and unable to face certain facts. I guess adults need fairy tales too. A lot of parents post ridiculous Instagram training videos to gain validation from cyberspace, while their child goes down the longest road to nowhere. These extreme approaches are generally undertaken without a contingency plan or any escape hatches in place. The life-changing decision to take a child out of school is too often made by a reckless parent under the spell of elite sport. There is no oversight or restriction on who should be allowed to leave the traditional schooling environment, and no investigation into whether the parents, or those in charge of the child's tennis career and/or schooling, are qualified to carry out their self-assigned tasks.

Parents seem to think if their kids don't become professional tennis players, they will just waltz into university unscathed by the past and be ready to move on with the rest of their lives. They assume the sporting experience will provide them with the necessary skills and leave them in good shape to cope with adult life. More often than not, the kid is left with the traumatising task of figuring out what to do without tennis, but with insufficient socialisation and a serious lack of life skills.

## School sucked but it was a holiday from my life

I was red lining when I was 12, averaging 50 hours a week of school and tennis. School really wasn't my thing, but it gave me an escape from the unsympathetic watch of my Dad and the competitive world of tennis. I was doing so much the State coaches came and warned him about the possibility of me burning out. But to Max, the terminology of 'burnout' was just a made-up word from a mediocre mind. 'The one that wants the fruit must be willing to climb the tree,' he would say.

Besides, I was overlooked by the state selectors in a come-and-try training session when I was 9, which started off my relationship with the federation famously. The rejection worked as rocket fuel for Dad. It drove him to drive me. Forgiveness wasn't Max's forte; he held onto grudges and resentments as tightly as he held onto winning TAB tickets. It made him biased and sceptical about anything they ever did after that. Besides, tennis parents seemed to produce the best players who got to the pinnacle of the sport anyway. Revenge in tennis is best served by winning, so he got his retribution a few years later when I became Number 1 in the world under his guidance.

Nothing was more satisfying to him than proving the establishment wrong. In fact, Max got so much out of it, he was prepared to sacrifice my emotional and psychological welfare in the process. Not that Dad was malicious, but he was emotionally stunted himself and seemed incapable of seeing things from a child's perspective. But nonetheless, him getting carried away with his own agenda meant my tennis turned into a sporting form of child slave labour. I was trapped on the tennis treadmill of continual commitments, rarely given a second to get off the eternal conveyor belt. When your life is spread so thinly between obligations, everything kind of loses its importance and meshes into one giant blur. You lose sight of why you are doing it, and now you're doing it, well … because … that's just what you do, I guess. It's a world of constantly running late, getting changed in the car, and having to scoff shitty pre-packaged food before the next session. Education and tennis didn't tango well together. You can only do one time consuming activity at a time. Dad was reluctant to pull me out of school, but the idea of having more time to focus on tennis proved too enticing to resist.

## My bubble had well and truly burst by 17

It was tennis or bust and I had well and truly busted by 17. After a disastrous trip overseas with Dad and best mate Langman, I fleetingly contemplated ending it all in a watery grave. In desperate need of a change in scenery from the tennis court, I tried to see what else may be on the horizon. People told me to make up this thing called a CV. What the hell was a CV? I found out it was a resumé of my prior employment history. For a whole afternoon, I stared at a blank Word document headed "Todd Ley Resumé", clicking my fingers and picking my nose.

Not only had I not had any working experience, but my education history wasn't looking too crash hot either, having been bailed out of school in Year 8 and with only a measly Year 10 completion credit. I had attempted doing Year 11 by correspondence but got caught bribing a tutor, who felt a bit uneasy about doing my work but needed the dosh so went along with it. I was unemployable. I'd wake up in the morning depressed, to find the classified section on the breakfast bench with potential leads humiliatingly circled, next to a list of daily jobs to do around the house.

Every lead or possible opening ended in rejection once employers got a hold of my resumé. Organisations only wanted to hire people with experience. Playing the Australian Open didn't automatically get you a foot in the door when it came to waiting tables or selling a Billabong bikini in a surf store. My sporting skills weren't transferable and were totally useless in this new world I'd entered—the real world, the working world, a life I wasn't sold on in the slightest. It didn't matter I wasn't sold on it, because the working world didn't fucking want me anyway.

A mate of mine received a full sports scholarship to a University in Indiana and pushed for the head coach of the school to sign me. But I had to complete Year 12 first, and with my lack of schooling and mental instability sabotaging my chances, I simply didn't have the capacity to study. Which became clear when I passed out halfway through the initial meeting with the head coach because I hadn't slept from the night before.

But I couldn't go back to tennis. It felt like trying to reconcile with an ex-girlfriend who'd cheated on me. Fool me once, shame on you; fool me twice, shame on me. Don't get me wrong, I've been known to enjoy rubbing salt into my own wounds, but not this time. This one stung. My pay-day millionaire lifestyle required more of a cashflow, so I took up work in a laundromat, a job offered by a tennis parent of a kid I coached.

I took offence to just about everything I was legitimately asked to do in the store.

My inflated sense of self would arc up and run rampant whenever I was asked to do something I felt was humiliating (like wash someone else's socks and jocks). I would get to work a few minutes early, park 800 metres from the laundromat, and catch a glimpse of myself in the rear-vision mirror in disbelief, wearing a stupid uniform and with dark circles under my eyes. The job was taking me to the cleaners. I chain-smoked Marlboro Reds and cried most mornings before walking in the doors, to then be told by the overzealous manager to put a smile on my dial for good customer service. I couldn't follow any orderly directions, and I felt staff were deliberately antagonising me by reminding me of the pettiest things, such as remembering to shut the lid on my lunchbox in the kitchen area, for occupational health and safety.

After I had been hired and fired in a matter of weeks, my self-loathing soared to new heights as I registered for the dole, which turned out to be even harder than working. Who knew not working could be so hard? This marked a new personal best rock bottom for me. It was only a bee's dick better than being broke, and I was officially going nowhere with nothing.

It was around this time I had the pleasure of being held hostage in a feisty ABC-like Q&A debate between my mother and older sister one night when they were drunk. That moment in time felt more like a moral and professional lynching than anything of the constructive kind. The debate topic: my future prospects. They didn't hold back, both swinging for the fences on what they thought I should do, while I sat there silent, leading head-first and chin-first into the oncoming verbal haymakers.

I was internally fuming when my sister told me she thought I should go and work in the mines, because what I heard at the time was all she thought I was capable of was digging a hole in the ground. I'll dig a hole in the ground all right and put you in it! Don't you people know who I think I am? My sister may or may not have been trying to rub my nose in it, but my pride and bitterness would take valid suggestions like this as unforgivable insults. I was greatly wounded from the slightest things and felt downtrodden and disheartened about my future.

The universe kept throwing me back into tennis. Maybe that was because nowhere else would have me, as I wasn't employable or capable of keeping a job for, well … ever! So, I became the thing I had never wanted to be, a full-time tennis coach. Not that coaching is a bad profession, but it just epitomised the title of failed tennis player, a label I was desperately trying to run away from.

### DAMAGE RECEIPT

| Fuck-Up (Cause) | Aftermath (Effect) |
|---|---|
| Prematurely home schooled | Limited career options after tennis |
| No contingency plan | A very hard fall and a substantial period of feeling lost and useless |
| Lack of life skills | Insecurity and low self-esteem |
| No support after tennis | Unhealthy coping mechanisms |

### THANK YOU!

## Comparisons corrupt the decision-making process

Elite sport can jeopardise parents' common sense and seriously affect their ability when it comes to making rational decisions for their children's future. Many parents are baited into making the wrong call regarding their kid's education, often basing their decision on what the child's sporting rivals are doing, instead of what is right for the individual. Comparing a child to other players is one of the most natural yet unhealthy things any parent can do to their kid. I think a lot of parents think it's okay to do the wrong thing for the right reason, but if they investigated their intentions thoroughly, they would find they are doing the wrong thing for the wrong reason.

I still find it mind-boggling that tennis parents try to palm off the decision to pull their child out of school on their kid's wishes to be a professional tennis player. Do you reckon if the kid wanted to eat ice cream every night of the week for dinner, the parent would agree to that too? Children can't speak for themselves, and they need someone who is protecting their best interests to speak up. To a lot of kids, what the real world holds for them is unconceivable, so it is vital a child has a rational adult to assist them through these demanding days. The number of times I have seen this decision go drastically wrong far outweighs the times it went right. The tennis eventually fails, the kid's schooling has gone out the window, and they are left with the insurmountable task of entering the real world, well and truly behind the 8-ball.

In the racing industry, horse owners choose to put stallions out of their misery when the horse injures itself in competition, rather than let it go through the rest of its life severely compromised. They cop a lot of flak from activists, but I understand their seemingly cruel thinking from my own experience of feeling like a broken-down tennis player, left to fend for myself in a world completely overwhelming. To this day, I sometimes feel I would have been better off if my trainer had sent me to the glue factory as well. I'm not saying correspondence school is never an option. But it is an option that should be treated with serious caution, as its repercussions can be extremely detrimental. Just because you pull your kid out of school, it doesn't mean they are going to make it.

---

```
           IT'S TIME TO PAY YOUR BILL.
        WE HOPE YOU HAD A PLEASANT EXPERIENCE!
```

| | |
|---|---|
| Subtotal: | Inferiority complex |
| Tip: | Seek professional advice |
| Total Costs: | Potentially unemployable |
| | Hopelessness |
| | Bitterness |

## Tennis academies—machines that exploit the dreams of tennis parents and their kids

Tennis academies are businesses that can be exploitative at the expense of kids and their gullible parents. They can provide a great service when it comes to tennis, but anything outside their sporting expertise simply isn't their problem. The extremely unforgiving environment serves a purpose for their business, which is to put out decent tennis players, but not necessarily decent human beings. Without guidance or protection in this testosterone-infested atmosphere, children are at risk of developing a warped sense of reality, resorting to unhealthy coping mechanisms as a way of survival, and cultivating a vindictive character for the remainder of their life. It is an exclusive cult-like world where the worth of young kids is measured in terms of their ability and their parents' bank balance. Players are commodities in a money-making machine and are dehumanised and used for the benefit of a larger operation. Academies are not held accountable for negligence and its after-effects, and it is the child who will have to live with the consequences.

Academies are like Disneyland to already besotted tennis parents. Their appeal is irresistible. Powerhouse academies are constantly plugging their product knowing their target audience is comprised of fanatical sporting extremists.

From the outside, these enterprises seem to have everything the young tennis player needs, but they lack two major components: care and compassion. The unspoken sink-or-swim policy emotionally separates the competitors from one another due to jealousy and envy. The disingenuous nature of academies reveals itself to a player only after their results plummet, cash runs out, or new blood arrives. Academies operate like a marketing funnel. The young players and their eager parents are pitched the dream of success and riches, but the academies only require—or rather, only expect—a limited few to make it onto the tour. A lot of academies house professional players at their facilities to give off the appearance they were created there, when in fact they trained somewhere else as a junior. This smart marketing idea influences parents into believing the same good fortune can be achieved with their child, but all the while the slim odds of making it remain the same. Actually, my bad; the odds do go up. The odds of you walking out of the academy broke, mentally scared, and in need of a good psychiatrist.

To keep this giant Ferris wheel going around, results and money are prioritised and player wellbeing is the last item on the agenda. I understand the need for money to run a viable business, but the chasm between greed and children's welfare is off the Richter scale.

*I could never handle my own freedom*

Athletes can come out of the academies with all sorts of neuroses and mental health issues, especially when they have had to live on-campus. For these kids, there is no escape from the relentless pressure, and once they are outside their personal Fort Knox, players tend to be completely unable to handle their own personal liberties and torpedo straight into chaos.

Of the multitude of talented players with whom I lived and trained with at academies many went on to face their own tribulations: my old roommate suicided, another acquaintance ended up in jail, and another friend has schizophrenia and is living on the street. These are just a few examples of the many children who have suffered; and there are countless others. The natural and normal development of relationships is also hindered, as socialisation between boys and girls is seen as distracting for players; so, players are shamed for seeking the company of the opposite sex.

For a child to fully reap the rewards of these unsavoury environments, it is crucial the tennis parent has their head screwed on the right way. And by that, I mean making sure they are adhering to their parental duties of being caring and compassionate towards their own children. Because academies will not provide this service. Even then, there are no guarantees a kid will come out of such a facility with all their marbles in check. Too many times, a parent gets locked in on the tennis, overlooking the human aspects of their child residing in such a fierce environment.

Player welfare needs to be monitored by an unbiased individual whose priority is the safety of the child, not the advancement of their sporting career. It's paramount that a player has round-the-clock access to a support system, such as a psychologist or a past player who has been down a similar path. Lack of empathy and the 'he just couldn't hack it' culture academies harbour is sickening when you look at the logistics about what some of these defenceless children endure.

## Abandoned at 12 in the compound of dreams and nightmares

It was 8 o'clock at night and I lay in bed, 12-years-old and living alone in a villa on the other side of the world at a compound for sporting extremists, the Bollettieri Tennis Academy, now called IMG. My agent was a shameless opportunist who kept a close eye on the foreseeable breadwinners within the fort, as these talented children were his potential meal ticket to a tastier feed. This talking brochure of a man promised my parents I would be well taken care of, so I got sent over to live on campus at the academy. However, the best assistance he gave me was a meatball sub after an airport pick up, before he threw me in the deep water, to see if I'd sink or swim.

I needed sleep, a lot of it to compensate for the energy I was expending in the 90%-plus humidity. I calculated I needed 10 hours of shut eye a night to refuel the tank and be able to go again. Florida is the only place I've known where the humidity is so brutal, and you sweat so much, after only 30 minutes of being on court, sweat would come out of your shoes. The monotonous and unforgiving demands of academy life was a Groundhog Day grind, where only the strong survived.

Down time was for conserving energy, as I needed to be at full capacity if I was to have any chance of staying relevant in the IMG hierarchy. And I could see I was already sliding down the pecking order, as fresh meat was continually flown in from around the world, and these players were receiving far greater attention than me. The psychological pressure alongside a relentless tennis schedule had me yearning for respite, but when I got what I wanted at the end of the day, I had no idea what to do with myself, or the time. I instantly turned into a neurotic insomniac who was terrified of being alone. Mountain Dew, Cool Ranch Doritos, and porn became my regular night cap. These vices helped kill the hours I spent alone before bed and distracted me from a default state of existential dread. But once the gorging had subsided, a growing sense of uneasiness surfaced, which made it near impossible to get to sleep.

Going out to a gruelling day's practice with insufficient sleep was sporting suicide. There was no real personal connection with my coaches, so there wasn't any opening to tell them what was going on, without them making it obvious they didn't give a shit and leaving me feeling like a wimp. It was a sweatshop for athletes, and they didn't care about workers' rights. Also, there was no shortage of players ready to take your spot. Competitiveness and cash contaminated the community, creating a sporting class distinction for the rich and ruthless.

Twelve is an intermediate age where you're halfway to becoming more independent while still being a needy child. 'You have to be mature beyond your years' was a constant motto thrown around which compelled me to suffer in silence and suck up my situation of living alone over the other side of the world. But my inept portrayal of being a 'real man' left me with a misery that was immeasurable. Most nights, a severe state of insecurity combined with an impending sense of doom would descend on me.

Hypervigilance was my default state and every creak and crack my villa made had me thinking the noise was a potential intruder. I was going to end up on one of those 48-hour crime shows, I just knew it. This heightened state of awareness made it virtually impossible to get to sleep, as my paranoia pumped pure adrenaline into my bloodstream, escalating my resting heart rate to occasional palpitations. The only trick up my sleeve was talking to myself in the third person. But while it made me feel better temporarily, it also made me sound crazier, as I could now hear the noise of my voice reverberating throughout the empty house as if it were an echo chamber. The hopelessness of the situation enraged me, and I became possessed by a poisonous anger. Once the rage had passed, an underlying feeling of abandonment sat heavy in my stomach like a litre of milk sloshing in my gut. By midnight, I was overcome with grief and desperately needed a cold flannel to put over my head. But I didn't like getting up and looking out of my window to where I was required to be training in exactly six hours. I would grimace and shiver at the thought. Living literally on top of IMG's centre court meant I was genuinely sleeping at the office. I was either playing tennis, thinking about playing tennis, or recovering from playing tennis. That was my life and my job.

Ironically, the 'caretaker' on campus didn't give a shit, and ground staff who were working as security guards would randomly check rooms to make sure kids were asleep. At IMG the victor got the spoils, and because I was signed with the management company, the rules for me were much looser and nobody checked on my room for weeks at a time. In the day and age when few mobile phone plans operated affordably internationally, I had a 14-digit reverse charge call card to get a hold of family. And on top of this inconvenience, the time difference between the US and Australia made it difficult for us to catch one another. In any case, the home phone was constantly engaged by my sister using the internet.

When my emotional state reached a certain temperature, my mind would short-circuit and shut down. I would get myself into what felt like a transitional state of consciousness, where I had a reoccurring hallucination, I was walking alone in the middle of Mars. The vision was neither scary nor happy, it was more alienating and obscure. When I clued on that the dream was like a metaphor for my situation, the vision morphed into a high-speed nightmare full of terror and fear. Suddenly, the experience would plummet into what felt like a slow-motion acid trip. This twilight zone continued back and forth between polarising tempos, until my mind would become completely distorted like an untuned television. Autopilot came to my rescue, and I'd sleepwalk around the ginormous facility on an oblivious exploration of the campus. I couldn't tell you how long these episodes lasted, but I remember coming to in the main pool on campus once, when someone came to my rescue.

Sometimes when I was having these mental breakdowns, I would resort to calling the mother of my doubles partner in the middle of the night. They lived two minutes down the road from the academy. Ever since Marcus and I played each other in a Final of a big tournament when I first moved to the states, the Augustine's opened their doors and took me in like a lost stray. Not only did they do that, but Marcus's mother Grace would regularly come down to the academy in the wee hours of the morning when I was having an episode to see what she could do to help. This empathetic woman seemed to be the only rational person genuinely concerned for my health and safety. Grace could clearly see the insanity of the situation; a petrified child living all by himself over the other side of the world from his family. You would have thought Dad would've been tickled pink about having such a caring family in my corner, only two blocks away from the academy who were willing to take me in when I needed rescuing from myself. But it wasn't the case, as my father hated the idea of me hanging out with Marcus. Max saw him as someone who wasn't invested enough in his tennis and would surely be a bad influence on my game. In his eyes, it defeated the purpose of sending me to there in the first place. For me to be allowed to go off campus with other people, my parents needed to authorise it through the academy. But for whatever reason, my folks never sent through their consent. My only shot at sanity was denied, as it seemed Dad would prefer me to go mad, while being locked in the sporting cage with the other tennis freaks, rather than spending time with domesticated normies. Despite my parents not authorising me to leave the academy, Grace and her family would regularly smuggle me off campus by having me lay down in the boot of their car whenever we went past the security guards at IMG's entrance. This bold woman took matters into her own hands despite the legal ramifications that might occur if she were caught giving asylum to a 12-year-old boy. A courageous gesture I've never forgotten.

I hadn't really spoken about my experience to anyone, so, years later, I found myself confused and disoriented when my psychologist listened intently to my story with a shocked expression, sympathetic reactions, and laughter about the absurdity of the situation. The whole thing had seemed surreal to me, and I only felt the pang after seeing him react to it.

I had become institutionalised by living at the academy and was negatively impacted by the culture and conditions. The problems I had mainly revolved around authority, people, and my perception of the world. I thought humans were just a bunch of innately bad creatures who should really be wiped of the face of the earth. Experience had taught me civilisation was made up of individuals who just wanted power and control over my life for their own gratification. Some did it forcefully, while others did it manipulatively. Some didn't even know they were doing it at all. But by and large, slavery was still a real thing, except now, it was just dressed up in a different way.

It seemed like everyone had an agenda or a bandwagon they wanted you to hop on. When I felt like I was being smothered or indirectly asked to comply with someone else's campaigns or crusades, I took that as a gigantic threat towards my personal freedom and individuality. Because there was always a hidden clause in there somewhere, I took it as my official job to smoke them out, like a social pariah. The curve balls kept coming, as I threw change-up after change-up, to test people's genuineness as if it was a major league sport. Ironically, the only characters I truly trusted were the slippery people who had visibly tasted the pavement, as the shipwrecked seemed to speak more of my language and were liable to look after their own kind.

Even though I was physically free, psychologically I was still imprisoned, and it made me adamant that I'd be the one who controlled life's challenges. The only way for me to solve my dilemma was to become god, but controlling the wind gets to be a tad difficult no matter how much practice you've put in.

## DAMAGE RECEIPT

| Fuck-Up (Cause) | Aftermath (Effect) |
| --- | --- |
| Neglect | Feeling abandoned |
| Obvious class distinctions amongst children | Low self-esteem, judgemental tendencies |
| Mismanagement; poor coordination of the child's life and whereabouts | Fear and feelings of impending doom |
| No oversight of academy life, lack of caretakers/ counsellors | Need to fend for yourself, not able to be vulnerable or rely on anyone else |

### THANK YOU!

My alarming behaviour still wasn't enough for anyone to do anything about, because this is the nature of academies. They don't care about an individual's wellbeing, only about their money-making potential. At a lot of these places, the business model relies on the exploitation of innocent children at the hands of their extreme parents. Of course, it's not sold like that; but if you look at it from the angle I've seen, the kids are pawns in an unethical business transaction between the wicked and the careless. Just because this isn't illegal doesn't mean it's not morally wrong.

## Hook, line and sinker

Let's just say tennis academies had my father at hello. No sales pitch was really required with my old man, as he was the perfect customer for the marketing representatives. It's almost impossible for a fanatical tennis parent to resist the allure of these powerhouse sporting factories. At first glance, they appear to be too good to be true. They've got the A list players, together with some of the best facilities in the world. It's all funded by the regular disbursing customers who pay top dollar to rub shoulders with sporting elites, while the grandiose coaches and money-hungry agents sprinkle fairy dust around the place to swindle the wealthy and disturbed.

All in all, parents don't send their kids to these compounds to have them come back as well-adjusted members of society. The establishments know this and are well-advised in what speaks volumes to their customers; and unfortunately, player welfare tends to be disregarded. Each party seems to assume the wellbeing of the player is the other side's responsibility, so children suffer psychologically in plain sight while no one bats as much an eye. You would think a responsibility like this needs to be established when dealing with minors in one of the most competitive sporting environments in the world. But it isn't, and players who are having trouble coping with the academies' rigorous demands are left to their own devices to survive their radical circumstances.

The bigger the academy, the easier it is to get lost. When I was in the belly of the beast, it felt like the most impersonal place in the world. Everyone had drunk from the Kool-Aid and had become desensitised to acts of child cruelty. I couldn't take my issues to the coaches, agents, or even the academy ground staff, for fear that I would just be prescribed more tennis. It was just a matter of time until most kids either burned out, ran out of money, or figured they were not good enough.

It's been said genetics loads the gun and lifestyle pulls the trigger.

Do I think living at an academy had an impact on me developing an assembly of unhealthy coping mechanisms and mental health issues? Absolutely. Did my upbringing also have something do with it? Absolutely. Each played a pivotal part in the sort of weirdo I turned into. I understand these academies are always going to want to make money, but more care needs to be taken to ensure children aren't put through what I went through. Unfortunately, I am certain academy life is still very much the same, even though it may be packaged differently these days.

```
        IT'S TIME TO PAY YOUR BILL.
     WE HOPE YOU HAD A PLEASANT EXPERIENCE!

     Subtotal:           Alienation
     Tip:                Due diligence
     Total Costs:        Fears and phobias
                         Paranoia
                         Abandonment issues
```

## How do you learn to be mentally tough?

Mental toughness is an asset spoken about and highly sought after in the tennis world.

The only chance players have to adopt this pivotal skill is if the parent has laid the foundations while their child was still young. Although it's questionable how much a kid listens to their parents, what's undeniable is how much they mimic them. The power of a parent's example works like osmosis in the initial stages of childhood, as a kid tends to become what they are most exposed to. So, the player's on-court attitude is generally a direct reflection of the behaviour they've witnessed within their household.

When a parent comes to me losing their cool over their kid not keeping theirs, it's obvious there is a massive discrepancy in behavioural expectations. The child stands very little chance of becoming mentally resilient on the back of their parent's hypocritical requests. Other parents resort to embedding their own version of mental toughness, using fear and abuse as their tools for the job. Many children are spoilt with equipment, lessons and attention, but are rejected and shamed if they do not get the desired result. Then there are the total silver-spoon kids, who are coddled in almost every way and never learn true perspective. Lack of perspective is a common issue in the tennis world, and the tennis parent often tries to overcompensate for the child's lack of life skills by trying to yell the lessons in. I am constantly flabbergasted by the audacity of tennis parents attempting to escape responsibility for their own behaviour, while demanding their children have total control of their own conduct and emotions.

Some years back, I was coaching a promising young junior named William, accompanied by his father, Jose. Jose was trying to be stealthy about his history of antics and deplorable behaviour at the local junior tournaments; however, word circulates quickly in the tennis world, and I soon found out Jose had been banned from all junior events for 18 months. This slippery man came across sweeter than pudding pie, with his cringeworthy handshakes ending up in weird and unnecessary hugs. Surprisingly, Jose's alter ego had slipped past my bullshit detector, and I was thinking maybe he was just a good guy down on his luck.

But when he saw there was a little competition on the horizon, it didn't take too long for his nice guy act to evaporate. Jose started acting like a scorned lover at the sight of me coaching anyone other than his son. Apparently, I was now his intellectual property, and he had the copyright legislation to prove it. He audaciously interrogated me about coaching other players as if I was being unfaithful to his son, citing he was here first, as if he was back in the school playground. Instead of allowing William to work with the other boys I was coaching, Jose snubbed every single one of them, preferring to isolate his son from the so-called enemy. Jose's competitive nature meant he was unable to grasp the fact that being a coach was simply my source of income and my loyalty could not be purchased. I couldn't live off the money Jose was paying me, let alone keep the electricity on, yet he seemed to think he had a say in who I coached and when I coached them.

The man's over-the-top outlook on local competition caused him to crack the whip harder than usual during William's sessions. As a result, the kid started spitting the dummy, ruining our lessons and sending his dad off on an emotional roller-coaster on the side of the court. One in every three sessions was ending in either tears, anger, or resentment.

I regrettably twisted Jose's arm into allowing William to play a set against one of the boys I coached and was secretly pleased when the kid dusted him up. Not that I wanted to see Will lose; I just wanted to see Jose eat his words and hopefully come down off his high horse, back to the planet Earth. But witnessing the aftermath of the scratch match made me feel unforgivably cold-hearted, as Jose terrorised his defenceless son from the match court to the parking lot, while I awkwardly continued to coach students nearby. After publicly humiliating his son on the kerb, he decided to give him some of his greatest hits in the car. The awful situation had an eerie similarity to episodes I regularly went through with my own Dad. Something had to be done.

What was I thinking? I knew what his dad was like, but I didn't think he would take it this badly. I became infected with emotion, wrestling with the idea as to whether it was my place to get involved in the altercation or not. But if not me, I thought, then who? I was the perfect candidate to do something given my resumé of similar suffering. I finished coaching and the Ford Festiva was still sitting there, parked two spaces away from my car. The closer I got to my driver's side door, the more my mind wanted the path of least resistance. But it wasn't to be, as Jose belligerently jumped out of his ride and got straight on the front foot, while his embarrassed son tried to make himself invisible, shrinking into the frontside passenger seat.

After five minutes of tennis parent psychobabble, Jose finally proclaimed, 'He isn't mentally tough enough! He's not able to control his emotions in between the points.' The outrageous statement reeked of hypocrisy and really got under my skin, so I volleyed back, 'How do you think you are going with that yourself, Jose?' This double-standard doofus wasn't used to anyone challenging him about his appalling behaviour while he waved his finger around at the rest of society from his high horse. My question made him come up with one of the most disgustingly hypocritical cliches there is in western civilisation: 'I want my son to do as I say, not as I do!'

## Never mind the body, what about the spirit?

The lifespan of a tennis player is relative to how long their spirit stays intact. Once the soul has been sucked out of a player, they're no longer able to withstand the relentless demands of a tennis schedule. Mental toughness is no longer relevant when a player is despondent and living in despair. Unfortunately, a lot of tennis parents can't differentiate between tough and stupid. Obsessive ambition makes a lot of parents yell offensive orders at children even army officers and boot camp sergeants wouldn't say to their troops. While this unskilled and outdated approach can have early success, it's generally just a matter of time until the player becomes internally depleted and snaps at the parent who's holding the whip. This type of cruel existence heightens disassociation. The children barely keep their sanity by clinging to unhealthy ways to handle thoughts, feelings, and emotions. In my own experience, when I was unable to leave unpleasant or abusive situations, or to fight back, my mind desperately wanted to divert the pain and I found reprieve in disassociating or self-repressing coping mechanisms.

When I was younger, my father would routinely fill a rubbish bin with ice, and I would put my legs in it for recovery. When we were at junior tennis tournaments, he would duck off to the petrol station a couple of times a day and come back to the courts with bags of ice to fill up the bin. Max was adamant to get his money's worth of ice, having me stay in the freezing cold water for as long as possible. It started off with me just putting my legs in, which I understood, then the arms had to go in too which I thought was somewhat reasonable. But next he wanted my bald head in the below zero water and started timing me to see how long I could keep it under. As strange as this event was; to be honest, I was fine with it. The problem with writing about developing dissociative coping mechanisms is I can't remember the events which triggered dissociation, precisely because I dissociated from them. This is just one example of an unpleasant situation I endured at the hands of my father which wasn't quite bad enough to cause damage, but it could have been.

As a coach, I have been in many scenarios in which the tennis parent has wanted me to get stuck into their kid to reinforce their unsympathetic approach. They would shamefully call their kids losers, faggots and soft bitches, while unbelievably asking the coach to assist them with the abuse. My heart goes out to kids in this situation, as they end up getting it from every angle possible. These tennis parents have no social discretion and typically overshare matters which should be kept in-house, abandoning whatever passes for unconditional love at a time when the kid needs their support the most. An accumulation of distasteful events can send a player over the edge. Coaches are frequently put in tough situations and can feel pressured to turn a blind eye to the appalling behaviour of parents in favour of the dollar bill and to avoid a confrontation with a lunatic. The heavy-handed approach is common and almost always backfires on the tennis parent, who misunderstands one of the fundamental components of mental toughness, which is emotional stability.

## Simple disciplinary measures at home set the stage for future success

Tennis parents are renowned for being unreasonable critics of their children, always far too harsh or way too lenient. Now, let's talk about the kids who are allowed to get away with murder. It's utterly unreasonable to ask a coach to teach mental toughness to a kid who has never even been required to carry out simple chores at home, such as putting the bins out or washing the dishes. In a nutshell, mental toughness is about abolishing self-limiting psychological barriers and learning to do things you don't want to do. If you have learnt self-discipline from your upbringing, you are more attuned and capable of grasping these simple but difficult concepts.

Tennis players live a privileged yet problematic life. They are exempt from a lot of day-to-day problems, and at the same time they are pushed to consistently perform and slog it out on the court. This polarising existence means athletes have a lot of doors opened and bags carried for them when they're not busy being ground into a fine powder. In this unbalanced existence, a lot of normal life lessons are missed because they are perceived as irrelevant to the tennis life. A lack of open-mindedness and fear of time missed on the court makes the parent double down on the sport as the tennis parent can't grasp activities outside of hitting balls could be seen as having any value.

Tennis has a snobbish heritage and there is a culture of putting junior players on a pedestal, freeing them from getting their hands dirty in other jobs or chores. In our society, and especially in the tennis world, it has been imprinted in us that it would be humiliating to find ourselves in certain undesirable jobs. What we fail to see is the lesson of hard work these jobs offer. A player's pride and self-image will generally be protected instead of them benefiting from some real-world experience.

The tennis parent's burning desire for their kid to do more and more tennis can turn into an obsession, a sporting illness of sorts. I refer to it as the 'disease of more'. Life lessons get put on the back burner while the disease of more takes over the tennis player's life, with more hitting, more screaming and more of the newest tennis attire. While the young child may be a tennis whiz kid, he or she can be left severely handicapped in other areas of their life. And instead of filling the underdeveloped minor in on some common life skills, the tennis parent prefers to yell them in rather than exposing them to the proper education. This lack of perspective seriously hurts a lot of tennis players, whether they make it in the sport or not. When you hear someone say, 'Think of what the children go through in Africa,' what they are really are saying is, 'Get some perspective.' I believe one of the biggest factors contributing to the lack of mental resilience in juniors is a severe lack of perspective, through no real fault of their own.

The degree to which I had been swamped in self-improvement material from a young age was nothing short of unhealthy. My bedroom walls were decorated with inspirational quotes and handwritten affirmations for me to ruminate over, as Max highly regarded success and pursuits of difficulty to be life's noblest vocation. If I lent him as much as an ear, Dad would have me hooked with elaborate tales about his football and army days, where he spoke about his battle scars like they were his lifetimes achievement. But beneath his fearless, storytelling exterior was a man grappling with the emotional void of unfulfilled dreams, teetering on the brink of losing it all in the pursuit of sporting excellence.

Not knowing how many hours a session would last was like a psychological form of torture. Just when the basket was emptying and I thought we were near the end, I would cringe when I'd hear Dad say, 'Right, let's do another bucket.' Morning turned into day, and days turned into nights. One time we couldn't get the flood lights on, and it was turning pitch black. Dad wasn't done, so he jumped in the front seat of the car and put the headlights on full beam, so I could continue working on my serve for another hour.

How I went in the session determined the sort of treatment I received once I was off the court. It seemed the only luxury I was awarded was in which way I wanted to suffer—at practice, or at home. The subtext was unmistakable: we can do things the hard way, or we can do things the really hard way. When I did well, I was treated like a messiah and pardoned from any chore or duty, leaving the housework to my family while they attended to my every need, like hardworking peasants.

One day, Mum did the unthinkable and had me doing my own dishes when Dad came home. He was appalled with what he witnessed. In his eyes, my hands could potentially get too soft, and I wouldn't be able to hold the racket anymore. His opinion was fine by me. I was being spoiled at home in return for the abuse I was copping on the court. I used this leverage to exploit Dad for the latest sporting gear, but his generosity always came with conditions. 'You can have this new outfit, if you play seven practice sets in a week.' Nothing was ever given in good faith.

I'd come to expect a certain level of absurdity from my father, so I was always ready for the unthinkable, and lived on high alert. My Dad's toxic relationship with his father seriously impacted ours. It warped the way he looked at our relationship as in comparison to what he'd experienced with his violent old man, in his mind we belonged on the Brady Bunch. Bad sessions seemed to stir up his past, bringing up his childhood, and I would hear how I was squandering an opportunity he would have given up a limb for.

Again, by comparison I was coming across as a privileged and entitled kid but how was any of this my fault? I was just dealing with my circumstances to the best of my ability and trying to survive in any way I possibly could. Not just me, but my whole family paid dearly for my 'poor' training sessions, as Dad's hostile energy pervaded the entire house. Once the switch was flicked, everything at home was gloomy and depressing, all because of a stupid game.

Was this meant to make me tougher? Was this meant to make me less entitled? Because all it did was make me angrier. This type of emotional blackmail went on for years, and dealing with myself became harder to contend with. Chewing on feelings was a regular occurrence, and I became accustomed to the taste of raw emotions trickling down the back of my throat.

Since I didn't have the luxury of quitting what I was doing, disassociation came to my salvation, as it was my only real means of survival. It was my mind's way of venturing off into the abyss and leaving my nervous system and subconscious to pick up the slack. This meant nothing was ever properly processed, and the boiling rage and well of unshed tears were just frozen for a later date.

Our training shenanigans could sometimes spill over into civilian territory, when brave onlookers dared to intervene while out for their afternoon stroll with their pets. 'Oi, leave him alone, he's just a kid—pick on someone your own size,' I would regularly hear. It immediately snapped me out of my daydreaming state, as I watched my father get into heated arguments with locals who tried to stand up for someone who couldn't stand up for themselves.

As a result of such confrontations, my human senses spiked, and I would rocket into a higher state of consciousness. People at the local tennis club would stop what they were doing to observe these verbal exchanges, while I stood down the other end of the court from my father, utterly humiliated and wallowing in a severe state of shame. But even though I was embarrassed by my father's behaviour, I still felt a heavy sort of obligation to my old man and wanted to take his side.

Once the uproar had ceased, I was left with adrenaline pulsating through my veins, and the only natural way to discharge it was to lift my intensity to a biblical dimension. The session would be spun on its head and go from a tragedy to a triumph. After some flawless tennis, Dad suddenly had a smile on his face that would light up an asylum. Max would bring me into the net and get me in a brotherly headlock, telling me how proud he was of the adversity I had overcome. He'd reassure me that he was just testing my mental toughness, as if the whole thing was a staged event. As the ordeal propelled me into a state of ecstasy, Dad would continue to tell me his job was to prepare me for some of the toughest players and conditions out there and if I wanted to get to the top of the tennis world, as I did, then this was required. I took him on face value, never questioning what he said. Besides, my mind wanted to purposely forget the unpleasantness, as the car ride home was always a highlight when I was rewarded with whatever I wanted, which was generally loud music, laughs, and McDonald's thick shakes.

The crazy thing about all of this was my father's extreme and unorthodox training methods actually worked. They just came with a huge price tag. When it came to playing matches overseas or against older players who were trying to intimidate me, it never really fazed me because Dad had been a far worse enemy than any other opponent I'd ever faced on the other side of the net.

Sure, for a short time I was match hardened, but the effects of the emotional damage caused by the constant drama soon started to tip the scale. As time went on, I became disenchanted with my father's conduct, and no longer bought the insinuation that his aggressive outbursts and harsh practices were for my benefit. The whole thing seemed like a convenient excuse to justify his inability to control his own emotions.

My fuse was running short from years of manipulation, and the impressive results I had early on in my junior career started to diminish. I went through a long period where I was emotionally unstable before taking to the court, ready to throw the towel in and tank at any sign of resistance from my opponent. As a kid, I would never have dreamt of tanking a match, and now it was a common occurrence. I couldn't comprehend it and I sure couldn't articulate it. I was beaten by myself. To not try on the court is known in tennis as a cardinal sin, and the people who knew me were in disbelief at the 180o turn my career had taken.

In the blink of an eye, my reputation went from a disciplinarian to a degenerate.

Something within me was trying to break through and say something, but it was going to require the opposite of mental toughness to stop this ship from sinking. It was going to require vulnerability.

## Being strong is easy, so how easy is it to be weak?

I knew how to be strong, but I didn't know how or where to let myself be weak. In a fiercely competitive, individualistic environment, the rules of the jungle apply. If you show weakness, you are eaten, so offence is the best defence to keep the wolves at bay.

But I was at a serious crossroads as I couldn't subdue my emotional issues under the fake bravado I was trying to pull off, and I was unravelling at a scary pace. I had zero idea of the personal liberation you could get from expressing your so-called weaknesses to another human being. I didn't even know it was a thing people did. I used to go to town on victims and complainers, as I thought it was the most unmanly thing I had ever heard of. Got an issue? Here's a tissue. I never thought in a million years it would be me needing the box of Kleenex.

I had never witnessed anyone speak about their issues within my family, but I sure had witnessed other people talk about their issues behind their backs. They either bottled them up or blotted them out with a drink. So, I followed in their footsteps and was caught drinking underage at a tournament, when I thought it would be a good idea to take an afternoon dip in the River Murray. I was reprimanded and made to see a psychologist at my national institute. This organisation was throwing my tennis career a lifeline by generously giving me funds to play the national circuit, as my other sponsors had chosen not to renew their contracts with me.

I was taking everything the wrong way and rolled up to the sessions in an 'I love beer' shirt as a 'fuck you' to the psychologist and the process as a whole. Maturity really wasn't on my side back then, and I couldn't grasp the concept of speaking to someone who looked like they hadn't experienced a bad day in their life. I took aim at the people who were trying to help me, and they inevitably and understandably stepped aside and let the hurricane vacate the premises. Looking back, the only thing that would have saved me from myself was doing the exact thing they were encouraging me to do—drop the mental defences, and talk!

'I love beer' shirt

## DAMAGE RECEIPT

| Fuck-Up (Cause) | Aftermath (Effect) |
| --- | --- |
| Contradictory example | Parent's word loses value |
| Spoilt off-court | Take things for granted |
| Mental toughness improperly taught to a minor | Unclear on emotions and feelings, constantly comparing to others |
| Avoidance from other family members | Extreme behaviour is excused until child burns out |

If a tennis parent was serious about instilling true mental toughness in their child, they might consider displaying some themselves. Parents ask me all the time what the difference is between the top guys and the rest of the tour players, and I get nervous about giving them my honest answer because I feel as if they always take what I say out of context. It's as if the tennis parent somehow wants to hear 'mental torment' whenever I say 'mental toughness'.

These people are biased auditors of their children's sporting careers, and generally too extreme in either the lenience or resilience column. On the one hand, spoiling a child is like a delayed form of abuse; but on the other, overkill is just plain abuse. If you saturate a small plant, you don't wake up the next morning to find a tree—you'll find a drowned plant. Trying to yell the lessons into a junior is as pointless as over-watering a daffodil. I believe too much psychological suffering leads a child to dissociation, as a way for them to escape from the cruel demands being made on them. Many athletes seem unable to see situations through a different lens because they've been type-cast as a tennis player for their entire life. This generally means the player's perspective on particular problems cannot be altered, because they don't have any other real-world experience against which to compare their issues.

```
              IT'S TIME TO PAY YOUR BILL.
          WE HOPE YOU HAD A PLEASANT EXPERIENCE!

        Subtotal:     A distaste for your parents
        Tip:          Congruency
        Total Costs:  Likely candidate for depression
                      Likely candidate for bipolar disorder
                      Unsocialised
```

## Summary

Misconceptions mean misunderstandings. This inevitably leads to people making mistakes. There are no second chances or restarts when it comes to the sport of tennis. The parent takes the risk, and then the child must live with the results. There is more on the line than just the child's sporting career, yet the tennis parent's ability to make rational decisions for their child is generally heavily influenced by hearsay or misconceptions.

A person's future usually depends on their education, and when tennis parents impulsively pull their kid out of school to do correspondence, they'd better pray the child becomes a tennis player, because life on other side of the coin normally isn't pretty.

Environment heavily determines what sort of personality a player develops, and becoming institutionalised at some of the money-making operations that pose as academies can very often negatively influence a child's character and their sense of normality.

And last, but not least: psychological resilience. It's hypocritical to ask a child to do something you cannot do yourself. Kids are visual learners, and they need examples from parents to properly show them how to do what is being asked of them. My aim is to get the parent to properly understand the massive responsibility on their shoulders, because if they don't tread carefully when it comes to the matters discussed here, my history could become your kid's future.

## Misconceptions—a side note

As you were reading this chapter, you may have noticed I left something out that needs to be noted, a little thing called confirmation bias. Now, it doesn't matter who you are or where you come from, if you are human, you are biased. And before you start ridiculing me or yourself for talking about this, just know confirmation bias generally happens unintentionally. Studies have shown people are biased towards confirming their already existing beliefs, and this natural human tendency stops people from investigating matters from a position of neutrality.

This theory ties in with my experience when it comes to tennis parents and their selective awareness. They almost always see what they want to see and hear what they want to hear. I've witnessed tennis parents inaccurately interpreting what I was saying to their child; and I only ever hear these individuals talk about theories that support their pre-existing beliefs. Because of this bias on the part of their parents, a lot of players lose freedom of choice and become passengers on the way to their own demise. This is excused because it is easily disguised as the child's own desire to be a professional tennis player. The culprits blatantly ignore any sort of evidence that proves their motives and desires are wrong. I have even seen parents' predetermined beliefs get stronger when faced with confirmation proving their existing ideas to be flawed. Which brings me to my next chapter on delusion! But first…

## Caught in the crossfire

Even people who aren't involved in the tennis journey can be greatly impacted merely by association. One big regret of mine is that there is a chance my sister got caught in the crossfire of my sporting career. The following story is my take on the turn of events. She may see things differently.

I thought the fact Tiffany and I both survived the family holocaust as kids would make us thick as thieves as adults. And it did for a while in an overly dependent fashion; but ultimately it ended up turning us into rivals. Well, that's how it felt to me anyway, and I can hardly blame her after a childhood where she was overlooked and underappreciated in comparison to me and my tennis talents.

When I walked off the sporting cliff at 17 and resurfaced back home, the tide had suddenly turned in Tiffany's favour. Not that I think she wanted to see me fail with my tennis, but its deterioration confirmed her case that our childhood was a colossal fuck up which she could hold over my parents' heads. Since my mother already felt terribly guilty about the treatment Tiffany had received because of my sporting career, Mum was terminally indebted to her neglected daughter and readily accommodated her quest for world domination. My Dad never paid any attention to the family politics and immediately went back to what he knew best, by coaching my youngster sister, Olivia, as she was now the new chosen one.

*who has the biggest trophy?*

I descended on the family home like an unexpected meteor from outer space that no one could possibly prepare for. Although I had a passport which said I'd been travelling around the world for the past six years, to me it almost felt like I'd been in the same place the whole time. The rinse and repeat cycle robbed me of any memories and all that remained were blurred snapshots of hotel rooms, arguments, and tennis courts. I was on a highway to a new freedom, so I thought, as normal life looked like heaven from my prison in the tennis world.

However, I came to find what I saw was just a mirage, and without the game of tennis masking our domestic dilemmas, resentments festered to unfathomable heights. It didn't take long for the family dynamic to disintegrate into smithereens and the consequences of my risky pursuit of sporting stardom became apparent. I guess my family felt it had already cost them enough, so they dodged the penalties and left me high and dry once again. Even though we were clearly on the road to ruin, Mum never quit when it came to keeping up appearances. God bless her, she was like one of those musicians on the Titanic who kept performing when the sinking ship was nearly fully under water.

A lifetime's worth of avoidance and artificial happiness for appearances sake had created a toxic energy, lingering like a black cloud over everyone's head. Small things turned into big things, as dirty dishes and misplaced socks could set in a full-scale riot. Having spent the better part of my life in weird and unsavoury environments, I could see I was going to need to upgrade my survival skills to ninja level if I was going to make it through this emotional minefield. Avoidance became my speciality. So much so that I could evade people in the house for weeks, even though we lived under the same roof.

Tiffany saved up $500.00 and bought herself a second-hand car. After being an uninterested father for most of Tiffany's life, Dad took just enough of an interest to be infuriated he wasn't consulted about the purchase of the vehicle. The household blew up and Tiffany was the first evictee to exit the premises. She went underground for a few months and finally resurfaced, asking me if I was keen to get out of the family home. After a few false starts, I gathered a garbage bag full of gear and started crashing with Tiffany at a rental she couldn't afford.

I had done my fair share of bouncing around from place to place, but nothing compared to this. Tennis was a professional endeavour, whereas this escapade was generated sheerly out of desperation and the need for survival. I was intoxicated by the illusion I was like the castaway character, Ryan, from the TV show The OC. Getting by was a day-to-day proposition which certified our bond in a co-dependent kind of way. But Tiffany most certainly was the ringleader in our army of two. In no way, shape or form was she willing to take a backseat to anyone, and I'd always been ruled or dictated to by something or someone, so being under the thumb of my sister felt familiar. Besides, I was a novice when it came to normality and needed a temporary tour guide to show me around the place.

As much as I loved my sister, Tiffany secretly scared the shit out of me.

She had a permanent scowl written across her face, and at times had dark hollows under her eyes that could easily pass for fading shiners. And underneath her brazen exterior resided a variant of her father's temperament which she would vehemently deny. Having said that, Tiffany was also generous to a fault and someone who you would always want in your corner if it ever came to blows. When I did as I was told, I was rewarded with all sorts of unnecessary gifts as a token for my obedience. Not having two cents to rub together meant I was happy to have a sugar mamma for a sister. Seeing I had leased out my soul so many times before, I saw no harm in being purchased once more for old times' sake. Better the devil you know, I thought, as my sister seemed like my only real lifeline if I wanted to start over and escape the wreckage of my past.

I'd been groomed to be the perfect Robin to an egotistical Batman and fortunately for my sister, all the wires and connections had already originated during my tennis golden years of chronic people-pleasing. Part of being a freeloader meant I was sometimes required to act as Tiffany's muscle, by doing all sorts of dirty deeds for her. She asked me to paint "Die pigman" on the fence of some guy's house in the city in the middle of the night. This was the maddest mission yet, but she was very persuasive and I, strangely, looked forward to showing off a newly borrowed streetwise persona. I waited till a few minutes after midnight and hopped out of the car wearing all black, with a couple buckets of paint like Picasso, ready to smear my masterpiece. Tiffany was the getaway driver/architect for my artwork, and she whispered her creative advice from the car. 'Put an exclamation point at the end of pigman,' she said. I remember thinking a couple of cans of spray-paint wouldn't have gone astray. Leaving the scene of the crime, we felt like a couple of career criminals who had just pulled off a dangerous heist. No longer than 48 hours later I was the lead suspect for the crime, as Tiffany's loose lips set off a sequence of events that got very hairy.

I've always tended to get into ride-or-die relationships. There is something more familiar and romantically dangerous about this kind of toxic scenario that's simultaneously scary and exciting. Having never learnt healthy boundaries, I had an overdeveloped sense of responsibility to matters that really had nothing to do with me. My level of understanding when it came to appropriateness was near non-existent. I would go in further than most and expect more than I probably should. Our Bonnie and Clyde relationship started to fracture when I began hanging around other people. I could clearly sense that outsiders weren't necessarily welcomed. It was played off as a bit of a childhood joke thing; but anytime I was getting close with a friend, it felt like Tiffany would try and sabotage it, in one way or another.

I put up with it as long as I could, but then other people I was hanging around with started to feel uncomfortable with the vibe they were picking up when my sister was nearby. The whole thing came to a head when Tiffany banned my first girlfriend from coming around because she said she was too boring. I think our childhood affected the way Tiffany looked at relationships. To her it was a contest of elimination, a fight to the end to be the most important person left standing. All those years of feeling second best to me and my tennis warped her understanding and outlook of what it meant to be a sister and a friend. It wasn't a competition or the survival of the fittest, and it wasn't personal, but that's how she made you feel about it. You either chose her, or she would kick you to the kerb so quickly it would make your head spin.

I began feeling like an unfaithful husband, lying about where I was and who I was with just to keep my sister off my back. The final conflict that ended our comradery happened on a disastrous night out when Tiffany stopped the car in the middle of a city street to throw a flurry of haymakers at me, because I was drunk and didn't want to go to a coffee shop. Whatever it was we had going on, it was over.

I immediately filled my garbage bag back up with my clothes

and hit the highway once again. I wasn't really seasoned for a life of eviction notices and baked beans on toast, so I went back to the family home with my tail between my legs. Sleeping in my own bed felt heavenly compared to the wiry and sheetless mattress at my sister's joint, but I did stay up all night thinking about Tiffany and wondering what she was doing. Her childhood didn't sit well on my conscience, and I felt I was partially responsible as my tennis got all our parents' attention, and then my sporting career went nowhere. I didn't get a chance to repay her for what she went through.

A few years later when my parents were divorced, Tiffany decided to move back into the family house. By this time, I was really clutching at straws in terms of establishing something looking even vaguely like a reasonable life. Tiffany, on the other hand, was now a corporate warrior climbing the ladder in the business world. In celebration of her newly found career, my sister did a victory lap at home and made up for the attention she once missed out on by suffocating me and our younger sister in her recent success. Business cards, office jobs and cubical slaves can seem like the pinnacle of maturity when you've grown up wildly unconventional. Tiffany fell into this train of thought, and influenced my mother into thinking the same, which wasn't a hard sell. Anyone who didn't measure up to Tiffany's idea of acceptability was societal trash, and I felt like I fell into the long list of losers who were snobbishly ridiculed during dinner service. Karmic forces had swung the pendulum in Tiffany's favour, and I was now getting a taste of what my tennis once did to her. I couldn't compete with Tiffany in a capitalist society, as I was busy dodging other bullets coming my way. Life had me against the ropes and I was just trying to survive the onslaught.

It is tough to agree on the best course of action to take with an alcoholic who is clearly ruining their own life. Misfired help can disrupt an addict more than you think and give them extra incentive to carry on killing themselves with death by instalments. I was astounded everyone had an opinion on what they thought I should do with my life, but never acknowledged my past or validated my pain. But rebelling didn't get me the apology I was desperately after, and in fact, they felt I owed them an apology for what I'd put them through when I was drunk. That's the great thing about blanking out from drinking—you don't remember it, while everyone else can't forget it.

I knew I drank differently to others, and while my immediate family weren't alcoholics, they sure did a good job of imitating them at times. Piss-ups were a usual thing, but all in all, I probably spilt more grog than they've ever drunk in their entire life. I guess the difference was they would drink excessively while I would drink compulsively. I must say, I was a little let down I was the only alcoholic to fly the flag for the Ley name, given the problem was littered though the male side of our lineage. And I thought it was laughably hypocritical that someone could hint at me to watch my boozing just because they could binge drink in a safer fashion than I could. I'll show them, I thought, and defiantly drank till I ended up 'liquor-dating' all my assets. I thought I was in control of my own actions and decisions, but I was merely a passenger. Alcohol was mercilessly controlling me from the safety of the bottle

*Half naked arm wrestling at a family Christmas piss up*

PART 3

# Delusion

**To be wrong is human, to be delusional is fatal**

Misconceptions and delusions may sound similar but there are big differences. Misconceptions are perpetuated by institutions and society, whereas delusion flies in the face of facts, and you believe dogma despite everyone and everything saying otherwise. We can forgive tennis parents for believing misconceptions, but it's your best bet to stay away from a delusional one.

We see many parents who fall victim to delusional thinking. These otherwise well-established and respected people in various areas of life, could be classified as clinically insane when it comes to tennis. Even when educated on crucial topics that are classed as sporting suicide, some parents' unrealistic dreams for their child's sporting career persist, as fantasy often wins over the universal truths of tennis. These delusional tennis parents continue to march to the beat of their own drum, and the child ultimately pays the price for the parents' fantasy.

In this part we explore some of the delusions of tennis parents, such as their unrealistic expectations of what federation bodies provide. The great forfeit. What is the cause of the significant increase in numbers of juniors withdrawing from tournaments and matches? And the on-court volume assault that has been a topic of conversation for decades.

## Is your child the best tennis player who never plays?

If I told you I wanted my son to be one of the best actors in the world, but I don't want him to act in front of people, what would you say? Dreaming, right? Well in tennis we witness this type of delusion everywhere; parents proclaiming their child's superiority and predicting their imminent success while not even participating in local tournaments. But why would a parent do such a thing when it's common knowledge that you can't become a professional tennis player without playing matches?

If you want to be Number 1 in the world, how about you try being Number 1 in your club first? There is nothing wrong with dreaming big, but at some point, the tennis parent and player need to get in touch with their own smallness in the tennis world. If the player had participated in local competition instead of thinking they were above it, they might have had the humbling realisation they were not all their parents had made them out to be. Losing tennis matches in your own state should serve as a constant reminder there is plenty of work to do if you are thinking about a career on the world stage. Unfortunately, many don't realise this until it's too late, when the player doesn't make the professional ranks after many years of now obviously pointless training.

Tennis has become an epidemic of forfeiting and withdrawing from tournaments and matches, to keep the fairy tale from being deflated. The saying 'the scoreboard doesn't lie' isn't lying. It gets difficult for a delusional tennis parent to swear black is green when their child is getting towelled up out at the local tournaments, although I have seen a few of these shifty parents try and put a spin on a 6/2 6/1 score line. 'Every game went to deuce' and 'it was only a couple of points here or there' are the usual analyses of a tennis parent who has their head in the clouds. Don't get me wrong, you can play well against a stronger opponent and be flogged, but ultimately 6/2 is not a competitive set.

These biased parents desperately want their children to avoid places of truth and reality at all costs. The tennis parent is swept up in irrelevant pressure-free training sessions where a player can appear much better than they truly are, creating a false belief. Practice becomes the new problem as all sorts of weird fascinations and nonsensical ideas start to appear when a kid is not playing enough matches. Tennis is one of the most skilful, competitive and psychologically demanding sports you can play, and unfortunately training sessions don't even scratch the surface when it comes to the level of pressure a player will encounter on a match court. Most of the gimmicky training players undergo is a total waste of time and isn't transferable into their match play. In fact, training so irrelevantly makes an athlete more anxious and less able to access the necessary tools required on the match court. That's why, in my eyes, practicing is for the pretenders.

But try telling that to Flavia, the tennis parent of a girl I was coaching. I had the pleasure of being Flavia's sloppy seconds once she'd made the rounds of every other coach in town. She was quick on the draw in telling me she was once a prolific handball coach in her motherland, so she and I were equals as sporting authorities. Her narcissism was already registering on my tennis parent Richter scale, and it wasn't long before it was clear she was the one coaching her daughter. We started to warm up with the mother standing on the side of the court with the ball tube, doing her absolute best to look casual and not show her fangs that would come out soon enough.

I look at tennis coaching like dentistry—some people need a clean out and others need complete dental reconstruction. It all depends on what they look like at the initial consultation. Flavia's daughter was mysteriously alternating between a one-handed backhand that looked as fragile as a house of cards and a two-hander backhand that you could tell was a more reliable and trustworthy shot. I brought the pair of them into the net to discuss the call to action. But just before I opened my mouth, Flavia said, 'I want her to play like Boris Becker.' As she got her iPhone out of her pocket, she continued, 'I want her to have a one-hander backhand and a two-hander backhand, just like this.' She showed me a video of her daughter walloping an unrealistic backhand on a rundown court. She then entered a delusional state, and told me, 'When my daughter goes over to the December showdown, where she will obviously win the U/18 final 6/0 6/0, I want her to be able to hit single-handed backhand winners and double-handed backhand winners. I want poetic annihilation. Can you imagine what this will do to the other girls confidence, Todd? It will smash their spirit.'

The only person's spirit this was smashing was mine. Flavia's daughter didn't know what her mother was advocating for was a death wish. So, to sober the woman up from her sporting psychosis, I played points against her daughter until I broke her backhand down in only a matter of minutes. People need personal evidence to awaken them to truth, and I was hoping this demonstration would humble the highly opinionated handball coach into using her eyes and her ears more than her big mouth. But Flavia's attachment to the images of her imagination didn't allow reality to intrude, and she became furious with her daughter for not hitting the shot 'properly' as she had done when it was just the two of them.

I told Flavia her technique needed to be realistic, and it needed to be repeatable. Flashiness and flare are the icing on the cake but tennis ultimately rewards simplicity. More for the dough and less for the show. Despite trying my hardest to reason with Flavia about her flawed ideas for her daughter's diverse backhand, she still couldn't seem to swallow it and defiantly disagreed. I told her the postman can probably hit a good ball if you feed it to him in practice, but it's in matches you find out if things hold up. The word 'matches' instantaneously triggered Flavia into playing defence, and she said, 'I can't force her to play any matches, Todd.' To which I replied, 'But you pulled her out of school to be a tennis player, Flavia. That's like me going to university, studying for the whole year and then purposely not sitting the exams.' Flavia's justification for why her daughter couldn't play any matches could have won her an Academy Award that day, as she came up with a litany of excuses. And her inability to ingest a slice of the humble pie on offer cost her daughter a career in the sport where she showed a lot of promise and natural ability.

A lot of tennis parents believe they can protect their sporting fairy tale by cherry picking stronger opponents and tournaments, instead of playing against comparative competition. They will often choose for their child to play above their age group, so the reasons for losing are seemingly justifiable. When faced with an equal or lesser opponent, a forfeit or withdrawal is always on the cards. Forfeiting is a symptom of fear. The child's fear that their parent will be disappointed, and the tennis parent's fear of being divorced from their grandiose delusion. Not playing is a clear tap out that no one believes, but it suits both child and parent perfectly. 'Tournament shopping' is now a thing. Players will enter tournaments and wait to see who is in the draw and only take the court if they are playing someone against whom it is okay to lose to. In the rare occasions matches against an opponent of similar standard are played and the child loses, the tennis parent takes the loss harder than the kid and can often be found still wallowing in self-pity 48 to 72 hours after the match.

Then there's the tennis parent's hypothetical match calculator: they compare scores and situations, to calculate where the child sits in their imagining of the scheme of things. Instead of playing and letting the results take care of themselves, the parent prefers a more illogical way of determining where their child is at and what they are projected to achieve: 'my kid beat this kid, and that kid beat this kid, and he got to the quarter finals of that tournament, so that means they should be here.' Despite these calculations being purely speculative, it allows for a delusional mind to get lost in never-never land. I wouldn't be surprised if a parent turned the idea into an app at some stage. This kind of equation is completely non-beneficial and irrelevant. It's like an extra in a movie saying they could be a movie star because they've been on set with Tom Cruise. Just because I beat Del Potro as a junior, and he then went on to defeat Roger Federer to win the 2009 US Open, it doesn't mean I could have won the US Open. But it sure is a good party trick.

A parent who needs their child to win, ultimately loses in the long run because this type of external pressure is too much for most athletes to handle. Truth be told, the freedom to fail, is the greatest gift a junior tennis player can be granted by their parents. But unfortunately coming across a detached tennis parent is as rare as spotting a white unicorn. With the high demand of tournaments and quality of competition, it is almost guaranteed you will take a loss every week on the professional circuit. So, there are plenty of athletes ranked in the top 50 who have never won ATP titles before. I obviously can't speak for anyone else but I'm sure these players sleep just fine at night knowing they are multimillion-dollar losers. So, it's fundamental to develop a resilience to matches and get used to different pressures if you are serious about becoming professional. In my opinion, the earlier the kid can take a bad loss to someone they are expecting to beat, the better, both for the kid and for the tennis parent. Because losing your way to the top is the only way forwards. Instead of avoiding competition, get some bad losses out of the way as early as possible!

## The dreaded dinner to dish the dirt on Dimitri's dream

It was time for the dreaded sit down with Dimitri to discuss his son's future. I had to break bread with the fickle father and try to meet him halfway on some of the terms and conditions for coaching his golden child. I'm a nervous wreck when it comes to meetings as communication has never been one of my strong points, and I find it difficult to say something contentious without becoming too emotional. Being a crippling empath means I tend to take responsibility for everyone's feelings, including people I don't necessarily like.

I've never belonged in a boardroom or felt at home in any office space for that matter. What can I say, typing keyboards, waiting rooms, and people wearing suits and lanyards tend to give me the willies. So, God only knows why I agreed to meet Dimitri at his engineering headquarters in the heart of the city. I got warmed up for the meeting as if I was about to square off against Conor McGregor in a UFC cage fight. The preliminary endorphins made me courageous in thought, but as the opening bell dawned, I felt myself reverting to my natural default, where I become verbally cautious and cowardly in action.

'Tennis Australia is going to give my son a million dollars,' Dimitri said, and I nearly choked on my piping hot herbal tea. Until this point, the somewhat level-headed, ex amateur fighter, had done a decent job of hiding his true colours, but this comment revealed the severity of his delusions. This was the first time I had a chance to find out his ideas and opinions about his son's future. I tried to educate him about the sort of involvement federation bodies have when it comes to funding junior players, but he disagreed. He declared his son was more talented than any other junior player in the country, and the national selectors would obviously notice that. 'He hits the ball bigger than Berdych, Todd.'

Frustrated and unimpressed by his bravado, I informed Dimitri Australia was the tennis home of hopefuls and has-beens and reminded him he had lost in the 2nd round of the consolation of the U/12s nationals just seven weeks earlier. He kept referring to boxing analogies that had no similarities to the topic or tennis whatsoever. The unrelated generalisations kept on coming, almost as if he was desperate to make me aware that he was worthy of my respect by trying to solidify his status as a former sportsman.

Dimitri was living in a world of delusional optimism, and he was inviting me to come and play in his magical playground full of irrational ideas and ridiculous opinions. His mannerisms and facial expressions altered when he was extrapolating his sons prospects, speaking in tongues like some sort of sporting mystic. But I wasn't buying a word of it. At this point, his son was just potential. He had no runs on the board as far as results go. He was no one from nowhere in terms of being on Tennis Australia's radar or the world scale. He was just a boy who was improving and benefiting from a healthy environment I had created at a local club.

But Dimitri's imagination seemed to see things differently. He was like an unchained kite that wanted to fly off into the wide blue sky and it was difficult to keep him grounded in truth and reality for more than a matter of minutes. Instead of processing the proposal I had come to talk about, he suggested a very different idea. Dimitri wanted to make a documentary about his son they could send around to management companies and potential sponsorship investors, promoting him as an Iranian immigrant living in the outback, as if we were putting in an application for a contestant on a reality TV show. He wanted me to source credible contacts to vouch for his son via performing monologues in his documentary titled The Last Ace.

Things were never the same after the meeting. Our failure to get on the same page saw Dimitri move back to an ex-coach for the third time, and he happily played the part of stage manager in the fairy tale of The Last Ace.

## DAMAGE RECEIPT

| Fuck-Up (Cause) | Aftermath (Effect) |
| --- | --- |
| Exceptionalism | A false illusion of self; unbreakable rules didn't apply to his daughter |
| Stubborn | Chased his own fantasy down a dead-end rabbit hole |
| Delusional | Wouldn't listen to professional advice about a professional path |
| Lack of humility | More important for him to be respected than open-minded |

**THANK YOU!**

This was one of my first experiences of extensively working with a junior, and the relationship going tits up. I had to walk it off for a long while. Once it was over, I realised I too had been delusional and living vicariously through Dimitri's son, seeking redemption from my own failed career. I was no better than he was. The delusion had us both acting out of character, falling victim to a fairy tale played on repeat in our own fantasy lands. My wishful thinking meant I had a reason to do the extra hour and charge next to nothing, as I wanted payback at the sport that chewed me up and spat me out.

We couldn't seem to marry his monetary agenda with my personal vendetta, and ended up duelling it out over a passive-aggressive text fight not long after he told me about his blockbuster documentary masterpiece. In retrospect, it was a crying shame the way the partnership ended, as his son's tennis existed but never progressed after the split. Spielberg and his son now remain in tennis's witness protection program, never to be seen or heard from again!

There is no point hitting a ball back and forth against a brick wall, dreaming of being the best tennis player in the world. To be a professional at anything, you need to put yourself to the test; so, in the case of tennis, the parent needs to be okay with their child losing the battle, for them to have any chance of winning the war. I could only imagine how depressing it would be to look back on a lifetime of purely training, knowing you never really laid it all on the line. It's better to shoot and miss than to live with regret. At least that way you have a story to tell and something meaningful to look back on, rather than bitterness and memories of hours upon hours of backyard training. Instead of aiming high and not playing local tournaments, it is essential to learn to set the bar low enough in terms of expectations and embrace the bumps along the way. A tennis parent's delusion will divert any true path to the goal and send their child sailing off without orientation. The bigger the goal, the smaller the steps, and not playing is NOT a step.

```
          IT'S TIME TO PAY YOUR BILL.
      WE HOPE YOU HAD A PLEASANT EXPERIENCE!

      Subtotal:      No chance of becoming professional
      Tip:           Play matches
      Total Costs:   Resentment
                     Confusion
                     An unshakable case of regret
```

## The problem with desiring sexy technique

When your child signs up for elite tennis, it is important to understand that it is a competitive sport that rewards one winner. The court is a lonely place where there is nowhere to hide and no one to pass the ball to; the buck starts and ends with you. Strategies and technique are fundamental to a tennis player expanding their capabilities, but they reach a ceiling once moulded. The philosophy of learn it, own it, use it is a great concept that eventually tests the practised skills under match conditions. Often the tennis parent spends too much time in the first phase and loses themselves to technique, disproportionately prioritising the polishing of technique that has already been polished. This tends to suit both parent and player perfectly, as practising more is the most convenient way of avoiding the ruthlessly unforgiving circumstances of competition.

'Talented' is one of the most over-used and unhelpful words in relation to tennis. While a player must possess a natural sense of the craft they are pursuing, talent always seems to be next door neighbours with complacency, which is in the same suburb as laziness and cool. It tends to signify a certain sort of sporting self-righteousness that often debilitates a junior's ambition to fight. A tennis parent can over-sensationalise how a player looks in comparison to their on-court demeanour. Aiming to have the Andy Roddick serve, or Stan Wawrinka backhand is not a bad thing when it's kept in context. However, in my experience, imitation tends to send the player down a rabbit hole of becoming an imposter. An athlete is much better off doing what comes natural to them, (within reason) rather than duplicating another player's technique. A failure from a junior to really grasp the grunt and grind of the sport generally leads to them making excuses when things go wrong under the bright lights of a match. Having spent too much time prioritising technique gives a player a false concept of what the sport is about, and when faced with adversity under match conditions, the technique stands up but their ability to compete lets them down.

Instead of just accepting defeat or taking personal responsibility after a loss, parents and kids look for someone else to hold accountable. The delusional parent will scapegoat, lie, justify or blame any other third party to keep the tennis fantasy breathing. Endless injuries, accusations of others cheating, denunciation of the coach, poor conditions, and the opposition's unfair strategies are just some of the consistent excuses endlessly used by a delusional tennis parent after a child's loss. The number of times I hear from a player or a parent complaining about how the opposition's family were supporting their kid during a match is absurd.

Let me spell this one out loud and clear. If you can't handle your opponent's parents clapping during matches, you shouldn't try becoming a professional tennis player. Instead of learning from the defeat, going back to the drawing board and improving what was exposed in the match, the junior simply takes their pick from one of the many excuses the parent has created for them to avoid taking responsibility for their own result. The delusional tennis parent goes around falsely making their child a victim of unfair circumstances to protect the sporting fairy tale, so much so that both become renowned around town for making enemies and stepping on people's toes. I use the expressions 'special snowflake' or 'terminal uniqueness' to describe this type of tennis parent and player; they both have a faulty belief system that makes them think they are somehow special or better than the rest of the players, without ever proving it on match day. They may look better technically, but tennis isn't figure skating, and you don't get rewarded for doing things prettier in our sport. Despite the evidence, this type of tennis parent continues to bang on about how naturally talented their child is technically. And while that may be, it doesn't change the fact the kid shows very little fight on the match court.

You generally find delusional tennis parents hanging around the local tournaments, taking a swipe at the federation coaches and state officials for their children not winning enough matches. It must be someone else's fault for their kid not winning, and the state coaches are always easy pickings for a parent who is looking for someone to blame. These parents have a surreal interpretation of what state coaches and federation bodies provide. The federation have eggs in many baskets, and run local squads for the masses, so they don't have the time to focus on your special snowflake.

I'm not flying the flag for these coaches, but I do think it's ridiculous to expect them to part the Red Sea and get your kid to walk on water. Not even the celebrity coaches would be able to get most of these kids to compete at a decent level, because parents and players have purposely fooled themselves into prioritising technique as they both fear the piercing reality of a match court. Even when the terminally unique kid makes it into the state program, the parent isn't satisfied, as they want their child to receive special treatment over the rest of the state players. The dissatisfied parent foolishly lets their tongue fly, ripping the state coaches to other people in the tennis bubble, and they inevitably pass this information onto the next person like a sporting Chinese whisper. The bad mouthing almost always finds its way to its target, and by the time the caning gets there, it generally has extra venom on it from the additional exaggerations other tennis parents have applied to it. With the odds of becoming a tennis player so heavily stacked against you, making enemies with people who can open doors is just about the silliest thing you could ever do. When the possibility of an overseas trip arises or a wild card into a tournament is available, parents go from bagging to begging national selectors.

## A permanent pitstop

'I don't want Regina to have the Kokkinakis forehand, I want her to have the Federer forehand' said Miguel the truck driver as he poorly imitated Roger's swing. His daughter was standing next to him with poor, sunken posture, totally humiliated by her father's antics, while being dressed head to toe in the latest Nike athleisure. Regina was a part-time tennis player, whose dad thought she should have a professional-looking game. But under no circumstances must her forehand look like Kokkinakis Miguel kept declaring. Ay, ay, Roger that, I thought. Regina was doing well for the amount of time she committed to the sport, but her father was making unhealthy comparisons with other players who were doing five times as much as she was. In Miguel's eyes, her forehand, which was technically pretty good, needed open-heart surgery then and there.

He then proceeded to crucify Regina's past coach and attributed her forehand fiascos to training at another club. 'Tell him, Regina. Tell Todd how much you want it,' said the tone-deaf truckie. But his withdrawn daughter just stood there with a deadpan expression on her face, while we uncomfortably waited for her reply. Finally, I blurted something out, just to kill the sheer awkwardness of the deadly silence. Now that Miguel was through putting his two cents in and interrupting the session, I told Regina to go back and try the type of forehand her father wanted her to hit.

Regina shuffled back to the baseline like a Southpark character and gave me a ready position that looked like a retired person waiting for a bus on pension day. Not wanting to be held responsible for Regina's utter disinterest, I overcompensated by turning my coaching voice up to max capacity as I yelled, 'All right, Regina, you ready for this?' The girl gave me a glare that suggested she may murder me somewhere in the future, but I fed the ball anyway because that's what I get paid to do. The next three forehands went in this very sequence:

back fence, back fence, bottom of the net. Miguel was all over her like a cheap suit as Regina stood there copping a mouthful from a bloke who looked like he would be more comfortable at the front bar having a punt.

I was caught in the middle of a Mexican standoff between an imaginative fantasist and an unresponsive part-timer. Miguel wasn't just intruding on my session now; he was practically running it by trying to teach the apple of his eye something he had no idea about and couldn't do himself. My affliction shifted from a sense of responsibility to rage at how little I'd decided to charge Miguel for my expertise. In this instance, a 15 percent tennis parent tax really should have been added to the total cost of the session. I pulled the night rider aside and him with a shit sandwich. That's a nice comment as a light entrée to whet the palate, followed by a main course full or rare facts and figures, followed by something sweet to wash down the residual taste of shit that may still be sweltering in his mouth.

'Miguel don't get me wrong. I really enjoy coaching your daughter and I can see what you're saying about her undeniable natural talent. The thing is, you have come here to pay me to coach your daughter, and you are now doing 90% of my job for me, which you're not good at and your daughter hates. How about this? The coach coaches, the player plays, and the parent does the parenting. For everyone's sanity, I'm going to have to ask you to watch from outside of the court.'

Miguel's bloodshot eyes dilated as he stepped into striking range and said, 'I've told you guys here, I don't want you coaching my daughter the Kokkinakis forehand, all right? I know you ruined his shoulder.' In a knee-jerk reaction, I threw my racket as far as I could over the fence and embarked on a long excursion to go and get it. Miguel started following me. He asked where I was going. I said, 'I am getting as far away from you as possible, mate.' Poor Regina stood by the fence stunned at what was unfolding. As I headed out the gate, I said, 'Good luck, man.' I grabbed my racquet and continued walking around the block to try clear my head before my next lesson.

I came back 20 minutes later with more of my wits about me, to see Miguel apologetically signalling a peace treaty by humorously waving a white towel above his head. He wanted to put out the fire, but both of us had crossed an ethical line that hadn't been previously imposed but should have been.

I put on my best adult voice, diplomatically telling Miguel I was no longer able to coach his daughter. No hard feelings and no regrets. Again, his bloodshot eyes became more noticeable, but this time they started to quiver and make moisture.

He put his hands on his knees in a fit of emotionalism, for what seemed like an eternity. I awkwardly moved closer to Miguel, unsure whether to console him or not. He looked up at me from a near-foetal position, with tears streaming down his face, repeating the same sentence in a remorseful tone: 'I only wanted the Roger Federer forehand.' As I uncomfortably waited for the hydrant to stop flowing, I looked over at his daughter Regina and shrugged at her, as if to say what should I do? Regina was a different kind of expressionless as she tucked her chin into her neck and inspected the pavement, while my next lesson joyfully walked through the gate with her usual greeting of, 'HIIIIIIIII TODDDDDDD.' Miguel's emotional meltdown showed no sign of ending and was now bleeding into my next client's session, so I intuitively sidled over to the sobbing transporter and decided to console him with a slow pat on the back. After a bit more waterworks, he and Regina finally jumped back in their semi-trailer and Miguel honked the horn as they left the local club.

Months later, just after coaching hours when I was packing up the club, I was surprised when Miguel the truck driver came, hat in hand, supplying kids from the club with super slushies and McDonalds Chicken Nuggets, for any damages he might have caused.

## DAMAGE RECEIPT

| Fuck-Up (Cause) | Aftermath (Effect) |
| --- | --- |
| Unfair comparisons | Unrealistic expectations |
| Delusional | Son stops playing tennis |
| Not allowing coach to do their job | No chance of change |

## THANK YOU!

Tennis parents fail to see when the likes of Nadal or Djokovic continually win tough matches, it's not their technique per se that gets them over the line, but their personality and character. These guys have cultivated their mindset through years of being healthily encouraged to compete as much as possible. What looks courageous from the outside is very normal to these top players on the inside. When you are exposed to a particular type of pressure and environment on a regular basis, the natural side-effect is it becomes easier, or the player just quits. And that is really a win/win when you think about it, because quitting something you're not cut out for will save years of wasted efforts on the training court.

Coaches are fully aware that parents and players are terrified of matches, so they avoid anything too competitive and end up perpetuating the problem by introducing new senseless technical trends to keep everyone in comfort zone city. Options and modalities that really should be considered insulting to the tennis player's IQ start to seem like revolutionary ideas. Because the parents/players are wanting to sidestep playing matches, overly technical and unrealistic options that appear to be innovative are welcomed with open arms as a diversion from genuine and serious competition. For this very reason, the coaching world has become saturated with insignificant drills, pie charts and PowerPoint presentations, as they are the sporting world's fairy floss that masks the bitter truth of their cowardice.

If you were unaware of names and faces and just watched players train from 400 to the top 10 in the world, you wouldn't be able to grade who was where. Everyone looks technically sound on the outside, but it's what's under the bonnet that matters. Match play becomes the medicine that needs to be taken voluntarily on a daily basis if a player is to have any chance of reaching their fullest potential. This is as straightforward as it comes. There are no shortcuts or elevators up to the top, and lots of trapdoors and pitfalls down.

```
          IT'S TIME TO PAY YOUR BILL.
     WE HOPE YOU HAD A PLEASANT EXPERIENCE!

     Subtotal:     Lack of resilience
     Tip:          Choose your words carefully
     Total Costs:  Unable to deal with turbulent
                   situations
                   Make excuses
                   Never get outside thecomfort zone
```

## The long buck!

Tennis is unquestionably one of the most difficult sports in the world to master. With so many facets requiring development, the internship can be a challenging and difficult process that takes a substantial amount of time. Depending on how players are tracking, there are different paths juniors will take. Players who need more time to grow and develop by around 16 years of age, in my opinion, should opt for the American college route, where they can get another four years of free solid training and accommodation while doing a university degree at the same time. Or if the player is already making their bones by getting ATP or WTA points on a regular basis and showing signs of transitioning from the juniors to seniors quite comfortably, maybe their decision could be to go out on the circuit instead.

Neither option is right or wrong, and each decision should be dependent upon the individual circumstances. Professional players have been made in both scenarios. The key to this decision is having someone who understands the junior's current level and their potential for future development, as well as their chances of survival at the initial stages of the circuit. This career-defining moment not only changes the trajectory of a young person's tennis, but also their life. Unfortunately, a lot of the time this pivotal decision is in the hands of a tennis parent who is wearing rose-coloured glasses.

Often tennis parents go with their own misguided instincts about this massive decision rather than doing their due diligence on the matter. What the parent figures is if their kid does more time on the court, they will more than likely not have to go to college and can go straight to the pros. So, they decide to up the ante with the hours on court, under the impression more equals better.

But that equation isn't necessarily true. When it comes to seeing a junior make a jump in standard, there are many variables at play such as physicality, maturity, emotional development, and the biggest one of all—time. If you go hell for leather in terms of training volume at the incorrect time, you won't see as much progress as you would if you waited until the child was more suited to be able to handle the increase in workload. So generally, the parent continues to overwork their child prematurely, which only puts invisible mileage on the odometer that can make the engine fail sooner in its career than it otherwise might have. If the parent is content with the process taking its natural time instead of speeding up the procedure to meet the expectations of the fantasy they'd created, many of these players could go a lot further with their tennis. In my opinion, it's not that a lot of the athletes who don't 'make it' weren't good enough, but they were being nurtured incorrectly by a delusional tennis parent. They likely could have made it via a different pathway.

### Weaving the camouflage that hides delusion

Elsie already had a couple bites of the tennis cherry with her two older sons, who were hugely unsuccessful according to the standards she set. This tennis parent seemed to look at it as a failure if her kids got a university degree and played college ball. How could Elsie possibly peacock her tennis parent prowess around the sporting fraternity if her kids never played on prime-time television? Her last roll of the dice was with her youngest boy, Sammy, and this time around she was a more seasoned tennis parent. So, what on earth could go wrong?

Elsie would have already been $150k in the hole from coaching and travelling expenses for her sons, and had totally burnt these two children out, but instead of cutting her losses and re-evaluating the gamble, she saw no harm in going for the trifecta by betting bigger on her final wager and trying to carve a pro player out of a boy who had Buckley's chance of making it. Vicarious glory was the only thing on Elsie's radar, and she would go all in for a chance to win some of that borrowed achievement.

With the huge time and financial risk involved in tennis, the return policy is virtually non-existent, and the price is a healthily functioning family and home life. Out of the blue, I got a call one Saturday afternoon from a disgruntled man accusing me of 'stealing Sammy's spark'. It took me a few seconds to comprehend the accusation as my working relationship with the man's son was a very good one. I held the phone far from my ear as the irate man lectured me on how I was ruining his family. 'I never see the two of them anymore. They are always at the tennis courts,' he complained. I tried to be as compassionate as I could and hear him out while not becoming a doormat, or worse, a punching bag for his disappointment. He made all sorts of claims about how I'd told his wife and son that Sammy needed to train seven days a week, so he could go straight to the pros and sidestep the US college system. The irony of it was I had told Elsie his son should be doing less, and the college route would be a perfect fit for Sammy once he completed high school.

Peter ranted, 'She lied the other day about where they were. I drove past the tennis courts and found both of them there, hitting serves. When they came home, I asked Elsie where they had been, and she lied straight to my face. She told me she took Sammy and a friend for some fat-free frozen yoghurt down at the beach.' Peter said he'd called Elsie out on lying, stating he had seen the pair of them with her own two eyes, but Elsie didn't fold under the intense questioning, and stuck to her guns.

While hysterically offloading about his altercation with his wife to me on the phone, Peter accidentally shed some light on a rumour circulating around the tennis community for some time, regarding the age of his son. Speculation had always circulated because Sammy didn't quite fit the description of an 11-year-old, with his budding goatee and the voice of a pack-a-day smoker. 'He's only 13, for god's sake!' Peter said. 'He should be out having fun with his mates, not chained to the hip with his mother.' The situation was getting weirder by the minute.

Peter wanted someone to take it out on, and a lot of coaches accept that kind of treatment from someone who is paying a decent chunk of money, which I totally understand. But I have a tendency towards impulsiveness and my tolerance for unacceptable behaviour is diminishing at a rapid rate, especially when my integrity is challenged, which means I have a high turnover of clients at the academy where I work. The departure of customers initially hurts the pocket, but ironically, I do my best coaching when I don't care about how I am coming across. Knowing it's probably just a matter of time until everyone leaves ultimately frees me up to do what needs to be done. But I do miss the boy, as he was my favourite kid out of all those I'd worked with. I hope he gets to college, because he would massively benefit from more time in the sport to develop. Even Elsie knows that. That's why she photoshopped Sammy's birthdate on his birth certificate. But with a mother motivated by the idea of sitting in the player's box at the Australian open as quickly as possible, Sammy doesn't stand a chance.

### DAMAGE RECEIPT

| Fuck-Up (Cause) | Aftermath (Effect) |
| --- | --- |
| Obsessed with tennis | Kid hates the sport |
| Rupturing family dynamic | Divorce |
| Fraudulently trying to get ahead | Humiliation |

### THANK YOU!

Generally, trying to speed up the process of making a should-be college player into a professional, ends in the teenager playing a season of tennis and then stopping the sport. The brutality of the future and challenger circuit eats underprepared players alive. There are endless amounts of seriously good nobodies out there, who never hit the airways of primetime television, but know how to fight and how to keep the ball going back over the net. Do not discredit how many great players don't ever get to play a Grand Slam but linger at the lower tier tournaments like unwanted termites. The tennis industry is infested with white ants who will gnaw at your immature game till it's completely dilapidated.

If the goal is to surpass the challenger events, an extra few years to develop a solid foundation without too much interference from such players can make all the difference in the world. Giving green behind the ears teenage athletes more time to evolve by going to an American college isn't the most romantic idea for a delusional tennis parent, but it's the smart option in the long run for a lot of players. Unfortunately, many juniors are mismanaged by their parents, who have a different agenda, and they are made to cram too much tennis in too little time. So instead of following the most likely path to success, the parent wants to fulfil the most glorifying trajectory possible. And that means it's do or die for the kid.

```
          IT'S TIME TO PAY YOUR BILL.
      WE HOPE YOU HAD A PLEASANT EXPERIENCE!

      Subtotal:     Injustice
      Tip:          Professional advice
      Total Costs:  Burnout
                    Festering resentment
                    A lifetime of living in the past
```

## Summary

A delusional person settles for never getting to their desired destination, so long as they get to keep living their fantasy in the cinema of their own mind. . A vast majority of parents and players happily waste their money and time, making it appear as though they are serious about the sporting endeavour through various forms of virtue signalling such as practice, rackets, grips, strings, coaches, sport scientists, conferences, new technique—you name it. The list goes on and on. To the untrained eye, the frivolous flag-waving looks legitimate, and it seems as if the player is on the right path to peak performance. But the journey never really starts because the player never had any true intentions to get anywhere. Since these training regimes and technical pursuits were generated purely for show, the player's career is purely pretend, and always destined to be just a figment of imagination. When a player and parent become serious about their craft, they start to view training and practice as secondary options to the game's holy grail: voluntarily immersing oneself in the messy and ugly process of pressure and competition.

I must add, given the nature of life and the state society is in at the minute, I'm all for people living in their own realities. Indulging in fantasy isn't a punishable offence and can be a somewhat healthy way of checking out of daily life, as most moments of the rat race suck anyway. No one is a bigger dreamer than me, but I draw the line when adults sacrifice their kids' childhood for their own psychological amusement. Before you go down that slippery slope, how about checking out what's playing at the movies instead?

## Praying for formidable problems

The cruelty I endured as a child, from playing tennis, was never going to be accepted by my father as a valid reason for me to be upset. Neither was witnessing my parent's domestic disputes, which happened so regularly the next-door neighbours started calling the cops for welfare checks.

But when I was 14, a problem was brewing within my family I felt would finally be a justification for exhibiting what I had been repressing for years. I was being used as a pawn in my father's twisted plot to catch my mother out, as he suspected her of being unfaithful. But if Dad had put half as much effort into his marriage as he did in trying to catch my Mum cheating, they'd probably still be happily hitched.

After Dad had given me his daily dose of discipline through the ruthless edge of his razor-like tongue, he would change and treat me as if I was one of his best mates. Nothing was diluted as he let me see the raw and unedited side of his life that most adults are desperate to hide from their children. And quite honestly, that's why I relished his company more than any other adult I'd ever been around. However, it also meant I was unnecessarily exposed to information that was completely inappropriate for a child to hear.

'I've got all the phones tapped and had a private investigator on your mother's ass for the last few months,' he told me out the front of Hungry Jack's in Traralgon. He then went down memory lane, filling me in on some of the scandalous behaviour that happened during their nights out, some of which sounded as if it belonged in the movie Boogie Nights. I found it hard to swallow, as my Mum was being painted in a light I didn't recognise; but if Dad said it, it must have been true.

As time went on, Dad still had no hard evidence of infidelity, so he raised the stakes once again by using me in another of his elaborate stings. Max made up a story that while I was walking around Next Generation (which is like my hometown Adelaide's country club), a friend of mine came up and pointed to a gentleman and said, 'That guy over there is having an affair with your mother.' He then said I had confided in him and was completely inconsolable about the rumour, and I was struggling to concentrate on my tennis because of it.

His imaginary story ruffled feathers in my family home and word got back to me (I was billeted in Melbourne at the time) that my parents had temporarily separated. Honestly, I was glad. I felt they had no business being married to each other, and my sister and I paid the price for it. The more I dwelled on the circumstances, the more I realised in the court of public opinion, I now had a serious cause to be genuinely upset. The only issue was that I wasn't at all saddened by the event. But this was a too good an opportunity to be sufficiently miserable, so I used the potential divorce as a convenient excuse to vent all the sadness I had accumulated throughout my turbulent upbringing. The seemingly traumatic event helped me channel what was really bothering me—the inhumane treatment of my childhood—as that issue was never going to be confessed and apologised for by my father. I never thought I'd see the day where people would ask Todd the human how he was doing, as it was such an alien concept.

A pattern of compensation and displaced emotion was to play out repeatedly until I reached my early 30s. I sought out toxic relationships so I could use the inevitable drama to channel my unresolved childhood issues. I gave money away to the less fortunate, to ease the guilt I felt for having nothing to offer my middleclass family for the suffering occurred at my expense. Then got annoyed at them when they only ever saw me as self-centred individual instead of an altruistic humanitarian, (even though they never saw a dime). I gave people profound life advice I inadvertently needed to hear myself and felt like it was a moral obligation to be onboard sinking ships, because no one was next to me when I was unmistakeably drowning.

In hindsight, I was dealing with the grief of a failed tennis career and the devastation it caused to everyone involved, as I'd never felt I had the permission to properly process any of it.

# PART 4

# Roles and boundaries

### Jockeying for position

What most people don't see in tennis is the power struggle occurring behind the scenes of a child prodigy's career. What appears on the outside to be a 'team' is generally just a group of individuals who secretly conspire to gain the reins over the player's career. In a way, the culprits have probable cause for wanting to seize the guardianship over the athlete's decision making, as a lot of young players aren't fit to order a cab from a taxi stand. Just because the athlete is the one with the ability, it doesn't always mean they are the one with the brains. So, the makers and shakers jockey for position, which creates inhouse quarrelling with parties who are supposed to be aligned and congruent. A lack of clear leadership means the throne can become occupied by an ill-equipped person, and nothing sinks a player's career quicker than poor governance. Here's a rundown of who, what, when, where, and why it happens.

There is a complicated yet crucial chain of command a tennis team needs to get right if the player is to stand any chance of reaching their full potential. When the junior is starting off on their tennis journey, the hierarchy should be: coach, parent, then player. During this initial stage, the player will be learning the fundamental skills of the game, while the parent is guided by the coach as to how the athlete is tracking. When the junior matures enough to become more accountable for their own sporting career, there should be a transition period to coach, player, parent, so the parent and player don't develop an unhealthy relationship that sabotages their family dynamic. Hypothetically, this changing of the guard should happen when the athlete encounters a coach's message, they will go to any length to undertake.

Allowing the teenager the space to absorb the teachings of an innovative coach from a digestible distance is the ultimate litmus test. This will show everyone whether the junior genuinely wants to pursue the path of a professional tennis player. But if adequate space is not given for this process, it will always be unclear whether the junior's desire to play the sport is an authentic gesture. It's true what they say: two's company and three's a crowd. If a buffer isn't allowed by the child's guardian, the coach's doctrine becomes ineffective; it won't sufficiently transmit into the psyche of the junior, as it would if it were just the two of them. However, for the biological middleman to step down the food chain, the coach must prove themselves to be a rare individual with a vicious level of devotion to the game. Otherwise, the tennis parent will be unwilling to demote themselves to a lesser rank.

However, it's during this reshuffle the tennis parent can try to snatch the top spot as the junior is starting to show greater aptitude—and the parent has always secretly believed they can teach better than the coach anyway. Having the hierarchy configuration land at parent, player, coach is a precarious arrangement that can see anything happen to the athlete's career. While there is substantial proof that an inexperienced tennis parent can steer the ship in the right direction, the number of talented prodigies who are crushed in the process never sees the light of day.

And even when the parent/player scenario does work, it tends to sever the parent/child relationship in the process. That ultimately has a negative effect on a player's career anyway. Since tennis parents have skin in the game, so to speak, detaching from their child's development and success seems to be virtually impossible—especially if they aren't truly sold on the coach's conviction to the cause. In an ideal world, the role of the parent should be more like a godfather in the mafia, working behind the scenes and getting a young hungry coach who's desperate to climb the ranks to do their dirty work for them.

The natural tendency is for the tennis parent to heavily rely on the coach while the child is still learning the fundamental components of the game. The coach is swamped with compliments and high fives by the parent, to maintain the illusion that the coach will remain the head authority over the player's tennis into the foreseeable future. But tennis parents know what side their bread is buttered on, and they will say just about anything to keep their kid benefiting from a situation that progresses their own hidden agenda: to one day be more than just a silent shareholder in the athlete's career.

For now, everything is functioning perfectly. The team set-up is right, the kid is progressing, and the parent is paying the bills and staying out of the way. It's only when the kid starts showing greater promise of becoming a professional player that things usually start going pear-shaped. Tennis parents can detour from a winning formula, thinking they have the golden goose, and they become lost in their dreams of a future world filled with fame and endless revenue. When a junior gets to a certain level, they attract more attention and more possibilities start to arise, which means managerial decisions now need to be made.

The inexperienced tennis parent tends to take it upon themselves to be the person in charge of making these pivotal calls, and inadvertently squeezes the coach from the top spot. Now, with the order of merit upturned and as the junior continues to progress, the priority shifts from development to scheduling and player management, as well as the athlete finding a healthy channel to air out their dirty laundry. This introduces a clear conflict of interest for both parent and player if they are working in close quarters. This is why it's imperative the person who fulfils the head role doesn't share the same genetics as the athlete. So long as they do, the player can and will remain emotionally suffocated, and anything is liable to happen. And more importantly, the bond between player and coach is severely fractured by the tug-of-war between parent and coach. The disharmony in the camp continues to grow as the coach is caught between a rock and a hard place and must make the decision to speak up and possibly get sacked or stay silent and watch the rookie parent make a catalogue of poor judgement calls. If the coach doesn't make a stand against the tyrannical parent, the player unconsciously loses respect for the coach and his words suddenly become comprehensively annulled.

To add another layer of complexity to this already complicated equation, there are agents, who always have an agenda on management that is tied to financial gain. Tennis players are too preoccupied with thinking they are Vince from Entourage to see an agent for what they truly are. This world of green lights and endless yeses is always a bad season away from evaporating into thin air. As the entourage continues to grow, the coach proceeds to plummet down the pyramid, finding themselves running errands and carrying bags. The demoralising downgrade leaves a sour taste in the coach's mouth making them want to see the player and parent secretly lose (I speak from personal experience). To their own dissatisfaction, coaches in this position generally tend to hang on for the ride for as long as they can, since they have invested so much time into the project.

After spending too many years under the control of a tyrannical tennis parent, the player waits for the day when they can finally seize the opportunity to become their own boss. And if this day comes before the player is mature enough to make good decisions on their own, chances are they will drive their tennis into the ground. The athlete's behaviour takes front and centre stage without anyone wondering why their chaotic outbursts are occurring. Subconsciously, the support team doesn't really want the player to examine the root of the issue, because the truth of the situation is complex and ugly and implicates everyone's motivations and wrongdoings. Instead, they Band-Aid their charges symptomatic behaviour while avoiding any culpability in the cause of the matter.

A child who has been under the thumb of an opinionated team devoid of ethics and compassion, doesn't come out unscathed. Being micromanaged and exclusively pardoned from participating in life is the perfect recipe to make an individual unfit to handle their personal liberties. The self-assuredness they have curated through their tennis abilities sabotages them, as it's unfathomable to the athlete that they are incapable of managing their own life. In a sport with limited opportunities, it can take someone too long to realise they probably aren't the best person to be running their own career. An accumulation of poor decisions makes sure the player never reaches their full potential. If only this chain of command was kept intact at the pivotal time in the player's career, things could have been completely different.

The tennis parent's thirst for pride and prestige down the road dismantles the correct hierarchal structure when they put themselves in the wrong role. Misallocating or overstepping boundaries generally sees a breakdown of trust within the unit and diminishes the coach's capacity to evoke radical transformation within the player. Overcompensation in some of these areas can occur when someone is trying to make up for something missed. In a sport where we train players to be arrogant, it is somewhat contradictory to place blame on a 23-year-old who thinks they know it all. The air of arrogance tennis lends itself to can turn around and bite players in the ass, seeing future Fortune 500 companies collapse into bust.

## Time to give the devil his due

While writing this section, I'm quite aware of just how many tennis parents have turned their children into elite players, and it makes me want to address the elephant in the room. How is it a parent who has absolutely no experience in the sport whatsoever can trump other seasoned coaches when it comes to making a professional tennis player? Should these autodidact parents be running our local programs instead of trained professionals? Seemingly, national institutions with unparalleled budgets and comprehensive mission statements can't hold a candle to self-taught tennis parents when it comes to the creation of elite players. In my opinion, this is because unconventionality is the only true way to the top. A parent who sees the world through a fresh pair of eyes, with a burning desire for brilliance, has far more chance of getting a player to the top than a local coach who's become accustomed to lowering themselves to a mass audience of mediocrity.

The upside of a person coming in blind and desperate is they're not familiar with certain psychological limitations that other coaches in the industry think are real. The world's an oyster to a narcissistic and culturally unaware human being. But before parents start rushing out to put their coach's hat on, I must add an important disclaimer: You are also far more likely to ruin your child's life than to get them to the top of the sport. It's okay to be a harsh critic of your child, so long as you're happy with being a terrible parent - a person must be willing to forfeit the other role because you can't have your cake and eat it too, with very rare exceptions. These are the laws of the universe, so choose your regret wisely.

Fanatical tennis parents are more than aware the coaching landscape is overcrowded with mediocrity, as bureaucratic systems must now adhere to a long list of rules and regulations. Society has succumbed to a state where everyone needs to be a winner, so the balance is tipped in favour of the unexceptional to appease a mass audience of campaigners and complainers.

While inclusion may win you a popularity contest with humanity, it certainly doesn't create greatness. All it does is cater to the lowest common denominator and neglect the few exceptions who exude rare qualities. It is therefore no real mystery this type of non-competitive, standardised training produces mediocre players by the dozen. Having to stand behind a politically correct credo disarms coaches and forces them to adopt an institutionalised philosophy regarding an extreme sport that instead needs a trainer to be unshackled.

*the self proclaimed "serve doctor" coaching a serve he can't hit himself*

A criterion of unworldly madness seems to be a prerequisite for extreme sport, so a crowd-friendly approach is an utter insult to the gruelling trade and those who are genuinely serious about pursuing it. Hyper-specialisation is created through a boundless exploration of extreme measures that isn't for the faint-hearted and can't be taught to the masses without a litany of lawsuits and societal condemnation. Since nice people coach shitty tennis, the right person to be quarterbacking this radical position is a deranged human being, and ironically, this makes tennis parents some of the best candidates for the role as they aren't imprisoned by such stifling practices and procedures as those tracksuit-sporting yes-men.

Sooooooo... my father would have been the perfect coach for me if he wasn't my own flesh and blood. But he was, so his coaching came at a price - I had to accept the absence of a caring father. The smartest thing a decent parent could do is hire a crazy coach, to save themselves from going mad on account of their own child. It also saves the player from the wrath of a belligerent and absent parent. Unfortunately, there are fewer and fewer daring coaches around, while the number of overbearing parents seems to stay the same.

## Cheers—I did my best coaching in the pub

When a professional player asks me to train or travel with them, I prefer to be very specific about what they want me to be. The word 'coach' is loosely used to describe a job where a variety of services are fulfilled, with coaching very often being the least thing that gets done. It's remarkable how many players hire coaches but don't really want their help. I was okay with being asked to crack some jokes, carry their bags, or have some drinks with them after a loss; but what never sat well with me was being asked to coach and then being looked at weirdly for doing my job when I tried to help the athlete on the court. A lot of players hire a coach, so they appear as if they are open to being helped, but then they blatantly ignore any advice given to them. It's all a game of posturing, which often leads to the coach playing pretend as well. Minding a toddler isn't too dissimilar to dealing with a tennis player. I sometimes look at my occupation as if I am a well-paid babysitter, except I'm not looking after babies, but instead looking after so-called professional athletes—like the time I was approached to coach a talented young girl, Aretha.

Anyone can teach a player how to hit forehands and backhands. The real challenge is getting a player to understand what an opportunity looks like, having them grasp what consequences come with certain behaviours, and opening their eyes to the benefits of getting real with themselves. They say when the student is ready, the teacher will appear; but although Aretha hired my services, she seemed to have no intention whatsoever of allowing me to coach her. The giant 'Fuck off' tattoo branded across her forehead looked strangely familiar, and it felt as if the two of us may have been emotional relatives.

Aretha's elusive father, Igor, was her coach/manager. I tried to feel him out on whether he thought the two of us would be a good fit, as she seemed standoffish and unapproachable on initial introduction. Igor reassured me I was the missing piece of the puzzle, and his daughter was itching to get started. I hate asking tennis parents their opinion on sporting matters, as it opens the door to their views and thoughts being valid; however, in this particular case the father had also been the coach, so I had to enquire.

One thing I've noticed since I started doing this job, is the parent's summary of where their kid is at is almost always wrong. What it sounded like to me was Igor had lost control of his daughter once she had come of age, and he was looking at ways of getting her back under his guardianship. I fished around for some information and got word Aretha was a talented swellhead with a chip on her shoulder. Apparently, she had been pushed to the brink by her old man as a kid, and was now more interested in long eyelashes, gaining Instagram followers, and attending frat parties.

I mentioned what I had heard to Igor over the phone to get the answer from the horse's mouth. Igor did a pretty good job of downplaying her rebellious reputation, putting it down to loneliness on the road, which in my mind was just a convenient half-truth exonerating him from any culpability in the situation. I was thinking to myself if there was ever a moment to show your hand, now would be the time, because it's hard tackling problems when we can't agree on the issue. But Igor refused to flip his cards over, and I was left to think about his proposition for a couple of days. I visualise situations in my mind so vividly it can turn me off experiencing them in real life, because I already feel I have done it. But in reality, it's all just a figment of my wild imagination. My gut feeling wasn't good, but when you're as lost as I was, even bad ideas tend to look like great options.

The arrogance instilled in Aretha made her a great tennis player, but it was also a debilitating trait making her reject outside information. She couldn't take constructive criticism, instead mistaking help as a full-blown attack and turning conversations into heated debates. Winning an argument clearly meant more to her than getting better, and it greatly impeded her chances of fulfilling her potential. She had much to work on and improve, but her abrasiveness made me hesitate and not pull the trigger on things that needed to be said. Aretha required rescuing from herself, despite her belief she had everything under control, and so long as she remained closed off to information from her coaches, we were all in trouble.

I realised conventional coaching methods are of no use when the player is on an incorrigible path and isn't willing to throw in the towel. Igor had his own agenda and was using me as a glove puppet to continue peddling his propaganda to Aretha, instead of letting me use my better judgement and deal with the situation. The proximity to her father was a clear problem, so much so Aretha even hated hearing anything come out of my mouth resembling Igor's old ideologies, and they could send her into such a manic frenzy that she would end up self-sabotaging to display her revulsion.

When a tennis parent coaches their kid using standover tactics throughout their formative childhood years, there is a price to pay.

And this price is to be paid in the future, which in this case had now arrived. Unfortunately, I had inherited her father's fuckups and was at my wits' end from the daily shenanigans these two brought to life on the road. Igor was an eleventh-hour individual who could overcomplicate buying a salad sandwich. His erratic behaviour meant a perpetual sense of anxiety was part and parcel of Aretha's existence. But Igor wasn't going to be denied, as he seemed to consider himself the Mark Twain of the tennis world and wouldn't get out of the road for anyone.

To make matters worse, these two hadn't held up their part of the agreement and were six weeks in arrears with my wages. Igor kept backdooring me and making it the tennis federation's problem, as they were supposed to be the ones footing the bill. No one was getting back to me, and I was running low on funds. My options were to quit and borrow some money from a friend to fly back home, or to see it out with the gruesome twosome for another five weeks on the road. I was banking on this money coming in, and felt if I left, I probably wouldn't ever be paid for the time I had done. I decided to stay, but I radically shifted my approach from being a devoted coach to being a disassociated one.

Luckily, I had lots of company as the coaching landscape is filled to the brim with head-nodding poodles who are more than happy to say whatever they need in order to guarantee themselves another night on the circuit. So, I picked up a few balls, manufactured a professional-looking coaching stance, shouted 'GOOD' a lot, and wore a bucket hat to blend in with the other degenerates in the travelling circus. But a sense of self-loathing seeped in as I began resenting myself for being another worthless sell-out lacking integrity. I needed to leave this situation pronto, before I slid into the depths of despair.

Every person has their limitations and mine was getting a mouthful from Aretha while I was sitting in the player's box, watching her second-round defeat against a qualifier. It's hard enough putting up with someone's dirty laundry behind closed doors, but when it gets aired in public, the job becomes humiliating. I felt drunk on rage and gritted my teeth until the match was over. My compassion for Aretha's situation had evaporated and I had now secretly turned into her opposition's biggest supporter. Igor was pacing up and down the locker room ruminating about all the things she did wrong, while the only thing I was contemplating was a cold beer. It would generally take hours to talk Aretha down from the ledge after a loss, and I wasn't interested in entertaining the thought of that after such a pitiful performance which had made a spectacle of me.

So, I bailed from the courts in a courtesy car and left Aretha with her dad, made a quick stop at the hotel to whack on some show-off attire, and then I was off to the nearest pub. The anticipation of the first drink made me feel as if I'd already had one, as I was giddy and ready to get amongst a crowd of people not affiliated with the sport of tennis. I found a pub so filthy that you didn't wipe your feet before you went in, but you did on the way out.

*the bucket hat*

Halfway through drinking myself to a personal utopia, I went outside for a cigarette, and saw Aretha walking down the main strip of the city with another player. Without hesitation, I yelled out her name from the smoking section where I was standing, waving at her for the two of them to come over. Drinking has always provided me with a radical personality shift, and I was interested to see how Aretha would handle one of the alter egos who lived behind my iron mask. I immediately started stirring the pot by throwing jabs about Aretha's awful attitude, with absolutely zero concern or consideration for how she took it. We were in my territory now and pub rules applied.

Aretha burst into tears when she was on her second mojito and ran off into the toilets while her friend preceded to call me a petty cunt. She was right, I was being an asshole and I was thoroughly enjoying it. This reoccurring theme of being an exploding doormat has plagued a lot of my interpersonal relationships. My avoidance of confrontation means the straws continue to build, making me feel weak for not voicing what needs to be said. I usually take this frustration out on myself with a spree of hellacious drinking, where the destruction inevitably works its way to the intended target anyway, in the form of a belligerent phone call.

After a smoke outside and another Fireball shot at the bar, I poked my head around the corner and found the girls on the back left table, looking a little worse for wear. Instead of coming in like a demolition derby, I shifted gears to one of genuine curiosity. I could tell the grog had softened them up and they weren't as edgy as before. A large tennis crew suddenly arrived at the shady pub, and we all danced like idiots in the neon lights for a few hours, helping clear the air between Aretha and me.

Later in the night, the two of us finally had a D&M where we got down to brass tacks like never before. The drink worked like a truth serum as Aretha told R-rated stories about her dad even Tarantino would find a bit gruesome. Sitting there listening, I realised my initial evaluation of Aretha was right, but it had been lost in translation as she'd triggered my own lesions of inferiority. I was dumbfounded that even I, who had been through an almost identical experience, could be brutally judgmental of a person who was cut from the same cloth as me. Aretha's bouts of arrogance and inability to take on actionable advice stemmed from a childhood of being severely overcoached. Now, even as an adult, she was still under the jurisdiction of her father, who was trying to disguise his tennis parent behaviour in a managerial role.

Aretha didn't need her father to be her agent or part-time coach. What she was clearly yearning for was for her dad to be her father, and only her father. It was the typical tennis story, where the parent prioritised the player and not the person. Suddenly, a stroke of genius hit me while I was under the influence. Since her dad had swapped roles from father to coach, I had to swap roles from coach to father. I disappeared into the dark of the night and sat at an empty bar till close, talking the proposition over with my friend Johnny Walker.

I woke up the next morning and my head was a hung jury. After some deliberation, I concluded the switch seemed too emotionally risky. I must admit, my ego was taken by the idea of rescuing Aretha and becoming a sage-like father figure who liberated her from a cunning oppressor. That sounded like a movie I'd pay to watch. But I would have just been crossing another boundary to make up for an earlier boundary incursion, which had already been made by her scheming father.

I'm almost certain we have not seen some of the greatest tennis players hit the centre courts because of power-hungry parents who placed themselves at the top of the tennis hierarchy. But then again, I also think we wouldn't have witnessed some of the greatest tennis players in history if some extreme parents didn't happen to coach their offspring. I believe the notion that parents can turn their children into superstars is such an alluring thought to a certain type of individual, that they find a way to rationalise the misconduct through the niceties of being a helpful and involved parent.

Each person has their own school of thought when it comes to the acceptability of their own parenting style. Is it fair game to traumatise a child with the hope of them becoming successful because of that conditioning? I guess that's up to each individual to determine. As for me, I can only speak as a traumatised child who wound up becoming unsuccessful, and I can definitely say the juice wasn't worth the squeeze. I've also spent a lot of time around successful athletes who were mistreated as children, and they're not exactly swimming in bliss either. If you want to go ahead and try this angle, then be my guest, as that's everyone's prerogative. But don't go trying to convince everyone you are a noble philanthropist. Instead, take responsibility for your decisions and be prepared to lie in the bed you made next to your now flattened child. That was the noblest thing my father did when my career went down the gurgler. Not that he ever verbally admitted his wrongdoing for his involvement in the sporting saga, but he was willing to get down in the gutter with me when I inevitably plummeted down into the sewer.

Dad's bed

## Romantic relationships: not encouraged but not surprising

In a bizarre sporting universe where it seems the real-world rules don't apply. There are all sorts of weird and wacky relationships among those who have grown up in the tennis bubble. The most common one is the female player and coach partnership that turns into a fully-fledged romance. Why does this happen, and should the parents of a young female tennis player be worried by this too common occurrence?

In an industry where it happens more than people would like to admit. The grooming of young female athletes is a silent topic not spoken about. It can very easily be overlooked in a one-on-one sport like tennis, where the coach spends significant time developing an emotional connection with a young person. Coaches who have been embedded in a sporting culture that blurs the lines between appropriate and inappropriate can lack moral judgement when it comes to acceptable ways to behave.

It is therefore imperative the parent oversees the working relationship between the female athlete and male coach, to make sure nothing inappropriate transpires. This can be a somewhat difficult line to interpret, as the coach is being paid to try and pull off the nearly impossible task of getting a young kid to the top echelon of an extreme game which requires an abnormal level of closeness and familiarity.

That said, a tennis parent's primary purpose should be overseeing the duo from an appropriate distance, which isn't an easy job in itself. If the parent is too close to the action, the coach's philosophies don't sufficiently seep into the bones of the athlete; and if they are too far removed from the situation, well, anything can happen. In the women's circuit, there is no shortage of predatorial parasites; and incredibly, after the bad apples are found guilty of wrongdoing, they still manage to find a way to coach somewhere else in the world, and parents willingly send their children to work with them.

Parents understandably look for ways to cut costs when it comes to their children's exorbitant sporting expenses, and they can opt for the player and coach to share the same room while travelling on the road. This frugal decision is a dicey one at best and is a clear breach of player/coach boundaries, which can massively warp the child's perception of what is rational. Now you add that to the fact a lot of players have a rocky foundation with their parents because of their tennis career, which can further complicate the relationship between the coach and player. Therefore, it's absolutely necessary boundaries are imposed, and living arrangements are the most obvious place to start.

In a lot of coach/player partnerships, the coach isn't really doing that much coaching at all but is more like a surrogate father who is filling the empty void left by the absent parent. The coach presents himself as an available person who can be trusted to listen without judgement, and as time goes by, this support becomes monumental for the emotionally wounded and socially deprived player who is in desperate need of understanding and connection.

### Looking for love in all the wrong places— avoiding Stockholm syndrome

Ursula was a 31-year-old walking resentment vending machine, delivering a sob story to anyone who paid her the slightest amount of attention. Tennis talks, and the grapevine whispered the only thing Ursula had been successful at lately was finding a way to bed her ex-coaches. And here I was, next on the job. Of all people, I shouldn't be playing God when it comes to judging anyone else's personal life, so I tried to take the information with a grain of salt and got locked and loaded and ready to go.

We were off overseas together on our first stint to Europe, but there was no honeymoon period at the start of this professional partnership. It always takes me too long to warm up to strangers, so I felt on the backfoot from the very beginning. An undercurrent of perpetual anxiety forced me into playing the 'job interview' version of myself, even though I was already hired for the gig. For reasons I do not know, I couldn't break away from this cookie cutter persona that in no way, shape or form resembled the person I truly was. But because I had committed to the role for so long, I felt there was no room for my real personality to come to the surface without Ursula thinking I might need a psychological evaluation.

Besides, she was already getting off on my fanboyish façade, as it was the perfect platform where she could hold her daily pity party. She was in a constant state of 'poor me-ism' which ultimately wasn't her fault, as she had been emotionally and psychologically damaged from sailing the stormy seas of professional sport. From a very young age, Ursula had been exploited and labelled as the potential breadwinner by her poor family, who were prepared to do whatever it took to get themselves out of a poverty-stricken existence. Ursula had been dispatched around the world like a human pass the parcel and ended up seeking refuge in a foreign country by marrying a man, looking for citizenship from a country who were desperate for decent players.

Everyone this girl encountered took advantage of her, either romantically, financially or emotionally. Her kindness was mistaken for weakness and made her prey to the underworld of the tennis tour. The soul without a compass had been used as lunchmeat and was now bordering on broke, after a topsy turvy career that hadn't earnt her the money and prestige she'd hoped. But tennis was all she knew, and time wasn't on her side as she rapidly moved towards the sporting glue factory.

Ursula didn't need to travel with a coach - she needed to travel with a psychologist. Actually, she needed to travel with about four psychologists so they could rotate when her non-stop complaining burned them out one by one. Despite being in the eye of the storm myself, I was still very disassociated and in denial about how royally the sport had ravaged my own life. Ursula's obvious and overflowing trauma was now splattering onto my raw and open wounds, which I only ever allowed to see the light of day when under the influence of alcohol. After a while, it dawned on me I was completely jealous of someone who was morbid and miserable, and I was agitated at how comfortable she felt disclosing her deepest and darkest secrets without a substance in her system. Let me have a turn at being a sook too, I thought. Ursula had the luxury of having these unadulterated whinges, while my personality was imprisoned to a lifetime sentence of being a yes-man. Not having my brokenness visible was starting to cause me a lot of grief. I resonated with Ursula's misguided attempt at trying to get her shit together, but now she was just looking at a massive pile of shit that was right in front of her. And with no proper way of disposing of her emotional waste, I continued to act as Ursula's daily dumping ground while becoming more resentfully envious by the second.

Incredibly, Ursula still supported her family, sending money back each week to people who clearly took advantage of her. She had been pimped out purely for her athletic ability. Her father was physically out of her world, but not out of her mind. Sadly, she was still under the thumb of a heartless and distant stranger who lived in a place that was a distant memory. People tell you their problems, and for the most part don't ask for any advice, and don't take any action. But Ursula had been so unseen and disregarded that she needed to be heard for a substantial amount of time, until I could bring any solutions to the table. She had a stockpile of misfortune and misery that had to be trudged through, and it was bringing up things in me I'd been desperately trying to keep down.

The calling for a drink became louder and louder. But I knew if I picked one up, I'd be toast. Apparently, Ursula had sacked her last coach for being a drunk, and I didn't need the extra misdemeanour on my overcrowded rap sheet. The idea of moderately drinking wasn't even a thought this far down the road in my alcoholism. The stack of undeniable proof I couldn't just have a few cold ones was indisputable. So, I went full savage mode; over-exercising, under-eating, and extremely reclusive, so I wouldn't be tempted to carouse the lively streets outside.

As the trip went on, the relationship grew deeper, and I'm no romantic expert but I know how to catch a vibe when I'm getting it. Invitations for late-night pie and facetious sexual innuendo were becoming more regular, and I let them go through to the ball boys as if I was oblivious to her suggestions. The connection she was craving was jeopardising our tennis relationship, which was surprisingly working well. It added a kind of weird tension to an already unusual situation. My inability to set healthy boundaries and be authentic from the start saw me retreat and become distant and cold, which threw gasoline on a fire I felt she'd started. Having to have awkward conversations with people because they can't read between the lines is draining, and I became increasingly annoyed that Ursula needed me to spell it out, instead of being able to put together what was going on for herself.

I'd done a decent job of putting the 'not going to happen' signs out there, but she still wasn't getting the memo. As in her tennis game, Ursula lacked awareness and the ability to abolish her tactics when they weren't working. I've always been melodramatic and tend to turn things into things that don't really need to be things at all. My avoidance of confrontation meant the awkwardness grew. It started to take a serious toll on the tennis side of things, in what could only be described as a very relationship-like situation, even though there was absolutely nothing going on.

When silence gains a momentum of its own, it's tough to break the cycle. It feels as if there is some sort of invisible force conspiring to make the situation worse than it needs to be. I have a bad tendency to suddenly cut people off and never see them again, instead of going through the difficult and painstaking process of talking the issue through with them. I can't imagine what it would be like for the wretched soul on the receiving end of that. Shit really hits the fan when you throw a first-round loss on top of an already fractured coach/player relationship. My 'last tango in Paris' with Ursula was well and truly over, and we never spoke again.

### DAMAGE RECEIPT

| Fuck-Up (Cause) | Aftermath (Effect) |
| --- | --- |
| Child exploitation | Psychologically and emotionally damaged |
| No emotional support | Festering and replaying resentment |
| Boundary crossing | Jeopardised professional relationships from a yearning for connection |

### THANK YOU!

The line between appropriate and inappropriate is sometimes hard to define in the warped sport of tennis. This young player had been so isolated, neglected and morally broken from her earlier years where she was poorly treated by her parents, that she desperately craved an outlet of connection to plug into regardless of how strange the situation. It was a bit like when a kidnapping takes place, and the person held captive may seek solace in the companionship of the person who is holding them against their will. Welcome to Stockholm.

Ursula needed help. She also needed help finding help. Getting the monkey off her back with me was the best Ursula could come up with, and although I tried my best to play the role of counsellor, it became clear I needed counselling myself. With her absentee parents not being of any support whatsoever, Ursula unconsciously and uncharacteristically looked outside the realm of normal to come up with a solution to her sadness and sorrows. Suggestively seducing coaches was her formula for companionship and closeness, despite the awkwardness and trouble it caused.

This type of story is not uncommon among the female athletes competing on the tour. A lot of female players tend to turn to emotional support from the coach if their primary support system (family) is in disorder. Because the lives of some female athletes have been such weird experiences from the get-go, sleeping with their coach doesn't seem to be such a crazy idea. And then there is the never-ending debate: who is suffering from Stockholm syndrome—the player or the coach?

```
           IT'S TIME TO PAY YOUR BILL.
     WE HOPE YOU HAD A PLEASANT EXPERIENCE!

     Subtotal:     Fragility
     Tip:          Psychological help
     Total Costs:  Inability to form healthy relationships
                   Overstepping
                   Fragmentation
```

## The problem with a parent picking up the balls

Tennis is the most dishevelled and disorganised sport when it comes to the chain of command. What is it about the sport that makes it so shambolic and disordered when it comes to adhering to appropriate roles and boundaries? I believe there are societal perceptions and a psychological element to this consistent breach of authority which dismantles order and destroys relationships. Let me explain further.

The tennis parent almost believes they can coach. This means that they don't totally respect the expertise of the coach, yet don't quite have the balls to try to do the job straight up. So generally, they are still willing to pay a coach because they don't trust themselves enough to take full ownership of the reins. They also desperately need a third party to blame when things don't go well, to avoid taking accountability for any liability or failure. So, the tennis parent spies on the training sessions, comparing mental notes of what they think with what the coach says.

Arrogantly confusing knowing a little with knowing a lot, many tennis parents totally miss the complexity of coaching and are unaware of how many years it takes to define those intricate skills. Like an award-winning actor doesn't just read the lines off the page to perform, the parent incorrectly thinks just because they have obtained the script, they are able to act in the movie. But top-level coaching is way more than that; it's about intuition and timing, understanding ebbs and flows, knowing when to be gentle and delicate and when to drop the hammer. When the tennis parent thinks they are armed with the same level of information as the coach, they start to creep further onto the court and into the territory of the coach.

Just because I wear sporting attire instead of a johnny pencil pusher 9 to 5 suit and tie, doesn't mean I haven't had to learn a very specific set of skills over many years to call myself a professional tennis coach. I have considered wearing a suit and tie to coaching to establish this societal status of reckoning, to clearly state in a materialistic fashion the title of 'professional'. My brother-in-law even suggested I change my car to get more parental respect. There are no real barriers to entry to be a coach, and because the coach's office is a tennis court that at times is often open for the public to walk on and use at their own leisure, it's not valued as a profession worth respecting. Parents feel no problem with walking off and not paying, as if coaches are running a sporting charity.

So, what is the role of the parent? Tennis parents have two golden rules to follow. They are amazingly simple but prove to be incomprehensible to many.

1. Unconditional love and support of their child.
2. Strictly leave the coaching to the coach.

These rules are put in place for the family to focus on, to assist them to be stronger together through a testing and trying journey for the child. Sadly, 80% of parents fall at the first hurdle of unconditional love, which should be the primary function of any parent. And that makes the whole tennis experience extremely painful for the child who suffers the consequence in adolescence and adulthood. Ninety-five percent of tennis parents fail at the second rule of leaving the coaching to the coach, and they don't stop failing at this rule until the child has completely stopped playing the sport. Their child has had enough of tennis because it hasn't been fun for the past two to five years; and if they have lasted five years, that means the child has just managed to go through hell longer than most.

I've come to believe parents picking up the balls is their gateway drug into coaching. This tennis catastrophe has developed from an early error of allowing the tennis parent onto the court during training sessions. If the parent is completely off the court when a lesson is underway, it defines a clear line that can be easily recognised when the tennis parent intentionally or accidentally foot faults. This is because when a parent is in the thick of the action, they tend to feel no hesitation in voicing their opinions on matters pertaining exclusively to the coach and child. With no wall, cage, or fence to separate and signify a healthy boundary of coach/player/parent, the parent doesn't feel a sense of shame when they intrude during the lesson, especially since they are the ones footing the bill. But this apparently harmless act only steps on the toes of the coach and confuses the child.

In the case where the tennis parent's opinion becomes valid, the coach automatically becomes subservient to the parent, which makes the coach's aura and message lose all its appeal. The best coaches are surgically uncompromising with their vision and aren't interested in a running a democracy. The byproduct of being unpersuadable is that coaches tend to earn players curiosity and confidence via sheer attraction rather than shameless promotion. Having a parent impede this process puts trainers into a coaching conundrum, as they are faced with the moral dilemma of asking the parent who pays their mortgage to mind their own business.

Not wanting to upset the apple cart, most coaches will allow the parent to do whatever they want in training sessions, understandably choosing to take the cash for their backyard extension with the money dropped by the insidious parent. An excruciating feeling of invalidation to the coach and injustice to the child causes the coach to hit back in a passive-aggressive counterattack, hitting the parent where it hurts most—the wallet. Adjusting the ethics settings from player progress to financial gain, the coach fake smiles and people pleases in favour of longevity, to squeeze every single cent out of the overstepping tennis parent, choosing to coach more for the approval and consent of the parent than to be truly beneficial for the kid.

## Confronting the offer that's too good to refuse

Lying for a living is one thing, but having to lie out loud is a whole different kettle of fish. On reflection, not all of what I was broadcasting to my longlist of coaching clientele was untrue. Most of it was just empty drivel for appearance sake only. Given parents' and players' lack of tolerance for the truth and my inability to deliver a difficult message in a digestible way, it got to a point where it was just easier to shout out sporting cliches and talk in bumper sticker slogans.

The insincerity of a day's labour left me with aches and pains in places I didn't even know existed. I used to dread waking up in the morning, sentenced as I was to another day as a used car salesman. What can I say? Alcoholism had hijacked my moral compass and demanded a fist full of fifties before every sundown. Drinking was no longer a summer of 69' by any stretch of the imagination. The degradation from my addiction was starting to become noticeable, (to everyone but me), as I was practically living from Thursday to Sunday in my unregistered and unroadworthy Mitsubishi Magna that had a shattered windshield from a beer bottle, I threw at it in a fit of rage, and a driver's side window that wouldn't close because my friend kept breaking into it. It was the start of a great depression, and my dog days had well and truly begun. Life was grim, driving to work in the middle of winter at the crack of dawn with a plastic garbage bag filling in as my driver's side window, to be paid by local hacks who weren't really interested.

Maybe if I have another crack at coaching a prominent young player again, I thought, maybe that will give me a sense of purpose and satisfaction? But the situation always seemed to end in the same result: I would just become a ventriloquist dummy to the tennis parents agenda. I was at the bitter end of selling my soul for something I wasn't proud of and wanted a chance to win back some of the credibility I'd lost not that long ago. The revival of myself could manifest through the emergence of a young, hungry junior, someone to whom I could be more than a coach, like a Cus D'Amato to a young Mike Tyson. If only I could find a way for the tennis parent to stop intervening with my process.

I've always loved the sound of my own voice, but I'd just about had enough of hearing the verbal diarrhoea spewing from my mouth on a minutely basis. Seeing my fantasy of coaching a young orphan probably wasn't going to come to fruition, I once again became interested in training a talented prodigy. But this time, it needed to be different, as every other attempt had ended in heartache and bad blood. My trusted confidant, booze, accompanied me on my fact-finding crusade, as I delved into my past to try and learn from my previous slip-ups and mistakes.

Naturally, my drunkenness takes me to town as the pulse of the city run through my veins when I've got grog in my system. Hostage-taking is a hobby of mine when I'm under the influence, as I bail up total strangers and offload the latest and greatest problems, I wouldn't dream of mentioning if I was sober. This winter night I got my violin out earlier than usual, rambling on about my working worries to as many people as possible. 'These fucking parents are always getting in the way.' And so on, and so on...

This one German backpacker had heard enough for one life-time and interrupted my never-ending monologue by bluntly saying, 'I don't know, man, just do it for free if you don't want them controlling you.' His comment immediately struck a chord, and something suddenly shifted. I had coached for fuck all before, but I had never coached for nothing. I thought about it, and then I thought about it some more. The only way to do it properly was to have the tennis parent do nothing at all, and for me to do every-thing for free. I could be the one who was in complete control of the situation. This crazy idea seemed to be one of my sanest at the time, so at the next sight of raw talent, I was going to hit the player with an opportunity of a lifetime.

I have a knack for picking the most challenging tennis parents to work with. Well, I don't choose them; the kid chooses me in a way, and the parent seems to come as part of the package. At the club where I was working, Sabrina was the only one on my radar who had the potential to become a pro. They don't come through in dozens. One Sunday morning, she caught my eye from afar, as I watched her ruthlessly denounce her father's coaching in an impressive fashion. That sort of ground-breaking defiance is a rare quality I generally notice in exceptional champions, so to cut a long story short, I laid everything out for them and offered Sabrina an opportunity that was surely too good to refuse. Free coaching, free transport, free everything. I almost found it offensive they had to think about it, but they eventually got back to me and were keen as mustard to start. I made it clear that everything surrounding tennis was my territory. Joseph seemed somewhat relieved he was finally able to step away from her tennis, to reclaim his parental duties. He proclaimed that he would go back to work full-time.

After a few weeks of promising practice sessions where the two of us were left to our own devices, the tennis parent pop-in began. Nothing drastic, just Joseph irregularly coming to training sessions and watching the action from the parking lot. A few days later, I got a call from Sabrina's Mum notifying me I wasn't going to be taking her daughter to school after morning practice anymore. This frustrated me, as I felt these car rides were the cornerstone for our working relationship to flourish. Feeling a bit weird about voicing my dissatisfaction with not getting to drive a young teenage girl to primary school, I chose to cool my jets and decided not to say a word.

For whatever reason, Joseph was now the new taxi service, which meant he was conveniently at every session we did. Inch by inch, Joseph kept encroaching further into enemy lines, as he'd now somehow moved from the comfort of his vehicle to the clubhouse. Don't get me wrong. I am more than happy with a cordial parent watching their child play from outside the boundaries of the tennis court, but there is a distinguishable difference between a person who is merely spectating and a parent who seems unable to refrain themselves from coaching.

Slowly but surely, Joseph had gone from the car to the clubhouse, to the court, and then he found immunity in a seemingly helpful gesture of picking up the balls. Joseph disguised his burning desire to be the next tennis parent extraordinaire through the noble act of lending a helping hand. I found this to be a massive invasion of privacy. It deviated from our initial verbal agreement but was not enough of an offence to really lay down the law. Now, I was watching the evolution of the tennis parent more than I was watching the development of the player.

Next, he started filming bits and pieces of our session, which was further evidence for my case that Joseph wanted to end up being credited as the architect of his daughter's tennis career. What happened to him getting a full-time job? He was now at the courts more than ever. I made a wisecrack that he was stealing my intellectual property by filming my lessons, in the hope Joseph would catch the drift of my joke and retreat to civilian territory. But it was too little too late, as he was now clearly under the spell of a sporting addiction. Because I had offered my services at no cost, my expertise was completely taken for granted. The entire thing backfired, and my unmitigated desperation dispossessed me of any of Joseph's respect.

One Saturday afternoon, I coincidentally drove past the courts and saw none other than Joseph, out there coaching his daughter once again. The ridiculousness of what I was doing hit me square between the eyes. I was sacrificing my sanity and financial restitution to train the daughter of a guy who couldn't hold up his end of what, I felt, was a ridiculous bargain. Even after being kissed with an opportunity of a lifetime, Joseph still couldn't divorce himself from his daughter's tennis affairs. And I didn't have it in me to keep pointing out the coaching boundaries, which I had made perfectly clear from the get-go.

The straw that broke the camel's back came on a wet and wintry day, where he kept peddling his irrational ideas. In a kneejerk reaction, I rather crudely asked him to stand down from his commentary duties and exit the premises in a timely fashion, so I could do the job to the best of my ability. 'YOU'RE FIRED!' he screamed. It was a first for me, as I'd been fired plenty of times, but never from doing free work before.

But dismissing me wasn't enough. Joseph dropped the ball tube and sprinted over to where I was standing, and started screaming at me like a furious baseball manager does at a referee after a shitty call. When I walked over to my belongings on the side of the court and hurriedly started packing up, he yelled, 'Where do you think you're going?' I stood up and saw Joseph running at me while lassoing a skipping rope as if he was in a spaghetti western. After ducking and weaving my way out of a royal lashing, I finally managed to yank the whip from his hands. Then he once again proceeded to charge at me like a bull at a red flag.

I grabbed his shirt and we pushed and shoved each other, until he flattened my beautiful nose with a cheap headbutt to the face. In a state of shock, I called out for the bemused bystanders to call the police, while I continued to try and fend off the brutish maniac. An undergraduate, who was meant to be having a 4pm hotshot class with me, jumped in to try and break up the tussle. Now the two of them were grappling on the floor while our clientele of horrified parents and pee wee players watched on in total disbelief. George managed to slip his way out of a figure four leglock, and got Joseph on the outside of the tennis fence and locked the gate to make sure he wasn't coming back in. Now, all we had to do was wait for the cavalry to arrive.

Unfortunately, Sabrina, who was an innocent bystander in all this, was locked inside the court with us, and it strangely felt as if we had taken her hostage. Her father paced around the periphery like a caged animal, broadcasting my incompetence to the shell-shocked audience and declaring he was going to kill me. Finally, the cops arrived and hurled Joseph off in the paddy wagon with his poor daughter, who also had to be taken to the cop shop with her old man. I made sure to sleep with one eye open that night and kept a knife underneath my pillow for safety measures. I was paranoid the deluded man would hunt me down and gut me like a fish. Thankfully, he only resurfaced in my dreams.

## DAMAGE RECEIPT

| Fuck-Up (Cause) | Aftermath (Effect) |
| --- | --- |
| Lack of respect for the coach's expertise | Thought that he could coach his daughter |
| Wouldn't allow the coach to do his job without overstepping | Made the coach and student uncomfortable by intruding |
| Confused and embarrassed his daughter | She moved interstate to start afresh |

**THANK YOU!**

Many quality coaches have checked out from doing any work with so-called elite athletes because they can't be bothered dealing with tennis parents. There also seems to be a paradox of value in the elite coaching domain, where trainers are almost expected to accept less money to work with a higher calibre of player. Legitimate coaches find this notion to be a total insult to their craft and personal expertise, so they don't even consider working with a lacklustre athlete who tries to portray themselves as serious for a peanut salary.

Since mediocrity is the order of the day, credible coaches have lowered themselves to the masses while continuing to uphold the illusion they are trying to produce pro players. The charade now consists of coaches banging their participation drum, competing for commonplace awards so they can swindle the local marketplace, and sitting in on regular coaching conferences where nothing of any real significance is ever created or even spoken about. I don't blame coaches for not trying to create the sporting superstar, as the only thing on the cards for an individual who does try is usually, headaches, treachery and potential court cases if the player happens to make it.

```
          IT'S TIME TO PAY YOUR BILL.
     WE HOPE YOU HAD A PLEASANT EXPERIENCE!

     Subtotal:      Unorganised
     Tip:           Parents off the court
     Total Costs:   Broken relationships
                    Treachery
                    Hostile environment
```

## Great coaches, shocking mentors

Tennis tends not to be the player's main problem. If it is, then they should consider themselves genuinely lucky, as for most players, it's what's underneath the game of tennis that really disturbs them. Though many within a player's sporting sphere are undoubtedly aware of the athlete's affliction, the general opinion is that hitting more tennis balls is the answer.

Unfortunately, coaches are conned into more coaching from pushy parents when the best thing would be to cease the pointless practice sessions in favour of providing the athlete with a safe place and an unbiased person with whom they can examine their difficulties with. What is really needed can forever remain unacknowledged and unaddressed when the true issues are avoided or misdiagnosed and, in fact, the prescribed 'solutions' exacerbate the athlete's problems. Outside counsel desperately needs to be consulted so the player has the freedom to explore the psychological avenues which the tennis world can't help but stifle. Sadly, most parents and coaches are apprehensive of the athlete talking things over with a professional, as they know what is happening is wrong and are afraid the player's eyes will be opened to the exploitation. In the egotistical jungle of the tennis world, coaches and parents want to be seen as having the answers to all the world's problems to solidify their stronghold on the player and increase dependency, hindering the athlete's chances of finding any solace.

Top coaches are generally fantastic trainers yet shithouse mentors. Many lack the emotional capabilities of dealing with the dilemmas of a child prodigy, and egotistical trainers are often channelling their own thwarted ambitions into their pupils' careers, by using the athlete's talent like a weapon for their own vicarious glory. However, there also seems to be this notion that a player must get along with their coach in order to work with them, but that is simply not true. Some of the world's most notorious collaborations in a variety of different arenas have come from dysfunctional duos, who could barely look each other in the eye. If the player gets along with the coach, it's a bonus, but in no way is it a prerequisite. Besides, the best coaches in the world tend to be the ones that are the least hospitable. It's not the job of an elite trainer to try to win a popularity contest, so if a coach is truly doing a sincere job, there will be a lot of times when the player goes home despising them. If the athlete isn't being constantly challenged or a little afraid of their coach's demeanour, no goal of any true significance may ever be reached.

In an ideal world, therapy would be compulsory for talented prodigies. And just before the tennis mad hatters misconstrue what I am saying, I am not alluding to sports psychology, where the player once again is coerced into matters that only pertain to the child's sporting career. Kids who have been pushed beyond their limitations by coaches and parents need an outlet who they can vent to when their disassociation finally wears off. A person who has been down a similar path and has significantly suffered, can often be the missing piece to the puzzle. I believe an ex-sportsperson who speaks the same language as an athlete could have more potential at winning their confidence over than a traditional psychologist. I am not discrediting psychologists as I think they are extremely beneficial, but it has been my experience that tennis players have real difficulty in going the psychologist route, despite there being clear psychological issues.

## Sinking into the dark side of normality

To live fast and die young seemed to be the coolest way to go out for someone of my stripe. The only issue was I happened to survive every close scare I encountered, by the skin of my teeth. Being alive in my mid 20s was a diabolical affair, as my tennis was well and truly over and my rioting and protesting for personal injustice was becoming embarrassing and sad.

I can't remember a specific moment, but when you see people moving on with their lives and you're still sleeping in the gutter outside your Mum's house under a mountain of cigarette butts, shame starts to become a close companion. I no longer craved the attention I once did but instead sought to fly under the radar in the hope of not outing myself as a raving alcoholic. Then it dawned on me I had two options to choose from: I could carry on with my wayward death march till the bitter end, or cling to the relatively conventional things in my life and try to present myself as one of the allegedly 'normal'. Being ordinary didn't whet my appetite, but since I was desperate to not feel the merciless scowl of public opinion again, I voluntarily put myself into the meatgrinder and reluctantly turned the lever, hoping I would no longer feel like a first-class fuck-up.

When you're mentally as unwell as I was, just sourcing a shrink should earn you a Nobel Prize. I don't remember what my quack and I spoke about on our first consultation, but what I do clearly remember is how ridiculous I found their solution. For 45 minutes a month I got to drip-feed a lifetime's worth of disaster to a sheltered and uninterested looking stranger. Then for the remainder of the month, I was left to chew the fat with my unplugged brain. By now, it felt like my mental health problems and addiction issues had joined in a swinger's orgy and I was left housing a family of squatters that had no intention of leaving. I got to the point where I had so many problems that I welcomed new problems, just to wash away the old ones. Having new issues felt refreshing, and when the new dilemmas started to stagnate, well, it was just time to make some new ones. Which was a problem I never seemed to have.

Walking the beaten path had some merit to it, but ultimately, it seemed trivial and uneventful. Colours looked grey and black, people appeared to be simple-minded and boring. I remember getting into a conversation one Friday afternoon with a couple, where they were talking to me about what they were planning on doing over the weekend. I couldn't understand their level of excitement as they explained their Saturday afternoon trip to Bunnings. I honestly thought my world would cease to exist if I were put through that sort of 'excitement'. I thought I might just collapse and have a heart attack from the sheer boredom.

The dark side was always whispering my name, going, Pssssst Todd, Todd, let's have a few drinks and talk this over. I was locked in a destructive cycle I didn't even know I was on, while trying to maintain the façade of a functioning human being. Everything was completely sideways, but I couldn't see it. Where most people rest and rejuvenate over the weekend and come back to work somewhat revitalised, I was just coming to the tail end of another tumultuous escapade on Monday morning. The start of my working week mainly consisted of fear and loathing, but as I slowly started to become more human, I noticed my colleagues were beginning to run out of puff. I remember thinking on a Thursday this must be the way normal people feel on a Monday.

But I didn't get to bask in the feeling of bliss for long, as come Friday the euphoric sensation of having pushed through another working week called for a well-earnt celebration. I was like a bottle of soda water that had been rolling around in the back of a car for weeks. As soon as the top was popped, my inner life would come spraying out all over the place, saturating whoever was in its path. Sometimes the contents would find its target audience and I could very quickly gain a cult-like following of wayward disciples to party with. It's true what they say, misery loves company, but I could get so dark I'd make depressed people seem joyful. My nearest and dearest copped the brunt of it and started to act like shift workers, partying with me in 8-hour blocks until the next person clocked on for drinking duty. Bad luck to whoever got me on the back end of a three-day bender, which usually ended in some form of psychosis and complete exhaustion. I tarnished everything I encountered, but this was my best attempt at being normal. A temporarily enjoyable slow-motion suicide.

Rock bottom had a trap door I painfully plummeted through, time and time again. Then I had a string of events that logic seemed in no way able to explain, with the last one being a rather lacklustre event in comparison to some of my other scrapes. I viscerally understood I wasn't just drinking because I wanted to, but because I had lost the freedom of choice. This match was a totally different game than I was accustomed to playing, and I realised I needed to admit defeat to have any chance of winning it. Internally bowing my head to my slave master alcohol, instantaneously turned my world upside down, as it was clear that almost everything I thought I knew about myself was a complete and total sham. Something had happened and I couldn't unsee what I saw, no matter how much I wanted to look away from it. An intervention from the divine guided me to a place that became my personal sanctuary and salvation—a roomful of recovering drunks.

The 12-step program suggested I should get a sponsor, but I was too shy, afraid, and judgemental to approach anyone. Besides, I had no interest in being someone's protégé or disciple. My transactional way of thinking couldn't comprehend the idea of someone helping me out for free. Anyway, my ego was also on the prowl for something more scintillating and upmarket than what I saw occupying these community halls and churches, something like a cross between a distinguished intellect and a risk-taking adrenaline junky. Someone more like me. Then I realised 'me' was the reason why I was in this predicament in the first place. Being beaten into submission seemed to be my greatest teacher, and I had to drink a few more times before I realised, I needed more help than I'd initially thought.

Finally, I came to see asking for help was probably the most hardcore thing I could do, and Harry struck me as someone who knew his way around a catastrophe or two. I was ready to finally pop the question to him, 'Will you sponsor me?'

*smashed.*

The whole ordeal felt weirdly like being back in school, when you're going to ask a girl out on a date. Terrified of rejection, my mind agonisingly thought through every which way the future encounter might unfold. I wasn't sure if Harry was seeing anyone else or not, so I got another alcoholic mate of mine to see if he was single and ready to mingle. Monogamy was a must if Harry and I were to become an item. I needed to be his one and only, as I had too many issues for there to be anyone else. Riddled with fear, I eventually proposed.

My life has mysteriously transformed since I began attending regular meetings and developing this peculiar relationship with a fellow wounded stranger. And I've witnessed other people's lives radically change in a similar fashion when they've undertaken a parallel road. Most alcoholics have experienced the luxury of having the bullshit almost entirely beaten out of them, so their inner apparatus is profoundly wired in such a way that speaking the truth is no longer a choice. It's either that or death. This honesty is incredibly refreshing and can heal someone back to sanity if they are desperate enough to be fearless and thorough from the very beginning.

## DAMAGE RECEIPT

| Fuck-Up (Cause) | Aftermath (Effect) |
|---|---|
| Human rights violated | Addiction and self-destruction |
| Pretending and avoiding | Issues were prolonged |
| Attached to self-images | Imprisoned within unhealthy personas |

### THANK YOU!

---

### IT'S TIME TO PAY YOUR BILL.
### WE HOPE YOU HAD A PLEASANT EXPERIENCE!

Subtotal:     Shambolic
Tip:          Seek outside counsel
Total Costs:  Career
              Mental health
              Reputation

## Hanging in with the hangers-on

Before I get into this bit, I must state this is my own speculative take on the events of being part of Thanasi Kokkinakis's support team throughout his Australian Open doubles win with Nick Kyrgios. This is purely my take on the proceedings, and other people's outlooks might be entirely different.

The circuit is like an upper class Contiki tour where middle-aged men and women can relive a part of their youth by joining the travelling circus as part of a player's support team. It's also a platform for people to gain recognition in their field of 'expertise', by getting a few selfies or carrying the bags of a somewhat semi-famous tennis player. So, it's the ideal gig if you're looking to clout chase or commit adultery without your better half finding out. In the mix of all the chasing and cheating are dedicated professionals who are more interested in the coaching side of things than which 5-star hotel they are going to next. But they are outnumbered and can easily get hidden among the hangers-on.

Being part of the coaching staff for Thanasi Kokkinakis during his and Nick Kyrgios's win in 2022, pays homage to this testament. During the warm-up of the Special Ks' first-round doubles match, the practice court was littered with leeches who were shamelessly willing to waltz around the edge of the court, soaking up an atmosphere that didn't belong to them. Jumping on this joyride were agents, coaches, fitness trainers, managers, statisticians, masseuses, girlfriends, and comedians, just to name a few. The overcrowded space gives very little room for the coaches to do their job, and seeing so many people sidle up to these so-called celebrities made me question my own motives and the way I interacted with the players. Was I just seeing my reflection mirrored in these professional parasites who were happy to sell their soul to advance their own agenda?

I was desperate to separate myself as much as I could from the rest of the sponges, purely to regain some self-respect. But in trying to break away from the bullshit, I was now just coming across as standoffish and withdrawn. In a perverse way, I felt I had to be rude to be respectful. While waiting for the women's final to finish so the boys could take to Rod Laver Arena, Kyrgios asked the question: 'If you replaced everyone in Barty's camp, do you reckon she would still win the Australian Open?' Everyone gingerly laughed it off, as no one knew how to answer the question, seeing it was blatantly obvious we were all just expendables.

*doubles win*

But the week before had a different feel, as Thanasi claimed his maiden ATP title in our hometown of Adelaide. I feel the support staff played an instrumental piece in getting him over the line, seeing Thanasi wasn't even going to take to court. But when it came to the Special Ks' AO doubles run, and the input these talented players needed from us coaches, it was practically non-existent. When they were both dialled in, they had enough game to clinch the hardware with next to no assistance. Not being needed as much as I probably would have liked made me feel as if I was just another hanger-on, even though I had been somewhat a part of Thanasi's tennis since he was a little kid. As I listened to the acceptance speech, I was irritated because the guys who had fought on the front line got bunched with the groupies who had been there for two minutes. I didn't feel comfortable being congratulated and praised for something I didn't play a bigger part in; in fact, I was annoyed at how empty and meaningless the whole thing felt.

It's strange accomplishing a massive feat you didn't have to try for, and the kicker is it's even weirder seeing people who have done even less bask in the glory that you are slightly more deserving of. What I was saying wasn't exactly music to the outfit's ears, as everyone wanted to pretend, they had done their part in getting the boys to victory. But in reality, we were nothing more than a bunch of glorified cheerleaders.

# PART 5

# Culture

### When it comes to assessing talent, you can't see what's invisible

Imagine being forced to run a race you have a 99.9% chance of not winning, but still having serious expectations placed on you that you will indeed succeed. Then, when you unsurprisingly fall short, you are branded with the stigma of being a sporting failure. Tennis has always had a toxic tradition of judging players prematurely instead of just seeing what naturally comes out in the wash. The sporting culture's obsession with player projection adds unnecessary pressure to an already gruelling game.

When a young and impressionable brain happens to reside in these extreme conditions, it tends to do more than just negatively impact an athlete's performance. Children are sold the dream of a sporting utopia, where they stand to become mega rich and adored by millions of fans, but they are rudely awakened when they find it's a lonely and psychologically agonising sport that in no way resembles the same game, they'd once been mesmerised by on their television screens. Coming so far in the sporting journey makes it difficult for players to just pack up and turn back towards normality. Or perhaps they should just cut their losses and go to hell in a handbasket, spending the remainder of their days walking the earth as a sporting loser.

Professional tennis works like the casino. Sure, there will be some lucky punters who hit it big and beat the odds, but ultimately, the house almost always wins. The tennis parent is like the delusional and optimistic gambler who thinks they've found a way to beat the system at blackjack. Through the perception of a determined truth-avoider, the possibility of becoming a professional player seems achievable. Romanticism gets in the way of reality, which can see tennis parents fork out hundreds of thousands of dollars to gamble on their children's sporting careers. 'WARNING' signs should be located all around the world in tennis facilities, like gambling and anti-smoking advertisements, to properly caution parents on their real odds. Although, my guess is that a lot of tennis parents would still be keen to wager most of their salaries on their children becoming professional. This is because parents tend to believe their children are special. Once a parent sinks a substantial amount of money into their child's specialty and invests time into believing their child is different to the rest, they become attached to their own ideas and are unable to see it any other way, despite how obvious the opposite may be. Don't get me wrong, your children are special, but they are special to you, which means they're not necessarily special at tennis (or the like) at all.

It's easy to be the best of the mediocre bunch at a local level and imagine yourself as great when there is no one great around for reliable comparison. Seeing how fiercely competitive it is to make a living from the sport, tennis isn't just a game of becoming the best against the average, but rather a game of becoming extraordinary among the exceptional. Unfortunately for athletes, most coaches and parents have absolutely no idea how hard it is to make it to the top of the sport. This underestimation of difficulty will psychologically plague the child, as the player will wear the unfair expectation of success while the miscalculation by the parent and coach is conveniently ignored.

It's so easy for parents, players, and coaches to get carried away by an athlete's potential and start living in a hypothetical world that doesn't yet exist. As mesmerising as the big picture may be, it will never actually arrive if the player doesn't emphatically immerse themselves in the day-to-day duties of owning their craft. While it may be temporarily comforting for the player to have their ego stroked by these meagre assumptions, all that forward thinking does is create a perpetual state of anxiety for the athlete on game day. Expectations burden a player with apprehension and corrupt their ability to perform under pressure. Optimal performance comes from a place of spontaneity, and in my experience, the tension and overthinking caused by expectation are the enemies of instinct.

Even when pundits do place expectations on players, there is still a major issue with how people tend to measure a child's potential. Quite often, the critics radically underemphasise some of the most important components involved in tennis. Coaches, agents, and parents generally look for the more obvious domains, such as ball striking, strength, results, and sheer talent. But in a game as multifaceted as tennis, predicting potential based only on these factors is not sufficient. A junior's desire and desperation, as well as their psychological nature and ability to undertake a solitary regime, are left out of the equation. Despite what the coaching fraternity says, tennis players can't be made without these innate attributes. Elite athletes are uncommon species who have a rare type of chemistry and ingenuity, making them more receptive to this peculiar trade and lifestyle. For example, I don't think anyone would've scouted Danill Medvedev as a Grand Slam champion when he was a junior player. And I spoke to a German sporting agent who had the chance to sign

Novak Djokovic when he was 13 but passed on the opportunity after watching him practise. He told me he could see Novak making it inside the top 100 but had no idea he would be a top 10 player. I believe that's because the hardest part of the sport is invisible.

The massive misrepresentation of what the game of tennis encompasses causes players to be discontented with the sport and the people who maintain the false facade. It's only when an athlete experiences the sports lethal blend of disappointment, isolation and competitiveness that they can fully grasp the nature and difficulty of the job at hand. A lot of players become so caught up in satisfying the expectations of others, that they can't be satisfied with themselves anymore. No level of success seems to bring players any everlasting value, instead, winning only provides the athlete with a temporary reprieve from their terminal state of dissatisfaction.

The tennis life can become an existence tormented by your merciless shadow—the person you are supposed to be but are yet to turn into. A sense of fraudulence can consume a player if there is a chasm between their junior potential and their current status. Next thing, it's lights, camera, match day and all that fear and anticipation rise to the surface, and how well a player is psychologically coping with pressure and expectations is on display for all to see. What almost everyone doesn't seem to understand is when players take to court, nearly all of them are suffering from varying degrees of mental illness. The evidence is right in front of us: athletes lecturing themselves schizophrenically; erupting in violent, erratic outbursts; and displaying obsessive compulsive behaviour for starters.

Some athletes even give their player's box a heads-up that they're going to direct some of the frustration at them, and some don't give fair warning but do it anyway. When a player is in this type of head space, it's extremely hard for them to win back control over their own mind. In a desperate attempt to avoid public humiliation, exit strategies and escape plans rush through their thoughts. In a bid to save face, players tend to make excuses, are mysteriously injured, and tank matches to avoid taking personal responsibility.

Some would rather not try 100 percent and be seen as a Mr Might-A-Been, rather than give it their all only to come up short and be labelled as a loser. Expectations cause players to act in ways unfathomable to the media and public, who just see two people playing what should be a cordial game of tennis. But the athletes aren't playing the same game everyone is watching. They are playing a game of damage control; a game of personal salvation which only outwardly appears like a match of tennis. To the untrained eye they appear as spoilt and disrespectful tennis players, when they are really just responding with knee-jerk reaction to outrage and unfairness.

## Myself versus my self-image

You know you've got some serious issues when your psychologist is excited to see you. Not that my shrink thought I was going to die (though he very well could have thought that), but what I mean is, he seemed fascinated to hear about my sporting career and the subsequent issues after it was flushed down the toilet. It felt weird, as if I were his own little lab rat or passion project; but at the same time, I was kind of chuffed someone was enjoying my breakdown and mainly used the sessions as my attention fix for the day.

A concept such as depression held no relevance whatsoever for the person, I thought I was. The diagnosis went over me like water off a duck's back, even though I could feel a deep and dark void that wanted to swallow me whole. Illnesses like these were for mental patients in institutions, I thought, not for sports people who once had the world at their feet. Medication was prescribed and I took it with my other regular concoction of lotions and potions for experimental purposes only. I can't say they worked, but then again, when you're mixing pharmaceutical drugs with your own stash, it's hard to really tell what's happening.

Tennis was now a memory of the past and excessive sprees of hellacious drinking became a happening thing. I was either bar hopping or bedridden, with nothing in between. Once I came out of that withdrawing cocoon, my bedroom looked as if someone had gone through an exorcism. I'd be laid out for days, shaking and rattling with remorseful flashbacks from things I had said and done when I was under my rulers' thumb. In fact, I was so mortified I couldn't even make it to the toilet, happily hoarding cans of my own urine behind my bed, trying not to get them mixed up with the full cans of beer I also hid there. Opening the blinds became a big deal, mortified as I was by what waited for me out there in the big bad world. And if my past was any indication of what lay ahead, it was not going to be pleasant.

Being under the lash of chronic alcoholism meant I desperately needed money to keep the train on the tracks. Conventional work wasn't even an afterthought, as I knew my limitations after being hired and fired from jobs on the same day. Not only was I axed from regular work, but I also found a way to be fired from my own coaching business, where I was self-employed. What I needed was a chunk of change, a lump sum, or a one-off payment to keep me afloat over the dreary Christmas period.

The local money tournaments seemed a likely option for me to dine out on, but the idea of reopening that awful coffin was enough to cause me to shiver in my shoes. As a connoisseur of emotional pain, I could tell the feeling wasn't my usual day-to-day gnawing anxiety, but rather a horrifying sense of shame and remorse, like the way I felt after a weekend bender. I could've been a candidate for biggest underachiever in the sporting world, and my sensitivity towards my own shortcomings grew exponentially whenever I revisited the old environments.

The massive expectations placed on me as a junior were still ruling the way I acted as an adult. When you squander your potential as completely as I did, a self-protection mechanism is automatically switched on to downgrade the cyclone to just a cool westerly breeze. I unconsciously overcompensated with an enigmatic self-image of sex, drugs and rock'n'roll, that gave off a vibe which said, 'I could've made it if I continued.' As far as the tennis community was concerned, I had detoured off the ATP path five years ago and taken a hiatus down Hindley Street, the preferred locale for losers of every persuasion, and I never came back.

But my overheads were starting to hang over me, so I signed up for the local money tournaments in hope of a quick cash injection. Going back and playing the tournament felt like showing up to a school reunion, where I had previously won the award as 'Most likely to succeed', but now rocked up unemployed and broke. Outside the sporting realms I had the freedom to be as big a loser as I pleased without too much prejudice; but at the courts, I was at the mercy of public opinion, and it felt like I had a complex legend to uphold.

Returning to the scene of the crime, it felt as if I was walking through a minefield of unwanted interactions with people looking at me as if they'd seen a ghost. Scrutinising athletes is fair game in the superficial world of elite sport, so tennis crazies just stared at me in the clubroom like I was a mannequin posing in a shop front window. The toilets have always been my grace and saviour, so I quickly rushed to the bathroom to straighten my tie. I found myself sitting on the back of the toilet lid overhearing a conversation between two random people who were taking a whiz at the urinals. A voice said, 'Have you been going out lately?' To which the other voice replied, 'Not as much as Todd Ley.' They shared a brazen laugh at my expense and left the toilets.

I was rattled at hearing my name being slandered by two strangers and completely forgot I had been purposely portraying the role of a disarrayed party boy for the past few years. The coincidental feedback should've been encouraging news for my self-image, but another portion of my personality seemed to take offence, so I couldn't wholeheartedly accept the criticism as a compliment. I walked out of the toilet cubicle like a shell of a man to wait in the clubroom corner until my match was called over the PA system.

Being underdone and overweight made beating the best of what the state had to offer harder than I anticipated. But dealing with my inner conflict wasn't a cake walk either, as my warring personalities were arguing over ownership of my behaviour, which resulted in various characters getting a turn behind the wheel. A lot of effort had gone into making it look like I didn't give a fuck. And since I couldn't win on cruise control, I needed to find another gear to get over the line. But trying hard was going to jeopardise the notorious reputation I'd so heavily invested in. I was in this constant battle of playing and acting, while critiquing my own performance through imaginary eyes that only existed in my mind.

I found myself not playing to win, or even playing for the money. I was still playing against what I thought these people thought about me. I didn't know it at the time, but my audience of practically none had captured me. This community I strongly despised still had the power to dictate my actions and heavily influence the way I felt about myself. After coming up so short from where I was expected to go, I felt naked and devastatingly ashamed, so my version of success became trying to make other people believe I could've once made it. Big expectations can cause unexpected behaviour, and clearly, I wasn't thinking straight by trying to win over people who probably didn't even think twice about me. But maintaining the illusion of my self-image was worth way more to me than money at the time.

## DAMAGE RECEIPT

| Fuck-Up (Cause) | Aftermath |
| --- | --- |
| Unrealistic expectations put on a minor's shoulders | Guilt, shame, remorse, depression, sensitivity |
| Not educated on how to deal with such expectations | Living in fear of letting people down if I didn't achieve these expectations |
| No support after leaving the sport | Addiction became a solution to an emotional problem |

### THANK YOU!

What's the best way to deal with expectations, seeing it's virtually impossible to avoid them in tennis? Great question, Todd. Let me tell you what I think. One of the best ways to deal with high expectations is to unequivocally accept the worst-case scenario is going to happen time and time again. Most players and parents pledge so fanatically to positive thinking that they would find this concept ultimately too hard and threatening to grasp. But if people are serious about not being held hostage to expectations for the rest of their entire life, this is what I advise for a practice experiment. Play a match to lose. Throw the thing on purpose.

Swing for the fence and lose to someone 6/0 6/0. Do it whenever you find yourself taking the game too seriously. Bring humiliation to you. Try it on for size.

So, wear the sport like a loose garment and stop looking for the game to award you with a self-image, because it has total control over you as long as you're projecting your sense of identity onto it. Being okay with looking stupid is a superpower that creates more room for an individual to relax and let their racket do the talking. If a parent gets on board with this psychological approach instead of chewing their nails off and riding each point as if an apocalypse depends on it, the player's potential is limitless. I recommend stepping into stupidity. That is when the idiot becomes braver to try the unthinkable, while the intellect stays imprisoned to the expectations of other people.

```
            IT'S TIME TO PAY YOUR BILL.
       WE HOPE YOU HAD A PLEASANT EXPERIENCE!

       Subtotal:      Failure
       Tip:           Open-mindedness
       Total Costs:   Self-esteem
                      Perfectionism
                      Inability to unwind and relax
```

## Learning to play on the dark side of the court

The tour is a circuit full of shameless opportunists who have all forgotten their morals and manners, with an impressive façade covering its narcissistic undercurrent. Everyone within the sporting fraternity stays tight-lipped about their secrets for success. In fact, tennis players are so competitive they don't even want you learning from their mistakes, even after their career is over. The dark side of competitiveness turns friends into adversaries and it's well-known between 'mates' that they don't wish each other well and are hoping that the other fails. Unfortunately, tennis delivers this same toxic environment all the way from the grassroots to the Grand slams.

Most individuals become so accustomed to the toxicity that they don't even notice it, like a fish not being able to observe the water because it's swimming in it. It's not unusual for a player to develop a spineless and deceitful character off the court, because of being raised in this extremely hostile environment. If coaches and parents don't make it their priority to teach children where the line is between competitiveness and bitterness, judgementalism becomes the players' primary way of thinking and behaving.

As soon as players start competing in junior tournaments, they put themselves out there to be judged by other people. Age offers no immunity in competitive sport; parents treat kids like adults and disgracefully disregard the fact they are mere adolescents playing a pointless game. These kids are subject to other parents' constant judgement and criticism in a way that would be completely frowned upon outside the tennis world.

A parent who continually criticises other kids in front of their child, inadvertently imbues their own offspring with self-esteem issues by reinforcing a message of perfectionism. Subconsciously, the kid knows they are under the microscope more than anyone else, and that can make a young mind catastrophise about not receiving much-needed approval from their parents. External achievements now define the child's self-worth, and success becomes the central measure against which to decide whether a person deserves their respect. So much for love thy neighbour. My own Dad encouraged me to ruthlessly interrogate players to extrapolate as much information about the enemy as possible, so I generally had my opponents pegged within the first few seconds of seeing them.

Instead of using local competitions to challenge each other and push everyone's level up, players are pitted against each other, and the atmosphere becomes psychologically poisonous for everyone involved. Keeping up with the Joneses—or to put it better, beating the Joneses—very quickly becomes the parent's and the player's new primary purpose for participating in the sport. This short-sighted and vindictive lens has significant consequences in the not-too-distant future. Nothing makes a tennis player and their parent more secretly satisfied than seeing one of their rivals go down, and the longer the child stays in this contaminated environment, the more this character flaw deepens. In the past, I've become fixated with seeing my supposed 'friends' fall victim to misfortune and bad luck. Perversely, getting my kicks from seeing players injured, mentally unstable, or losing matches they should have won, became a personal hobby of mine. News of a comparative rival going further in a tournament or scoring a wildcard was like having a spear thrown into my icy heart.

This selfish and self-centred type of mentality is the wrong attitude for life. While it might help your game, it certainly won't turn you into a decent person. Tennis is such a lonely existence, it's already an individual game, and the divisions grow with people's nastiness and spite. It is too difficult to have meaningful relationships in such a sterile environment. People could come back and say, 'Well that's just the way life is.' But it doesn't have to be! This is why I caution players about spending too much time at the tennis courts: because unfortunately, I believe a human being can't help but become their environment.

## Character assassination

An individual basing their opinions on first impressions is simply someone waiting to be proved wrong. But I didn't believe my Terminator x-ray vision made any mistakes, as I was a deadeye dick when it came to evaluating everything and everyone around the Australian tennis scene. All the compliments for this immoral trait must go to the chef, my judgemental father Max, as he knew how to give you someone's biography before they even opened their mouth. See, Dad believed his thoughts unequivocally, despite them being based on unfounded assumptions. If his brain thought it, it was real. I guess I inherited the skill of condemning someone, prior to investigation, from one of the best.

Having all but conquered the national landscape, I was now looking for bigger fish to fry. The European dirt was calling, and a select few players were sent over to compete in some of the biggest 14/U junior tournaments in the world. Bad blood simmered within this god squad, as all the athletes had become accustomed to duking it out on home soil for national titles. It goes without saying that our tennis parents were tangled up in those heated matches, which ultimately turned into personal vendettas. So, watching them all wave us off at the airport sure made for some interesting viewing. Since we were such fierce adversaries, it was hard to become close mates with my fellow comrades despite the transient brushes of comradery and companionship. We didn't need to necessarily play each other in the draw for there to be a contest going on, as bragging rights for who went furthest in the tournament was always a game worth competing for.

In Europe, differentiating the players from the coaches was challenging, as the sheer size and strength of some of the international specimens made me wonder what was in the water in certain parts of the world. The change of scenery was uncomfortably congested with bulging calves, deep grunts and 5 o'clock shadows. Little old me was still a pre-pubescent 12-year-old runt, who could have easily squeezed his entire body into his own tennis bag. Moreover, we Aussies had come from a sacred spot over on the other side of the globe, making our names against local hacks nowhere near the pedigree of these swollen goliaths.

Rumour and inuendo quickly circulated around the locker room, as the players frantically tried to distinguish the contenders from the pretenders. Amid the trepidation, the draw was finally released, and everyone held their breath as they eyeballed the A4 piece of paper introducing them to their ultimate fate. I was comforted seeing I was up against a Chinese boy, and not some backyard brawler who was homegrown on the red European clay. My attention quickly shifted onto the draws of my fellow compatriots, where I was livid to see my stablemate, Gazza, was served up the match of a lifetime by the sporting gods above. He was due up first against a French wild card at 9am. While these cryptic entrants have a whimsical title, they generally were nothing more than sacrificial lambs over on our side of the pond. I completely forgot that social norms may be lost in translation, now that we were all navigating in new waters.

It was five to nine and the tension was building. Neurotic players loitered around the tournament desk like mental patients in a psych ward waiting room. A friend of mine whom I knew from Bollettieris gave me a nudge, pointing out the guy Gazza was up against. I immediately thought it was a joke when I saw a lanky and lethargic-looking tourist ever so slowly making his way to the tournament desk. I reflexively said to Lars, 'Come on, you're taking the piss, aren't you?' But he had already jogged off to finish his warm-up. I stood there in disbelief, totally jealous at Gazza's luck to have drawn such an amateur, then I ran over to him with a disingenuously pleased face to inform him of the good news.

The crackling PA system started calling out players' names for the 9am matches, instructing them to assemble at their designated courts. Since my match wasn't on till later in the day, I gave Gazza moral support, walking with him to his battleground, which felt like a short flight away. We stalled a bit to let the Frenchman walk first, so we could dissect his mannerisms. It was legitimately hard to take him seriously as he looked like the spitting image of Steve Urkel, a character from the '90s comedy show Family Matters. He wore RUN DMC glasses, rocked op shop clothing, and carried a one-zipper racket bag as if he was a Sunday afternoon picnic player. After a matter of minutes, Gazza and I were assured we had the Frenchman pegged, and hypothetically moved onto his next opponent. I didn't even bother to wait around to watch the start of the match, because in my view I'd already seen it all, so I wandered over to keep an eye on Gazza's next opponent. After 30 minutes of watching two South American dirt rats grind it out as if it was desert warfare, I moseyed back over to Gazza's match to catch the tail end of the slaying. The unorthodox-looking tennis player was giving my mate a lesson he wouldn't soon forget.

The Frenchman was like a Formula One race car driver who was testing out his new turbocharged engine for a practice run. He'd purposely let Gazza's shots get as far away from him as possible, then would put his foot on the accelerator and sprint the ball down at max capacity with a death-defying slide to break. Revving his motor in such an extreme fashion meant the Frenchman looked gassed in between the points, and I was sure it was just a matter of time until he blew an alternator. He dawdled around the backstop as if he was about to conk out, then finally parked his ass on the fence to return serve. But as soon as the point started again, he would shift gears and go from zero to a hundred in just under two seconds flat.

This guy wasn't just a compelling tennis player, he was a full-blown entertainer, showboating to the few people there by defying the laws of physics with his freakish athletic ability. I continued to support my sparring partner till the bitter end, trying to hide the spiteful smirk written all over my disingenuous face. All in all, there was no shame in losing to this dude. He was an unprecedented freak of nature who went on to be a top 10 ATP player in the world.

```
                    DAMAGE RECEIPT

     Fuck-Up (Cause)        Aftermath (Effect)
     ----------------------------------------
     Judging people       | Superficial
     prematurely by how   | tendencies and not
     they looked          | giving people a
                          | chance
     ----------------------------------------
     Believing my         | Isolated and
     assumptions of       | lacking connection
     people were right    |
     ----------------------------------------
     Inauthentic and      | Self-loathing
     two-faced            |
     ----------------------------------------

                       THANK YOU!
                    ||||||||||||||||
```

Being fake and judgemental isn't something you generally grow out of; it is something you grow into. In fact, it progressed to the point where I had a habit of looking down on people from the gutter, and disliking people I didn't even know yet. Not for a second do I think tennis players are the only creatures on earth who judge others, but the more cut-throat the line of work, the more judgementalism there seems to be in the industry. I can't imagine librarians and cleaners have such a vested interest in seeing their rivals come apart at the seams.

Constant exposure to fierce competition tends to fill an athlete's inner world with insecurity and fear. Expectations are added by outside influences from those who haven't spent a second living under the scrutiny they are condemning. Humans are hypervigilant to imminent danger, which the athlete comes to unconsciously associate with tennis and the players in it, so athletes see other players as a serious threat to their own safety and survival. Unfortunately, people generally tend to handle these feelings of doubt and insecurity by pointing the finger at someone else, instead of facing what is going on inside them. How many people do you think want to really face the malicious part of themselves that is triggered by the sport they are supposed to be in love with, and audit the people who got them into it? Athletes simply project what they are feeling onto other players and then condemn them for doing the same thing.

```
           IT'S TIME TO PAY YOUR BILL.
     WE HOPE YOU HAD A PLEASANT EXPERIENCE!

     Subtotal:     Poor character
     Tip:          Stay away from the courts as
                   much as possible
     Total Costs:  Judgmental
                   Hypocritical
                   Inability to develop
                   meaningful relationships
```

## The intergenerational difference in culture

The younger generation seems to have two mentalities when it comes to tennis. Some players seem to love the sport and wear the title of tennis player as a badge of honour. Others could take it or leave it, and at times they seem to resent the sport and the two-dimensional identity they can't seem to escape. The mix of abuse and privilege, coupled with the lack of life experiences, can leave athletes trying to build a more three-dimensional identity by adorning themselves with tokens suggesting other interests. There have been numerous instances where top players who have struggled with the rigorous demands of the game in their earlier years went out to the real world to explore other options. These supposed breakdowns have often been breakthroughs, as the athletes have come back later with a different perspective and found a way to reach ultimate success.

On the other hand, there are players whose freakish ability, rather than passion for the sport, found them at the top of the game. And though it has always been the older generations understanding that you must love and respect the game in order to play at the highest level, we now see another tennis generation, some of whom seem to find success regardless of them despising the sport. But if the sport has seriously damaged and affected the lives of some of these individuals in the top tier of players, is it a fair expectation for them not to show signs of dissatisfaction and unhappiness after many years of anguish and torment?

The legends of the past keep an eye on the sport from afar and are infuriated at the sad state of affairs tennis has turned into. Watching some ungrateful players represent their country, that they bled for, devalues the mark they made in the sport. So, when it comes time for these two different generations to coexist, they don't seem able to meet halfway. The times are very different today. Kids are now heavily influenced by social media and have more reach to see how other people live their lives. This can lead to players unrealistically comparing themselves to celebrities from other fields such as singers, actors, and basketball players. Unfortunately, tennis isn't a sport that serves you up fame and fortune on a silver platter, and the sacrifice players make to become professional is more noticeable than ever.

The old-school generation wants players to earn their stripes and show respect for the opportunity at hand, instead of constantly complaining and looking for shortcuts. But some of the new wave players are showing more allegiance to sincerity than heritage. They want to be able to be authentic and pay homage to the side of themselves that tennis takes away from them. In a nutshell, they want to be recognised as more than just tennis players. This intergenerational difference in culture becomes a public mockery as both sides seem to handle the situation in the wrong way, with the feud broadcast over breakfast television where the morning hosts get to put their two-cents in. The rift created puts up a wall, stopping a wealth of knowledge and information from getting to the new wave of players who would greatly benefit from the wisdom.

A failure of compromise seems to be the issue, as legends aren't willing to get off their high horse, and the younger generation lack respect for prior champions who paved the way before them. Instead of extending an olive branch to the misunderstood, a civil war goes on behind the scenes among countrymen who sadly can't seem to see eye to eye.

## Some questions you should NEVER ask your Mum

'What's a rim job Mum?' I asked. Her face dropped as if she'd seen Satan in the flesh, and I could immediately tell by the look on her face it was something that shouldn't be coming out of a 12-year-old's mouth. Here I was thinking it maybe had something to do with gardening, when in reality it meant… well, you know what it means. I had heard the term loosely thrown around the locker room by Davis Cup players earlier that day. I had been given the honour of being the orange boy for the team when they took on Germany, in Adelaide in 2000. My mother, Sharon, the passive silent type, furiously yelled at the top of her lungs for my Dad to meet her in the bedroom at once. The two of them nattered it out loud enough that I could clearly hear what they were saying, despite the door being slammed shut. I never did find out that day what a rim job was!

Davis Cup was the mecca for me when I was growing up. I wanted that green and gold jacket more than anything. Australia had a reputation for being extremely patriotic when it came to the Davis Cup, and I was overwhelmed at being initiated, even if it meant I was just peeling the bananas. During the practice week leading up to the tie, the team seemed to have good chemistry in training sessions, with the usual back-and-forth tennis banter. I paid close attention to the flow of the operation, picking up on small details such as players' nicknames and practice routines. Desperately wanting to be part of the club, I started encouraging team members by using these sobriquets but was quickly told this was not permitted and only certain people could call the players by their special nicknames. Bit weird, I thought, but whatever. Their names, I guess.

As the week went on, the shit talking increased, and I realised certain players wouldn't practise with certain other players. The team started to operate like an artificial stepfamily who'd inherited relatives they didn't like yet had to find a way to get along with come Christmas time. Watching people on TV achieve things you could only dream of automatically makes you put these people on a pedestal, and you forget they are exceptional tennis players but not necessarily exceptional human beings. Instead of seeing my desire to play for the green and gold growing, I was somewhat uninspired and disappointed by some of the scenes that went on during the tie.

The Aussie team had sealed the deal and won the tie 3-0 after the doubles on the second day, leaving the dead rubbers to be played on the third and final day. Celebrations kicked off on Saturday night once the result was finalised, and a couple of players were a bit left of sideways the next morning. Only the real die-hard players were still keen for the dead rubber, as pride was now the last thing left to compete for. I was sitting courtside barracking for the Aussies to sweep the Germans, when I got word to go and get something out of the locker room for one of the athletes. I waited till the change of ends and scooted off underground to run my errand for the team. I opened the changeroom door and was hit by a front bar fragrance and saw one of the marquee players still in his suit from the night before, laid out on the bench under his locker. Holding his forehead from an apparently vicious hangover, he yelled, 'Who the fuck is that?' I froze and timidly replied, 'It's Todd, the orange boy.' He said, 'Hurry up and get the fuck out of here.' I was pretty shaken up after being cussed out by one of my childhood heroes. Meanwhile, the Germans found a way to reclaim some of their dignity by snatching the last two rubbers of the tie, which sent our locker room into complete disarray. A racket was demolished into tiny pieces while the rest of the team stood around in an eerie silence as if it was a funeral.

Even though it was a team environment it still had a real individual feel to it, and it didn't seem natural for some of the star players to be a part of a group setting. Which makes sense, as tennis is an individual game, for the most part. It was a good eye-opener for me, as I no longer cared to play Davis Cup for Australia and became more self-oriented than ever.

### Say hello to Hollywood!

While I was living at Bollettieris I became Americanised, which was cultural suicide for a young Aussie touching down on home soil. My new place of residence was Victoria, as I had been selected into the Australian Institute of Sport, which meant I was required to be in Melbourne when I wasn't abroad. While living in America, I had adopted some of the slang and swag, and dressed to impress the biggest show-off all, which was none other than super coach, Nick Bollettieri himself. Ironically, it wasn't my taste in fashion that caught his eye, but rather my touch of flare. I disobeyed orders one humid afternoon while doing a mundane cross court volley drill, and instead hit an audacious drop shot winner that viciously spun back over my side of the net. He screamed out, 'Hollywood!' From then on out, 'Hollywood' was what I went by.

Nothing was too jazzy for Nick as he was a trendsetter in his own right, continually defying the status quo of the tennis world. The cult leader's lawlessness meant the academy was a place for pundits with supersized personalities, and for this very reason everyone there seemed to share a quiet but common concern they weren't being flamboyant enough. It was a distinct contrast to the tall poppy syndrome we have back home in Australia, where you are condemned to plead the fifth about your gifts and graces, because taking yourself too seriously is considered a cultural sin. I immediately rubbed people up the wrong way in Melbourne with my unabashed confidence and unsociable personality. The word 'arrogant' and my name were generally used in the same sentence. But I felt like I could walk the talk, as I was being hailed as the 12/U king of the planet.

Because I won some of the biggest tournaments in the world, the federation body was forced to grapple with my father Max, who was ruthlessly unreasonable at the best of times. Dad was looking to strike while the iron was hot, as he felt my junior results gave him enough leverage to barter with sponsors and organisations to get me more opportunities. And he was right. However, the broader tennis community becomes bitter when they see a junior being offered finances, free clothes and rackets, and you almost immediately turn into public enemy number one. But I was still too oblivious and naive to pay attention to any of the sporting politics, so I continued walking around the National Tennis Centre like my shit didn't stink.

It's so easy to take things like this for granted. But for me, being showered in non-essential things didn't seem out of the ordinary. It just felt like it was all part of my destiny. To say I was spoilt infers I didn't fully deserve the rewards. I definitely earned what I got with my blood, sweat and tears, but I just don't know if it was all necessary, or if the frills were at all even helpful. I was too immature to understand these opportunities would be gone as quickly as they came if I didn't keep working extremely hard, and unconsciously the spoils disillusioned me into feeling I had made it before I'd even really started.

Dad could see I was getting too big for my boots and tried to counteract it by throwing out empty threats such as getting me to work at the local butcher's, which of course he never pulled the trigger on. I wish he had; it would have been the best thing for me. But he couldn't stand to see his masterpiece off the court for that long, so he tried his next best tactic, which was yelling. But yelling only amplified my behaviour, as a reflexive fuck you. Not only was my unsavoury attitude getting under my father's skin, but the tennis community at large seemed to want my head on a stick. I was now regularly receiving online death threats from people within the sporting sphere.

I didn't like the role of social outcast, but the more abuse I copped, the more I embraced the role of the villain. Being judged by people who don't know you at all is a weird thing to get used to, and since I was being vilified and accused of being a certain type of person anyway, I thought I may as well lean into the persona instead of letting the situation swallow me whole. Even though I despised a lot of Dad's decision making, I always revered the psychological make-up that allowed him to make such brazen choices. My portrayal of an antihero was laughably inauthentic, whereas Max played the part like an Academy Award nominee. Dad owned all his oddities and really didn't give a flying fuck whether he was resented, rejected, ridiculed or despised. I was in awe of the guy for happily standing on the opposing side to society and not letting what people thought of him get in the way of me achieving my sporting goals. The only problem was, I couldn't remember what my dreams were anymore, although I knew they certainly weren't this.

Nothing infuriates an old school coach more than an entitled kid who is taking an opportunity for granted. They know the wank gets in the way of the work, so my coaches hated seeing me being handed stuff prematurely. It also spits in the face of their attempts at playing the sport, as they probably would've walked across hot coals to get to training when they were my age. And now, they were forced to work with a braggart who would pull up stumps at any sign of adversity. As my passion for the sport came into question, I started to look like a spoilt brat in the eyes of the coaches. They couldn't fathom being given the opportunities I had received as a youngster and behaving in such a lousy fashion.

The superficial rewards I received blinded them to what was going on beneath the surface. We came from totally different generations, and these guys weren't practising psychologists, they were ex-journeyman tennis players who had turned to coaching by way of making a buck. They had no time or sympathy for the soft. On paper it looked like I had been given every single bit of good fortune, yet I was frequently half-arsing practice sessions by acting out as either a manic clown or a whinging sook. I used these performances to try and entice the coaches and other onlookers into the circus tent that was my life, because behind the thin veil of teenage angst was a lost kid in a foreign city who was self-harming as a way of feeling anything at all. My existence was a sad kind of alienation, where I felt uncomfortable within my own skin and out of place wherever I went. I spent a lot of time alone, wondering what the hell was wrong with me. It was clear I was no longer interested in pursuing the thing I had sacrificed my childhood for. Slowly but surely, I was disregarded and thrown into the too-hard basket. I got kicked off Australian teams, sent home from overseas trips, and even tried blackmailing my coach's wife.

My coaches and I were at a stalemate, and we couldn't find common ground for connection. A mutual understanding was non-existent and the communication, which wasn't great at the best of times, totally collapsed. I wasn't responding to the typical hard-ass, finger waving in your face, if-you-can't-hack-it-fuck-off mentality. But the new intern, Paul, was the missing link. He bridged the gap between the new wave player and the old school coach.

It takes a certain individual to discard personal differences and be genuinely curious about where a player's outlandish behaviour might be coming from. Since I was a peripheral citizen, whose identity wasn't rooted in anything solid, I could easily transform from looking like a rock n roller, to a rapper, to a wrestler, all in the space of a week. I changed, and I changed often. Thankfully, Paul was the type of person who didn't find my cultural appropriation and overall weirdness as offensive as the other narrow-minded coaches. Coming from the US college system himself, Paul was more attuned to American culture, which I had humiliatingly claimed as my own. Throughout a difficult period where I was seriously struggling, Paul's presence impacted my life for the better.

Despite being given the role of just a hitting partner, Paul ended up being a more influential figure than most of the other trainers, who seemed to feel as if their faces belonged on a coaches' Mt Rushmore. His philosophy of 'connection before correction' went a long way when it came to dealing with the disenfranchised youth. Tennis seemed to be Paul's secondary concern, and for someone like me, who had been treated like a 'human doing' rather than a human being, Paul's approach was rescuing. Instantaneously, my results improved and enthusiasm for the sport returned. Paul didn't necessarily have an illustrious CV like the other coaches, but what he had far outweighed all their sporting experience put together.

Those skills can go a long way to assist a kid who has been seriously depleted of TLC.

## Squeezing into the impossibly tiny, tall poppy box

Australia's tall poppy syndrome curbs this country's potential, instead of allowing it to push out and grow as far as it can. If you want to be a professional athlete, the nation wants you to live your life according to a bunch of twisted and contradictory stipulations. We want you to try your hardest, but don't be a try hard. We want you to be great, but not to really admit it. And we want people to show their personalities, but they can't tell their personal truths. It's a difficult ask to try and get someone as undomesticated and raw as a young tennis player to fit into this tiny box, and it's generally a death sentence for any athlete who tries to follow these cultural norms. The public don't understand that a lot of these guys aren't looking to win the Australian of the Year award, they just want to win tennis matches and make something worthwhile out of the brutal years of oppression and mistreatment.

The older generation around me couldn't see past some of the benefits I was receiving for my sporting career. It never occurred to them to think about what I had to do to receive that assistance. What do you think is the price for being the best 12/U junior in the world? If anything, the sponsorships felt like renumeration for the emotional abuse and social deprivation I had suffered every day since first picking up a tennis racket. Just because you're good at something doesn't necessarily mean you love it; it doesn't even mean you enjoy it. Very few players continue to have the same love for the game as they get older, and some never really loved the sport to begin with. The fact that young children are often coerced into doing something against their will isn't something the sport willingly exposes, regardless of how obvious and well known it is.

If a junior is rewarded with a handout because of their sporting career, they have essentially earned it from child slave labour, whether the public wants to acknowledge that or not. If a kid working at the Nike sweatshop got some free attire after slaving away their childhood years behind a sewing machine, you wouldn't be vilifying them. Are you comparing yourself to a kid working in a sweatshop, you say? Yes, I am, if we are talking about the hours of labour put in for no return. People seem to easily overlook what appears desirable on the outside without truly understanding what it costs.

And that's one of the reasons we're now left with a generation of misunderstood players who divide the nation.

### Time to square the ledger with Langman

I've never quite known the grounds on which friendships are supposed to be built, as all my close friends have been people I've tried to crush and destroy on a regular basis. When competitiveness is the key component of kinship, you find the connection comes with its fair share of conflict. And my relationship with Langman has been no exception.

I call him Langman because we share the same first name and I want to be the only Todd in my circle. Langman was twice my age, three times my size, and four times uglier when we met. He was by far the loudest and proudest of the local Thursday night squad I trained in, and after the session was over, he was the only one brave enough to take my Dad up on his offer of playing practice sets with a 7-year-old. We duelled until the owner called last drinks, then Langman dropped a bombshell that was to change my life forever. Langman told Dad and me that he had a floodlit tennis court in his backyard, and it was literally two minutes away from my house.

He didn't think twice about jumping in the car and hitching a ride with us, who had been complete strangers to him until just a couple of hours earlier. I wanted to keep the same score from where we left off, but Langman demanded a clean slate so he could have another bite at the cherry. But that's the way Langman was once he stepped over the white line; he was a cunning provocateur who would try to antagonise you into an early submission with his bag of confrontational party tricks that weren't always legal. Despite his on-court antics, Langman was by far the biggest character and most entertaining person I had ever come across. He truly was a first ballot, hall of fame shit stirrer.

Finally, the match was adjourned at 12:15am, when Langman's Mum, Janet, came out in her nightgown, saying the next-door neighbours had put in a noise complaint. 'Doesn't Todd have school tomorrow?' Janet asked my Dad. She recognised the situation as strange. The look on her face said she had been expecting to see a gang of teens drinking on her tennis court, not her 14-year-old son happily playing tennis against a 7-year-old with a 50-year-old bystander as the referee.

The three of us shared a fanatical taste for tennis, so this sort of behaviour instantly became normalised. It wasn't long before school was well and truly out for both of us. Langman was expelled and I got home schooled, if you could even call it that. Once Langman got his licence, he practically became my part-time chauffeur and right-hand man, driving me around from obligation to obligation and taking the occasional power nap in the front seat of the car.

It may sound like Langman didn't have a life outside training and trafficking me around, but that couldn't be further from the truth, as once his daily duties with me were over, the rest of his life began. I was too young to consider how bizarre the situation must have looked from the outside, as the age difference had people perplexed as to whether Langman was my coach, bodyguard, brother, chaperone, or friend. Truth is, he was all those things. But it wasn't a paid gig, and we weren't blood related. In a way, I think the job worked more like an apprenticeship for Langman, as he had to earn his stripes from his messiah Max, while getting an all-access look into what was required if you wanted to have a serious shot at superstardom.

Our relationship was built on admiration. He put me on a pedestal because of my sporting ability, and I loved the way Langman could defuse a stressful situation by using his quick wit and larger-than-life personality. At the time, most people saw Langman as just another a local joker, but ultimately his buffoonery and lack of self-awareness were his biggest strengths. In fact, Langman had the perfect amount of dedication and absurdity to make him a valuable participant in the travelling circus. He could learn what the experts knew, but they couldn't hold a candle to his desperation and natural gift for showmanship. In an industry contaminated by unhealthy pressure, Langman's outrageous sense of humour cut through. But just because he was a natural stand up, didn't mean Langman joked around when it came to his conviction to the cause. He didn't operate under the slightest hesitation about whether our tennis dream would come to fruition. Even if it didn't, he seemed happy trudging the path of high performance anyway, as extreme competitiveness was in every fibre of his blood and bones.

I was learning from him just as much as he was learning from me. Our car rides were a form of education. We'd stop at Subway, and he'd shout me double-choc cookies and refill our communal cup until the store manager said, 'That's enough.' Once, he persuaded the girl behind the counter to give us both some free yellow Subway visors, which we proudly wore during our club matches on Friday night. Langman was spending so much time with Max and me that we changed his name to 'Leyman'. Janet felt as if she was losing her child and would regularly call up Max late at night, asking him if he could please return her son. My father was raising us like a couple of ferocious pit bulls, and if Langman ever saw someone messing with the meal ticket, he didn't wait for Max to say bite.

Like the time we were in Italy playing Futures just before I was due to compete in the Wimbledon juniors. Langman was deep in the third set against a lefty local, and Max and I were doing cheerleading duties from the grandstand. The opponent's father was starting to get awfully edgy, giving me death stares every time I clapped in support of my brother from another mother. Langman clutched a crucial cat and mouse point, bellowing out another massive 'come on', to which I applauded as usual, when the fiery Roman father stepped towards me as if we were gladiators back in the Colosseum. I immediately felt sorry for the other guy, as he didn't know what he'd just walked into. In the blink of an eye, Langman dropped his racket and jumped into the stands as if he was Ron Artest in Malice in the Palace. My Dad had beaten Langman to the draw and was already ready to rumble, while I had the difficult job of trying to get these two savages to not eat this poor guy alive.

Langman always stepped in, always supported me. When things got rough at home with Dad, Langman opened his doors and gave me a place to stay. Towards the end of my dying career, he even offered to pay for some of my training sessions, which I couldn't possibly accept.

But when the wheels came off my career, everything changed. My world suddenly stopped and Langman's life kept going, which I took as an offence. I wasn't mature enough to understand that people had their own lives to live, so I took our separation as a kind of abandonment. Langman had become desensitised to child cruelty and indoctrinated into a world of self-discipline where you take ownership of your own results, and he placed the responsibility of the end of my career squarely on my shoulders. It felt as if the people who knew the most about my tennis seemed to understand the least. Langman seemed more interested in using me as a sparring partner for his next batch of protégés, than concerned about my mental health and well-being. When the aftermath of my downfall wasn't being validated with any sort of consideration, I started to retaliate with tongue lashings to give the insensitive son of a bitch a piece of my mind. My mother confronted me and demanded I apologise to

Langman immediately, but I wouldn't as I believed I was the victim, and he was the one who owed me an apology for jumping overboard when the ship got leaky.

Years went by and then I ran into him at my local watering hole on the back of a four-day bender. He was having dinner with some friends, and I sent my drinking buddy over to his table to whisper in his ear that a guy named 'Todd' wanted to speak to him in the side smoking area. It didn't take long until I burst into tears, remorseful for my behaviour and being such a failure. The air was somewhat cleared, but the crying wasn't well received. You might not get a heart-to-heart with Langman until he's on his death bed with stage four liver cancer. I've only ever seen a single tear fall from his face on one occasion—when his engagement ended because his fiancée couldn't fathom how he wanted to spend more time with me (a teenage boy) than with her. Maybe the armour will come off one day, but since real men don't show their feelings, I'm not going to hold my breath.

These days I find myself wanting to know the man behind the mask, not the version he shows in his over-sensationalised coaching sessions, which put mine to shame. But our relationship, unfortunately, has been built on earning respect by bulldozing through life's tasks rather than helping each other see what's causing us to constantly be swimming against the current. His vice of workaholism is conveniently more camouflaged and socially accepted than my alcoholism, so he has been allowed to wave his finger at my behaviour, which is just a different presentation of an issue we both share. No one ever thought they'd see the day when I'd give up the booze, but when I did, I felt a silent thread from Langman pulling at me saying, 'You can get sober, but don't go getting successful.'

Seeing how people react to me trying to turn my life around has been an eye-opening experience. At times I've weirdly felt ashamed for trying to be a better human being. It seems like some people just want you to stay where they want you. Rewiring my brain to disidentify with some of my flawed core beliefs is proving to be one of my hardest mountains to climb. Langman and I are running a tennis academy together, but we are becoming ever more different people. Where seems to be chasing wealth, an immaculate front lawn, and the accolades from his tennis success stories (not that I think these are unworthy ambitions), I have become more interested in pursuits of creativity, fathering my son and trying to figure out who the fuck I really am. Yet I'm still so competitive I get annoyed at him for thinking he's winning the greenest grass contest, when that's not even a competition I'm participating in. I've come to realise that a rivalry against a best mate is a match where both friends end up losing. But I'm not sure the poker game will ever conclude.

Step 9 in the AA program requires me to apologise to the people I have hurt with my destructive behaviour, and Langman's well and truly at the top of my list. Not wanting to give him the satisfaction of rounding everything off as my fault to have over me for the rest of my life, I've been unable to make the amends to Langman in person. So, I thought I'd deliver it in pen so it's on public record.

So, here goes.

Langman, I apologise for being unappreciative of everything you have done for me. Witnessing other people take advantage of you first-hand has made me realise that I, too, have taken our friendship for granted. I've been unfairly cruel to you, especially considering how much you've put yourself on the line for me, time and time again. For this, I'm truly sorry. And I'm grateful to call you a friend and a brother!

Todd

P.S. I put you on the map.

## Ladies and gentlemen, the trainer has been called to the court

Tennis commentators seem to be judge and jury on distinguishing what a legitimate reason is for a player to take a break during a match. I have heard them consistently question how genuinely a player needs to go to the toilet in the middle of a match, but they don't query a player's integrity if, out of nowhere, they conveniently need a medical timeout to get their calves massaged when they're 5/4 down in the third set. Why do they scrutinise the legitimacy of a player's need to do a wee or a poo more than they do a sore leg or shoulder? Isn't it more obvious players would need to go to the toilet more than they are likely to be injured? And if someone could lie about needing to do a number 2, couldn't they also lie about having an injury? What's the difference? That says it's okay to disrupt your opponent's momentum by getting your fake injury massaged during an injury time out, but you'll be considered a cheater when you call for a toilet break, even when you genuinely need one.

# PART 6

# Complexes

### Finding the formula for unconditional love—or something like it

If disgruntled tennis players hate the game and what they have been put through so much, why wouldn't they just quit the sport? They are adults now and in charge of their own lives, and no one is stopping them from going and working in another profession. If you hate the sport, just quit!

There are several obvious reasons why players stay in the game, such as financial reward, status and a lack of anything better to do. But generally, there is a deeper issue at play that goes unnoticed, and it goes all the way back to childhood parenting.

In many tennis households it has been taught from early childhood that love is conditional. This is obviously never stated out loud, but nevertheless the child gets the message loud and clear from their parent's behaviour. While the English language is certainly a powerful medium, it's been reported only 7% of communication is interpreted through words, while the other 93% comes through behaviour, body language and vocal tone. Therefore, even though parents know the 'right' thing to say—like 'it doesn't matter if you win or lose'—children are well versed in the fact that this statement is pure nonsense, as the cat's out of the bag the second a kid loses a tennis match. The incongruency of the parent's verbal message and contradictory behaviour creates confusion for the child, and it can seem to them that they are only loved if they are winning, even though you'd hope the parent unconditionally loves them.

In order to feel the love most children are awarded automatically; the pursuit of high achievement becomes a necessary component in a player's life. But unconditional love is permanent, and fundamentally deeper than the temporary validation the tennis parent gives their child. When a player runs on a love deficit, they become an emotional busker, willing to sing for their supper to get a momentary hit of validation to spike their internal bankruptcy. This theme of misinterpreting love for admiration can play out for the entirety of an athlete's life. They may remain a hostage to their adolescent need for approval from external sources, because they feel a deep sense of incompleteness and are desperately searching for ways to become whole.

The outrage of it all is this type of emotional blackmail works wonders in getting results early in a player's life. The supremacy a parent holds over their child often leads to them using this power in a corrupt fashion because kids have a biological need to be loved by their caregivers. I believe one of societies biggest human rights violations is caused by parents who make their children work for recognition. The crime is that if a kid can't safely attach to their parent, their human development and very survival are in jeopardy. So, children are at the mercy of their parents and will do anything for their affection.

Ironically, to me, some of the worst forms of abuse come from parents who worship their children so much that they subject them to being their own personal mascots. Instead of the adults fulfilling their primary role as a provider and nurturing caregiver, they idolise their kids' talent and put them on a saintly pedestal. Magnifying someone's abilities isn't the same as loving the individual, so parents who hero-worship their imperfect children only ever end up devouring them in a scrupulously debilitating fashion. And to make matters worse, today's society and culture rewards high achievers without any curiosity about where the child's drive and desire are coming from. This societal message only confirms the tennis parent's 'you have to achieve to receive' philosophy, which has been drummed into the child since day dot. The apparent absence of love leaves a gaping hole in the make-up of many tennis players, and very often leads them to making all types of misguided attempts to obtain temporary relief from a terminal problem.

As the player gets older and transitions from the juniors to the professionals, their public profile begins to grow, and another solution becomes available to soothe this deep yearning—attention. To someone who has been ostracised from normal society and hasn't received unconditional love from their parents, attention has the potency of heroin. Instead of chasing the ranking, some players chase the attention as it provides a similar feeling and effect their achievement once did. When it comes to youth these days, being 'known' is an achievement of sorts; they want to be famous more than they want to be respected.

When a player reaches their later teenage years and gives up on acquiring the approval of their parents, the need for attention pervades into other aspects of life. Many players seek this attention through bad behaviour. Unfortunately, good behaviour doesn't get you the audience negative behaviour can. Take someone like the American rapper Tekashi69, who was once a broke dishwasher and became an overnight sensation despite being a terrible lyricist. Instead of trying to get better at his art, he marketed himself as a musical villain and asked for and invited as much negative attention as possible, while using Instagram to show himself doing the unthinkable on a regular basis. Some tennis players adopt a similar strategy and apply it to the sporting world, attracting attention from immature teenagers and tennis fanatics to soothe the internal deficit.

The problem arises when the day comes for the tennis to come to its conclusion, or when the fickle Instagram followers abandon ship. How on earth does someone succumb to the reality of being just another brick in the wall? Living anonymously is too agonising for a lot of players to manage, so they sign up for activities where they can still bask in the glow of a fading limelight.

### A hole in my soul—a dull ache you couldn't touch but couldn't ignore

Whatever you don't transform, you transmit. But Dad didn't think there was anything wrong with him. In fact, he felt he had the formula for survival and success. Making it out of a grim existence with all his faculties intact provided my Dad with a faulty sense of self-assuredness about his life methods and extreme philosophies. This, he felt gave, him a license to teach at the university of life.

Our household was all intensity, with zero intimacy. Maybe love (whatever that means) could have connected my mind, body, and soul to each other, and enabled these faculties to live together in holy matrimony. It seems when a vital human need isn't on offer for a child, their psyche goes on a boundless exploration to find a surrogate option. Remarkably, I stumbled upon something even grander and sweeter than love, but an almighty catch came with it: you had to devote your life sincerely to becoming a master or a messiah. Then, and only then, would you be showered in an awe so glorious that it made love seem like a trivial pursuit. And since unconditional love from my father was clearly off the table, being worshipped as a titan of tennis was something seriously worth striving for.

Immortality seemed to be the only way forward and luckily, I had an inexhaustible amount of underlying anxiety to propel me towards that much desired superhero status.

My father supplied me with most of the drama along my hero's journey, by continually testing my emotional pain threshold. Sometimes the emotional suffering was applauded, and I was showered by Dad's praise in the car ride home, telling me how proud he was of my efforts. Other times, usually when I had come up short in a tournament or shown too much emotional anguish, the commentary wasn't so pleasant, in fact, it was downright abusive and cruel. Just knowing this type of incident was only a lacklustre performance away was a petrifying thought.

On the other side of the coin, I knew the exact opposite could happen if I won, or if I slaughtered myself senseless in the pursuit of excellence. In the instance I won a close match on the tennis court, Dad tended to celebrate me as if I was a Grade One Stakes winner at Flemington. Max was so temporarily intoxicated by the triumph that his victory speeches weren't just confined to my ears only but were given to any living creature game enough to give him some of their attention. Not that he was bragging or boasting, but Dad was so drunk on the glory he needed to vent about it to someone to get it out of his system. Witnessing my father having these euphoric episodes because of my ability to wave a racket around was a conflicting experience. It was like that episode of the Simpsons where Homer starts showering Lisa in praise because she has a natural talent for predicting who will win football games. After all, Dad's affection was what I wanted more than anything else in the world, but I didn't want to be condemned to barter for care and decency through my performance. As much as I lapped up the adoration, it also intensified the feeling within me that I had very little intrinsic value. I had the horrifying premonition I was nothing more than a human spectacle, needing to perform for the gratification of others. This shivering suspicion made trying to relax almost impossible, as I knew imminent danger was on the cards if I couldn't compete at the highest level.

Dad's hyperfocus on my tennis career and the lack of consideration he gave to anything else sabotaged everyday life and most of his relationships, although those were the least of his concerns. But just because they weren't his concerns, didn't mean the situation didn't bother me. I felt an inexplicable sense of guilt towards the desertion the rest of my family endured because of his serious involvement in my life. In my eyes, I was now indebted to everyone and the only redeemable way I saw of paying everyone back was with the riches and fortunes of my pending tennis career. Since I was still years away from making any real money from the sport, I continued my torturous quest of winning and destroying myself for hits of affection. Watching Rocky fanned my sporting flame into a ferocious fire, as the movie exemplified a romantic theme of beating yourself to a pulp, which was contagious to my impressionable brain and consolidated my father's core philosophies.

So, I upped the ante, getting up at super-early times of the morning to go through my own workout routine, which usually ended with me running to school with Dad driving behind. He didn't give a shit about the people who were hustling to get to work behind him in peak hour traffic. They'd honk and yell out profanities, while he stubbornly went 15kph in a 60 zone with one eye on me and the other on the stopwatch. But my escalated efforts didn't seem to bring me any more reward. Ironically, the validation went down, and the whip cracking went up.

Mind you, he was still a constant mouthpiece for my sporting achievements, by praising me to other people in the same way he idolised his champion greyhound sprinter, Dirt Bird. But even Dad's usual hero-worshipping had changed, and it was now moving more towards megalomania. Max would constantly forget his audience and go off on lengthy tangents about random players and the inner workings of the tennis world.

Our family understood conversations needed to be steered away from tennis territory, otherwise Dad would drivel on all night about about biomechanics and wrist pronation on the serve.. But because he was so charismatic, Dad tended to come across as an eccentric sports nut, instead of a self-absorbed man who was busy living in his world of one.

I was starting to become disillusioned by the romantic idea of hard work, as it seemed like nothing more than societal farce. My constant overtime wasn't earning me any more emotional backpay; it was just making my ringmasters portfolio look more impressive to his imaginary audience. Dad was judging each day on its own merit anyway, as he believed you couldn't get full from yesterday's food.

*#1 in the world trophy*

There comes a point where you literally can't work any harder or get any better without it being seriously damaging and frankly psychotic. Dad's allegiance to his empty ideal meant he got lost in the hyper-productive black hole, where every minute of every day was devoted to discipline. I couldn't just watch TV; I had to be stretching on the Swiss ball. And now, instead of getting ice creams and compliments on the car ride home from tennis, I was being forced into using my hand squeezer to strengthen my wrists for the backhand volley. Eventually, I made it to the top just to try and get away. But not even becoming the Number 1 junior in the world was enough to quench my old man's voracious desire.

Who did you have to be to get some recognition around here? Since working hard wasn't working for me, I became resentful towards any activity where I was required to lift a finger. I was bitter at the measly exchange rate that came with this laboursome pursuit, and I entered a new rebellious phase, where it was lame to even try. This brought my inner and outer worlds to a crossroads. Obviously, professional sport and hard work go hand in hand, and now I was being berated by my father for not giving my all on the court.

Knowing validation from my father no longer satiated my emotional thirst, my psyche went on a voyage to find a suitable alternative. Having given up on the golden rule of hard work, I started to gain a notorious reputation around the tennis traps for being a bit of a recluse. Infamy was far easier to attain than affection and praise, so seeking negative attention became my new vehicle for emotional wellness. But this coping mechanism turned out to be no different than the other one—the same busking, just in a different show. Attention is a hard habit to kick when you've been raised to be a performer, and by the end of my tennis, I was clutching at straws for anyone to give me as much as a side eye.

When I crash landed back in the streets of Adelaide after a failed tennis career, I was plagued by the same characteristics. This meant romantic relationships were doomed to fail, as brutalising yourself isn't a love language most people can comprehend. I was still perversely hardwired to obliterate myself for the of the approval of others, and I was going to extreme measures to acquire the missing feeling. But inflicting unnecessary suffering upon myself was always met with a mystified look from outside parties. Once again, I couldn't understand how assaulting myself wasn't winning me a standing ovation from my partner. *I'm killing myself over here,* I'd think. *What's the matter with her?*

Ironically, I was repeating the same pattern from my childhood, and I ended up bitter and resentful when my romantic 'acts of love' weren't being celebrated and worshipped to the standard I was accustomed to. Unbeknownst to me, I didn't need to nearly kill myself and become utterly miserable to win the approval of another person's heart, because the love was apparently already there. But I just couldn't accept this love in blind faith without inflicting damage upon myself to make it feel warranted.

Attention once again became my daily jam. I was a devout exhibitionist who tried his best to conceal his show-off nature, pretending I didn't like the limelight while wearing aviator sunglasses inside on a wintry evening. Since my tennis was no longer a means of recognition, I had to come up with new ways to get it. Being highly emotional and a crippling empath, I thought the arts seemed like the perfect point of call. I wasn't an artist, but I certainly felt like I was an artist type. And I was desperately searching for a location where I could behave like a lunatic without winding up behind bars in a jail cell.

I didn't genuinely care about the craft or have the tolerance to be a theatre student, I honestly just wanted a standing ovation. Besides, introducing myself as a performer sounded way better than a tennis coach. But when my acting fantasy collided with the sobering reality of being cast as an extra, I turned my back on tinsel town too.

Pivoting left, I wound up in a modelling agency strutting my stuff on the catwalk for a few months. Incredibly, the fashion world made my vanity look like child's play. One night before a runway gig, the spiritual leader of the modelling clan was giving the boys a pep-talk to pump us all up. In true Derek Zoolander fashion, Filip said, "Just remember, boys—the girls want us, and the guys want to be us. Now, hands in." I shamelessly put my hand in the huddle and yelled, "FINESSE" with the rest of the prima donna's. I ended up being blacklisted by the owner of the modelling agency for getting into what I thought was an open relationship with her best friend, which turned out to be a clear misunderstanding on my behalf.

Next on my quest for eternal flattery was the music scene, but I'd never strummed or plucked a G chord in my entire life. Deejays were like local celebrities in the town I lived in, and I wanted in on some of that C-grade status, thank you very much. I befriended a DJ called Danny Depressed and strongarmed him into giving me a trial set at a dive bar called Supermild. But it didn't take long for the open bar to beat me in straight sets.

Next came the convertible car I couldn't afford, and the body image issues resulting in over-exercising and under-eating. Time after time, I kept looking for a life seeming sparkly on the outside, while I was completely and utterly bankrupt on the inside.

Drinking as I was destroyed my ambitions, and very quickly everything was stripped right back. I knew I was down for the count, no longer able to chase grandiose goals, so I downsized, developing an even deeper interest in entertaining strangers. Weekends consisted of drinking from breakfast to blackout while busking for donations of attention wherever I could get it. I much preferred the cheap and seedy bars where I felt like a millionaire in comparison to the rest of the regulars in the place. That way I could preach from my bar stool while looking like a poor man's Keith Richards, without feeling like my audience could see through me.

I paid my way out of regular problems by bribing the bar staff with tasty tips, and would throw money at any other related issues by telling the people I'd offended to put their drinks on my tab. This turned into a rather expensive hobby as I became a renowned drink shouter at my local watering hole. But the generosity was nothing more than a selfish and desperate attempt to buy other people's admiration and company, so I didn't have to suffer the agonies of my low self-esteem.

The stakes were high with this new coping strategy, as I was now getting attention from some suspicious characters. Dabbling in the dark arts with some of society's undesirables made me feel like I was breathing on borrowed time. I was too bad to fit in with the goodies, and too good to fit it with the baddies. But this bar was my sanctuary, and probably the only place on planet earth where I was safe from my feelings of inadequacy. At the same time, I was at a real risk of drinking myself to an early grave or getting myself offed on the way there. Desperately needing something that's clearly killing you is a baffling predicament to be in. But I just couldn't deal with being average, and I had no external qualities to hang my hat on but the persona of a loudmouth after too many Hotty Toddys—a shot the bar named after me.

But even in the seediest bar on earth, I could still feel as insignificant as a prop-holding extra. Not only was I livid at the people who I thought were better than me, but I was envious of the people in the bar who looked comfortable in their own skin. The relaxed and content ones who didn't need to perform to earn admiration from an anonymous crowd. The ones who could simply be themselves and enjoy the night.

```
            DAMAGE RECEIPT

    Fuck-Up (Cause)      Aftermath (Effect)
    ....................................
    Didn't smell the    | Not able to look
    roses along the     | back on massive
    way                 | achievements
                        | with pride and
                        | happiness
    ....................................
    Conditional love    | Seeking
                        | admiration,
                        | approval and
                        | attention from
                        | exterior means;
                        | low self-esteem
    ....................................
    No rest or          | Inability to chill
    relaxation          | out and constantly
    promoted            | needing to be busy
                        | to feel worthy.
    ....................................

              THANK YOU!
          ||||||||||||||||||||||
```

It was always my understanding that when I gained a certain level of self-awareness, I'd be able to change my own behaviour. That then, I'd be able to drift off into the sunset and live happily ever after, without a worry in the world. But that certainly hasn't been the case. Even though I can now clearly see how my life has been utterly terrorised from seeking validation, I still can't seem to get off the emotional merry-go-round. My newly gained skill of self-awareness has felt like a form of psychological torture at times, as I'm now able to see myself wanting the approval of others, whereas before, I had the luxury of not knowing I was after it at all.

It's difficult having a mind that swings between grandiosity and depression with absolutely nothing in between. Since I'm plagued by a sense of incompleteness, a part of me is always on the prowl for ways to make me feel either better or numb. It's ugly stuff, looking at the driving forces behind some of my hobbies and behaviours, as they are often performed from a place of self-hatred rather than for satisfaction. Ambition turns into obsession and everything else in my life gets neglected from the full-throttle pursuit.

Constantly scrambling the earth for a few measly drops of admiration leaves me in a state of the exhaustion blues. But since I see no other way of feeling neutral, I'm compelled to continue searching for an everlasting ovation. It's taken me sometime to realise this type of adoration isn't within my grasp anymore. I've been chasing a carrot that's not even dangling. So, now what? Well, my rather 'healthy' mental health issues surface, as I try to numb myself in the most wholesome way possible, since I'm trying to give up all my life-threatening vices. Unfortunately, self-destructing on a low carb salad doesn't quite hit the spot like a bottle of scotch and a 40-pack of smokes. So, when my over-exercising and nutritious bingeing ceases to distract me from my inner turmoil, a deep and dark depression overwhelms me and makes me feel like I'm a lazy and worthless piece of shit.

Truth be told, peace and serenity scare me, and I wouldn't have the slightest clue what to do with it anyway. I'm not ready to sit on a blanket near a lake and listen to Cat Stevens all day. I figure there will be enough time for that if I get to 80. However, in saying all that, I am in the process of trying to wean myself off attention seeking dependencies, and something tells me this is going to be my hardest habit to kick yet.

```
            IT'S TIME TO PAY YOUR BILL.
        WE HOPE YOU HAD A PLEASANT EXPERIENCE!

   Subtotal:      Workaholism
   Tip:           Smell the roses
   Total Costs:   Self-annihilation
                  Unfulfilled
                  Unhealthy emotional dependence
                  on validation from outside sources
```

## Taking a risk on intimacy to get close to the truth

Intimacy, the skill of honestly sharing your true self with another human being and experiencing closeness and connection, whether it be intellectually, emotionally, or sexually, is a subject rarely discussed within the sporting world. Intimacy is something that I've personally struggled with, and I believe it stemmed from my conditional upbringing and years in the tennis sphere. I can't speak for anyone else because people don't regularly disclose this type of personal information, but I will go out on a limb and guess that other athletes have experienced similar issues.

    Some players may be comfortable letting themselves be vulnerable and exposing themselves to the world, or at least to trusted friends and family. However, the issue tends to arise when a relationship become too close or intimate, even though intimacy may be something the player desperately wants. If you are not in a relationship, it's easy for intimacy issues to be disguised through one-night stands and partying, because it all happens in a dark nightclub and alcohol is usually involved. Lust is also a different beast from intimacy, and we'll get to that later.

Tennis players' lack of trust in others seriously jeopardises their capacity for intimacy, and many of us prefer to keep people at an arm's length. I think this fear may stem from a childhood blighted by conditional love, where the kid must constantly earn affection to feel a sense of wholeness. It sets a faulty baseline for the child because it says, 'You are only worthy of intimacy if you are good enough.' With tennis players, personal standards are so ridiculously high from a very young age that we are destined to project their unrealistic expectations onto other people as well as ourselves. These standards aren't exclusive to tennis, and generally manifest in many different areas of life, such as beauty, success, status, and image. This way of life turns into perfectionism in all facets, and it comes into play when selecting a suitable partner, as they are seen as an extension of the individual and therefore must also be perfect. God forbid the partner isn't faultless and brings in any extra scrutiny from outsiders. These expectations generally sabotage relationships, because the player is more insecure about how their partner makes them look, which ultimately gets in the way of them developing a deeper relationship with their significant other.

In tennis it's fair game to almost objectify players as puppets rather than people. It is common for spectators to pick apart athletes' physiques—his calves are a little small or she's stacked it on—and justify it as relevant to the game, which in many ways it is. But I can't imagine this objectification does wonders for players' body image or self-esteem; in fact, I know it doesn't. Athletes can become morbidly obsessed with their own reflection and can develop eating disorders or body dysmorphia because of the continual scrutiny. Through no real fault of their own, tennis players can turn into some of the vainest creatures who walk the planet, just from being in such a superficial environment for so long. Players take serious issue with the scrutiny they receive; but despite not wanting to be judged themselves, it doesn't stop them from judging others. Conversation among players generally consists of shallow slandering of rivals' physical features, like: 'Did you see how low his nipples were through his shirt?' or 'That sock tan is fucking hideous!' Even if it's not a conscious decision, players are quick to deflect scrutiny away from themselves onto easier targets, as a way of self-preservation.

Being conditioned by such a ruthless environment naturally makes a player look for ways to lessen the damage. Since copping continual criticism on the chin would cause a nervous breakdown, athletes tend to seek refuge behind self-images instead of being their authentic selves. An excessive reaction to a feeling of inferiority can make an athlete forfeit their true life, in replacement for a fabricated persona. But this solution only creates more problems, as dishonouring your own individuality tends to erode a player with inner conflict. But I still don't think this is the primary reason that players safeguard themselves with personas and façades.

While they are certainly protecting themselves from relentless objectification, I believe they are more importantly protecting themselves from themselves. What I mean is, players are quietly desperate to avoid painful realisations that will confirm their underlying suspicions surrounding their own self-worth. And nothing acquaints someone with who they really are better than a relationship or intimacy. The truth doesn't always set someone free; it can also be earth-shattering and extremely bad for a person's health if it catches them by surprise. So, intimacy becomes a strip that could potentially reveal more than just a player's privates.

## Pretending to know but not having a clue when it came to intimacy

No one enjoys losing in qualifying and waiting around to play doubles, as the courts are all occupied by main draw matches, so you start feeling more like a tourist than a tennis player. The tournaments earliest losers were having some beers in Room 246, and when in Rome, do as the Romans do, I thought. Thankfully, my relentless shadow of a father wasn't with me. We'd had a fight, and I went on hiatus momentarily, so now was the perfect moment to make up for lost time by getting a taste of what I had missed out on for years.

I was an old 16 in tennis years, but a young 16-year-old when it came to life. But I didn't want to come across as a lightweight to the rest of the ratpack, who were old enough to rent a car and collect unemployment cheques. Tennis doesn't discriminate when it comes to age, especially when you lose early in a tournament. The rule seemed to be: if you can take a loss, you can take a beer. I hated the taste of alcohol but loved its effect. The agenda for the night was straightforward: drink till you've erased the day's loss from your memory and then hit up a club in town to make the most of a shitty situation.

But I was a featherweight and on my last legs real early. Trying to look like a tough guy and keep up with the experienced drinkers it didn't take long for the toilet bowl to become my close companion as I vomited up most of the Melbourne bitter that I'd consumed. Mid-chuck I heard a couple of familiar female voices coming from outside.

I looked in the mirror, saw three of me, so dusted the middle one off and re-joined the piss up, to see the lineswomen who'd called my match earlier in the day, each with a whiskey in their hands. It turned out they were sisters, and the older sibling was showing the younger sister the umpiring ropes on the tennis tour. They'd made some shocking line calls in my last round loss, so I made sure they didn't hear the end of it.

Three-quarters of a bottle of Wild Turkey later, everyone was on the floor of the dingy hotel room playing strip poker. I was a total prude, a virgin in fact, but I wasn't letting anyone in on that little secret. I wanted to fit in. Besides, I had the chaos under control, I thought as I stripped down to my worn and torn tighty whities.

'Just deal the fucking cards,' I said to the dealer, Chris, who was only shirtless with jeans on. 'Fuck.' I was the first one out and the crowd was calling for my cock. I got up and people started trying to yank my undies from me as if I was male stripper on a hen's night. The pressure got to me, and I panicked. I quickly grabbed my gear and bolted for the hotel stairs. As I was sprinting for the exit, I heard someone scream out something I couldn't make any sense of. I didn't stop to ask any questions, as I charged up the fire escape stairway, desperate not to give anyone a flash of my privates.

I made it back to my room, wearing nothing but the essentials to cover up John Lennon and Paul McCartney. Yes, I nicknamed my nuts after The Beatles! I won't bother telling you what body part I called Ringo Starr. My roommate Jack was also drowning his sorrows, so I began telling him the bizarre story about the lineswomen drinking with the players, when I realised, I'd left my phone in Room 246. 'I'll come down with you.' Jack said. He grabbed his cans of vodka Smirnoff, broke one off and threw it to me.

By the time we made it back to the room, the game of strip poker had escalated to more of a Boogie Nights kind of vibe, and people were drinking and shamelessly hooking up. By this stage, the Cruisers were seriously catching up with me, and I was in and out of blanking out as things turned into what could only be described as a Roman orgy. But this wasn't like the orgies that I usually strangled the goose to on Pornhub. For starters, the room was pitch black and you didn't know who was where. Sound was the only sensory receptor available, so logistically you were guided by moaning and whispering pillow talk. My mate Jack wound up getting a handful of something that he wasn't interested in holding. He went nuts and turned the lights on, to everyone's dismay. 'TURN THE FUCKING LIGHTS OFF!' the sexual deviants yelled as I peered around the room trying to get my bearings.

A lineswoman beelined it to my direction and we started fooling around on the foldout. I had no intentions of taking anything further than some innocent hanky-panky, but she had different ideas, as she jumped on me and forcefully put her hands over my mouth and said in an umpiring manner, 'Quiet please.' I always planned on the first time being with the one. The girl of my dreams, where I would be wearing all white, with candles in the windows and rose petals over the bed, and Barry Manilow crooning romantically in the background. Not in a rundown hotel room with six nymphomaniacs, two of whom were the lineswomen who had to call my doubles match the next afternoon.

Maybe this story has something to do with my intimacy problems, but maybe it doesn't. Honestly, my behaviour in relationships has been just as big of a surprise to me, as the person on the receiving end of it. Looking back, I pity the ones who dared to try and make a decent man out of me, as some hearts were broken in the process. I may very well hold the Guinness World Record for the most relationship break-ups with the same partner. In fact, the cycle would repeat so frequently that I never knew when we were on or off anymore. It was like watching a movie I'd already seen and hoping it somehow had a different ending. But since neither of us changed, the ending remained the same and we were doomed to circle in the same drain forever. These relationships were soul sucking and incredibly disruptive to not only our lives, but everyone who encountered them. Even though I could clearly see the damage these things were causing, it felt like I was being manipulated by a gravitational pull exceeding my own freedom.

I didn't know just how much my wellbeing was dependent upon other people, as once a relationship was broken off, it felt like a life-threatening blow. Caught in a swirl of emotional grief, I desperately wanted another turn on the merry go round, bewildered as to why I got off the ride in the first place. This sent me scrambling back to someone who I'd found completely incompatible just a short time before, ready to announce my undying love for her (though I never would). Going through the baffling process of trying to explain my incomprehensible actions was weird to say the least. I questioned whether I was either psychopathic or sociopathic during these encounters, where I felt absolutely nothing in the face of a distraught person. Since I simply could not share myself in an intimate fashion, I was forced to dance around the truth by muddying the waters with verbal nonsense. Sometimes my poetic word salad was given the benefit of the doubt, and a reunion would occur. But the second I was let loose out of the doghouse; my perception shifted straight back to a fatalistic view over my partner's inadequacies. My mind couldn't help but pick away at imperfections like a picnic platter, so I could find fault in things that were damn near perfect. This pattern of push/pull became a regular tendency in my romantic relationships. Once the honeymoon period fizzled, I would crash back into normalcy and feel as if a random stranger was now occupying my personal space.

Women have questions for all types of things and require a certain amount of affection to help them feel comfortable and safe. Because I didn't feel like conversing and cuddling with someone who seemed so off-putting, I was compelled to withdraw or overcompensate with an exaggerated persona to avoid the threatening discomfort of closeness. Intimacy seeks to disrobe you from any artificial pretences you may be clinging to, and I had no interest whatsoever in stripping down to this prerequisite, as it would mean I'd be forced to face the real me. My gut feel: myself and I would not get along swimmingly.

It's so easy to give an external excuse for an internal problem when you're completely unconscious. It's even easy to do it when you're totally awake. Some people will go to whatever measure necessary to avoid certain truths, and since I was so adamant my girlfriend's disproportionate amount of mayonnaise on her turkey club sandwich was our main problem, I didn't once stop to look at my side of the street.

Judging women from a shallow criterion just isn't cricket, so obviously I couldn't broach such trivial matters and out myself as a narcissistic hypocrite. Especially since I ordered the schnitzel, chips, and gravy myself. How could I possibly expose the innermost parts of myself, when these traits were downright hideous and in dire need of as much concealer as humanly possible? I couldn't express any of this to another living soul, so the madness continued to revolve in my mind like a never-ending rotisserie, while I was clamped in a daily routine of trying to uphold the façade of upstanding citizen.

If I was ever sexually propositioned, my response would be weird, to say the least. Even though I was a toey young man full of impulsive desires, I could strangely feel angered and repulsed by the suggestion of intimacy. Whenever the deed did happen to go down, I resorted back to disassociation and fantasy as a way of coping.

### DAMAGE RECEIPT

| Fuck-Up (Cause) | Aftermath (Effect) |
| --- | --- |
| Limited interaction with the opposite sex | High turnover of relationships |
| Broken trust from parents in childhood | A sense of feeling unsafe and requiring superficial defences to guard myself from being hurt |
| Power of example was dysfunctional | Couldn't see my behaviour as abnormal |

### THANK YOU!

Intimacy was going to bring the house of cards down on my fractured beliefs about who I thought I was. To avoid the discomfort and possibility of earth-shattering realisations about myself, my tendency was to cut and run or push the other person away. The closer I got to someone, the more I awoke to the fact I wasn't really who I was pretending to be, so I would adjust my position and retreat to a more comfortable distance. Sometimes it was as far away as the Himalayas.

When I thought of sharing my innermost self with another person, the likelihood of them not running off seemed slim to impossible. While society probes men to be more vulnerable, no one enjoys having to shoulder a sobbing mess. And I knew I wouldn't survive disclosing such humiliating information, to then just be abandoned by a person spooked by my oversharing. Instead of the relationship growing deeper, it would turn into a more personal competition, where my partner became my biggest rival. I would project my perfectionist ideals onto her, so I could potentially gain self-esteem from other people by using her as an accessory for my benefit. Just as a new pair of Louis Vuitton loafers or Dolce and Gabbana shades would do. Not holding myself accountable to the same standards I expected of my partner, I reeked of hypocrisy.

```
         IT'S TIME TO PAY YOUR BILL.
    WE HOPE YOU HAD A PLEASANT EXPERIENCE!

    Subtotal:      Intimacy issues
    Tip:           Please let me know if you find
                   something that helps
    Total Costs:   Objectification
                   Perfectionism
                   Projection
                   Likely to develop intimacy anorexia
```

## Wild coupling is the reward for years of denial

The tennis parent sees no room for young romance. To them, such business is trivial and an unnecessary distraction that can only lead their child down the wrong path. So, they tend to put the player on a leash and exclude them from normal scenarios where interactions with the opposite sex can occur. A guilty conscience for oppressing a kid's natural urges can often lead the parent to make up for this deprivation by showering the child with alternative spoils.

But this compensation doesn't come with good convertibility as the child becomes accustomed to a particular type of lifestyle that bolsters their sense of self-importance. For a lot of people, being placed at the centre of the universe makes the player believe they are fundamentally better than the rest of society. This feeling of entitlement also makes the kid believe their needs are more important than anyone else's and can unsurprisingly make them exceptionally selfish and self-centred. As a result of this extreme conditioning, it's very common to see tennis players show strong traits of narcissism in adulthood. This type of personality may work wonderfully in a fiercely competitive environment such as tennis, but it causes havoc in interpersonal relationships, and comes to a head when the player is ready to start dating.

Trying to repress a child's natural instincts has heavy repercussions as they age towards adulthood. Allowances need to be made so the athlete can have some social flexibility, as they are swarmed by adolescent urges that get stronger by the second. If the parent doesn't understand the magnitude of the situation and fails to give their child enough leeway, the player's career is in jeopardy of burnout. Not from too much tennis, but rather from biological deprivation.

On the male side of the sport, parents generally compromise. They tend to allow the player to philander, in a trade-off that sees the kid stay away from other damaging vices such as alcohol and drugs, which will certainly ruin the sporting dream. This unsaid understanding seems to be a reasonable one for the player, considering he has been subject to a lifetime of abstinence. Hedonism very often becomes the new form of religion as the player tastes the fruit formerly forbidden to him. The parents' gesture still mostly protects the interests of the player's tennis career, but not his personal development when it comes to forming healthy relationships, as he is given a green light to consort with as many women as he can.

To get the results they need, the tennis player has generally been trained not to care about other people's feeling, despite the damage it does. Their career and needs are of the upmost importance and anyone or anything intruding on that right gets tossed out the window. This is how the player has been trained, from cancelling on friends and family at the last minute, to getting the $50 rib eye steak while the rest of their support team starves. Players become desensitised to thoughtless acts of selfishness and disloyalty. They lack empathy for the people they hurt, putting it down as the price to be paid to become a top tennis player.

### When it comes to love, the first cut is the deepest

My girlfriend Erica said to me, 'If I buy you a pair of jeans it will hopefully stop you from taking them off with someone else.' What do you say to something like that when you are a part-time cheater and a full-time bullshit artist? In my mind I was a good guy because of how little I cheated. I mean, I didn't go rogue all the time,

just when I got on the gas. Which was every weekend. My ability to compartmentalise my life into separate worlds meant I didn't even feel guilty for the scandalous behaviour I carried out under my alcoholic alter ego. Because my personality change was so dramatic when I drank, it literally didn't even feel as if I was the one doing my own drinking. It also meant the behaviour that came with it didn't belong to me, so there was no real thought attached to my dishonourable actions. I didn't even stop to consider what I was doing.

Todd the person no longer seemed to exist, as I was now one half of Erica and Todd. I couldn't just blow around in the breeze anymore, as Erica was a high achiever with big plans for her future. Our relationship had stemmed from a playground romance during my short stint in high school, which was ultimately interrupted by my deportation to the sporting sausage factory in America. The problem was, my previous experience in relationships was childlike in comparison to this one, because this adult relationship had adult expectations. It was too serious for someone of my immaturity, but after plummeting from the sporting solar system back into a foreign society, a steady woman provided me with some much-needed emotional consistency. Unfortunately, this relationship didn't cancel out my belief that I was also permitted to indulge in guilt free promiscuity when I was drunk, as a sense of emotional and sexual entitlement had me feeling I deserved the best of both worlds.

Erica was the most overwhelmingly normal person I'd ever met in my entire life. I don't say this in a bad sense, I just mean her level of accountability and the things that she wanted to do with her life legitimately terrified me. For example, Erica wanted me to join the mixed netball group, socialise with her school friends, and thought the two of us should backpack overseas for a few years. I, on the other hand had never endured such conventionality and couldn't manage enough change to buy a bus ticket to her house on any given day. Instead of seeing me as a deadbeat boyfriend, Erica kept looking at me like I was her knight in shining armour, which I initially relished but ultimately found completely unbearable.

Seeing my parents had a marriage that made dying alone look appealing, my perspective on relationships was quite warped. My mother was very domestic and tried her best to juggle my father's uncontrollable emotions and, since the apple didn't fall far from the tree, I was interested in recreating a similar type of relationship that could help me, save me, from myself. So, Erica and I clearly had different interpretations of what a relationship was all about. I couldn't grasp why she kept trying to get us to do everything together. Mum and Dad never went out on dates or travelled anywhere as a couple, so the idea that Erica and I would globetrot around the world just seemed like the most ridiculous suggestion I'd ever heard. I didn't think there was any room for gallivanting around the place; I thought you were meant to suffer and strive. Besides, I'd done all that, and the world I'd seen wasn't a place worth revisiting. Looking back, I guess we both ironically wanted the same things, but the holiday I was keen on taking was a getaway from myself.

Little did I know, when you're dating someone, you're practically dating their folks as well. My inner reaction to being around Erica's family was difficult to interpret, as I couldn't put my finger on what I hated about these nice, respectful people. I came from a household which lacked any semblance of normalcy, so a pervasive bitterness engrossed my soul when I was around anything or anyone who was natural, normal, or well-adjusted. An obvious disgust towards Erica's loving family was now written all over my face, as they continued to talk to each other in pet voices and show their gratitude to one and other through endless displays of public affection. Supper time meant everyone was required to sit at the dinner table and talk eloquently about the day's happenings. Which immediately made a liar out of me. What was I supposed to speak about? I had a vague suspicion Erica's English-majoring father might not enjoy hearing how Dad wanted me to help him sell pornographic calendars door to door with his housemate named Balls. I was learning more about the dysfunctionality of my own family, the more I was around someone else's.

Erica was more of an adult than I've ever been, yet there were curfew rules to obey, and restrictions surrounding me going into her room. Her lack of independence under her family's roof drove me up the wall, and I hated blind compliance in matters I thought demanded protest and needed change. But worse than that, I felt scorned and degraded that I came off second best to Erica's family and their silly guidelines. When I didn't win her all to myself, I felt even more entitled to behave in a hedonistic fashion.

Erica wanted to make a man out of me, but I was too selfish and egotistical to be a good person's other half. Ironically, they were the exact traits that made me excel for a brief period in an individual sport. And because I had trained to be so uncompromising for such a long duration of time, flexibility and easygoingness seemed like characteristics of a spineless coward. I was accustomed to being catered to and always getting my own way when it came to particular things, and that heavily contributed to my immaturity in early adulthood. My needs were always more important than anyone else's, so even a person merely stating their own desires seemed to come across to me as inconsiderate and rude. I was easily dissatisfied and the more comfortable I felt, the lousier I became as a boyfriend.

Despite all my pet peeves, I did really like Erica and she was my first love. However, our emotional bond hardly made a dent on my adolescent desires when I wandered into town. Erica started working weekends at a pub, which I took as an insult to my company. Boredom meant trouble, as I immediately gravitated towards a gang of undesirables who dabbled in an extreme banquet of self-indulgence. I felt right at home amongst these narcissistic degenerates, and my reckless behaviour occurred without a conscious thought.

To cut a long story short, I was caught red-handed making out with my mate's sister at a seedy bar on Hindley Street. I was caught by Erica's sibling on the same night she gave me the jeans. When I got the tap on the shoulder, it didn't even compute what I was doing was wrong; it took a while for what I was doing to even register. I was dialled in on another station and I couldn't locate the decent side of me that could see what I was doing was unacceptable. I eventually took off the jeans, but only to give them back to Erica. She dumped me the next day.

**DAMAGE RECEIPT**

| Fuck-Up (Cause) | Aftermath (Effect) |
| --- | --- |
| Encouraged womanising | Serial cheater |
| Over-entitled as a kid | Believed my needs were above others |
| Lack of socialising with the opposite sex | Overwhelmed and insecure |

**THANK YOU!**

Elite tennis is a game where narcissists need only apply. If you want to get to the top, it pays not to care about other people's interests and needs, and to place yourself way above them. In fact, the more empathetic I was of my team's sacrifice and struggle, the worse my tennis got. When I stopped to think about how my behaviour and performance was hurting them, I was overwhelmed with tremendous guilt and shame I hadn't previously been aware of. Empathy was, in fact, the enemy.

There are no part-time narcissists. You can't draw a line in the sand on this characteristic, and when I finished playing tennis, the sport left but the entitlement stayed. If I wasn't acting narcissistically, you can bet I was thinking narcissistically. Me, me, me. Even my friends used to joke that whenever I was around the situation inevitably turned into 'The Todd Show'. I've always been my favourite topic of conversation, and when someone isn't interested in my solo performance, I just move on to another audience in hope of finding a paying customer.

Since I didn't make it to the top 100, I wanted to be admired for being the greatest player of all time who never made it. The guy with all the raw talent at his disposal who was unjustly victimised by poor management and politics. I was riding out the rollercoaster of bad fortune by trying to extract as much pity from people by delivering well-rehearsed sob stories. This would then mean that people would be sympathetic towards my narcissistic behaviour and exonerate me of all my disorderly conduct. I thought I was superior and squeaky clean, despite behaving like a poor man's Hank Moody, the serial womaniser from the TV series, Californication, played so convincingly by David Duchovny. At least Hank knew he was a piece of shit. I couldn't see it about myself. My unsubstantiated way of thinking inflicted pain and suffering on innocent people who cared about me more than I realised.

```
              IT'S TIME TO PAY YOUR BILL.
        WE HOPE YOU HAD A PLEASANT EXPERIENCE!

        Subtotal:      Narcissism
        Tip:           Tread carefully
        Total Costs:   Lack of empathy and regard for other
                       people's needs and feelings
                       Burnout
                       Terminal sense of uniqueness
                       Poor sense of self-awareness
```

## Lackey Langman supersedes Messiah Max

Langman was wise enough to know that you either hit the ground running or you hit the ground and rot. So, while Max and I were both flattened in the aftermath of my sudden sporting demise, Langman was already busy getting on with his Plan B. When my botched career didn't get Langman the coaching status he desired, he became even more desperate to prove to the tennis society and my Dad that he was more than just a local hack with a big mouth. This level of devotion meant Langman sent shockwaves through the local market, which attracted a swarm of students who wanted his time and expertise. The ones who were sincere and willing to work stayed, and those who didn't ultimately left, but not before they shit canned him to the rest of the tennis world about being a sporting Nazi. Funnily enough, this worked in Langman's favour, as he developed a ruthless reputation within the tennis community for only working with the most serious kids in the state.

After I stopped playing, the relationship between Langman and myself changed. We naturally drifted apart, as I felt his obsessive tennis talk rudely interrupted the pity party I was throwing over the loss of my sporting dreams. Because I overpromised and undelivered with my miserable career, anything tennis-related now came with a severe sense of toxic shame. Unfortunately, it didn't take long for me to come to the painful realisation that I was practically unemployable without the game, and that money didn't grow on trees. So, I begrudgingly accepted the role of a local tennis coach despite the job feeling like a form of prostitution. Lack of options accompanied by a side order of alcoholism led me to do a deal with the devil and sell my soul for a couple of measly bucks.

Unable to fully grasp my precarious situation, Dad was still unrelenting with his tennis talk. He was now harping about how I should become a Tennis Australia coach and work for the national federation. Not only did these continual suggestions infuriate me, but further, they showed me just how delusional and blind Dad was when it came to my tennis and the trauma surrounding it. Besides, this was the same mob wanting me to fork out thousands of dollars for a Level One coaching certificate, after I'd been swinging a racket around since I came out of the womb.

In tennis, athletes compete against each other as players, and if they go down the coaching route later, compete against each other as coaches. Langman was always a bit apprehensive when the idea of us sharing a couple of his clients came up; but he knew I could provide an invaluable service that would benefit some of his top kids, exactly as he did for me not that long ago. My track record, however, showed I was a big question mark, liable to cancel at the last second or just not show up at all.

Despite the occasional hiccup, my regular clients were pleased with the service I provided, as I could still hit a reasonably good ball, and was more than happy to play points with the kids while trying to talk them through it. I started to take an interest in a couple of promising juniors, but the closer and more involved I became with the elite kids in the tennis industry, the more I questioned my involvement in this familiar world. Was I not now just recreating the same thing that had happened to me, but for some other poor little kid?

By now, Dad had gone from being fixated on my tennis, to being fixated on the tennis of the kids I coached. Max's intensity about what he thought these kids needed to be doing, and when they needed to be doing it by, clearly reflected the severity of my own childhood and astonishingly showed me he hadn't learned anything from the car crash that was my career. It felt as if my own horror-show of a childhood was being played out in front of me and, to my disturbance, it was all in slow motion. Dad was only helping in the best way he knew how, but with my wounds still so raw, his assistance was triggering and dangerous. I wanted a relationship with my father, and I wanted him to be proud of what I was doing, but I didn't want to have to pretend to be interested while he lectured me about the figure-8 forehand in his rundown apartment decorated with tennis post-it notes scattered all over the walls.

Instead of sternly telling Dad I no longer wanted his unsolicited advice, and likely causing a scene, I would sit and agonisingly listen like I had always done. I'd eventually self-destruct and go missing for a few days, and Max and Langman would send the search party out to find me. Langman was forced to apologise to the people we worked with on my behalf, and the show rumbled along. Nothing was going to get in the way of his dreams of becoming coaching royalty, and he managed to crack the code with one of his protégés trending on the world scene, who went by the name Thanasi Kokkinakis. I had been an inclusion in Thanasi's career since he was young kid, but on a much lesser scale than Langman, who did 95% of the heavy lifting. 'The Kokk' had surpassed my curbed career quicker than a greyhound coming out the gate. He transcended the tennis scene at such a rapid pace that it was new territory for Langman.

Despite being a part of the team when Thanasi was in town, it was evident I wasn't anywhere near stable enough to be looking after a multimillion-dollar kid on the road. Being left out of the equation had quite a sting to it, but I only had myself to blame. Dad, God bless him, rushed to my defence and was quietly furious with Langman because there wasn't more of a position available for me. Max felt the success Langman had with Thanasi went to his head and made him famous in his own mind. But after coaching a kid from the ground up to 69 in the world at 18 years of age, which is something only a handful of people have ever done, I think it's warranted to feel that you're the top G.

However, Dad didn't see it this way, and his disdain towards his once-upon-a-time lackey grew in stature. Maybe it was because he was jealous Langman had done something he hadn't, or maybe it was because I was left out of the Thanasi situation. It could have been both. Either way, Max was unimpressed and unwilling to give Langman the credit he'd always wanted from him. But in failing to give Langman his praise, Max also missed the recognition Langman regularly awarded my father, by acknowledging that Max was the mastermind who showed him the ropes and gave him the blueprint. Langman never claimed to reinvent the wheel. He just applied what he learned, and what he learned worked.

# PART 7

# Burnout

### It's a long way to the top if you want to be No. 1

A lot of people know a lie can become real in your mind through the power of belief. Even though most parents don't fully believe some of the programming they are instilling in their children, it doesn't mean the highly susceptible player won't think it's real. It's a known fact that belief directs behaviour. Whatever a person believes about themselves, they tend to embody those beliefs in their actions, be it positive or negative.

Once a tennis parent is content with the psychological programming they have instilled in their prized possession, the adult may take it as their life's mission to protect the player from jeopardising this indoctrination, by keeping their kid away from the rest of society whenever they aren't on the tennis court. The biggest difference between the top players in tennis is generally in their mindset. The athletes who get to the top usually share the belief that not only is what they are striving to achieve possible, but it is their birthright to accomplish it.

As the child becomes a self-fulfilled prophecy and makes their way through the tennis rankings on their sporting quest, they may see no reason to question any of the beliefs they hold. If any friends or acquaintances suggest something that doesn't align with this narrative, they tend to push them away. Allegiance to the cause is far more important than companionship, and there are countless instances where athletes abruptly turn their back on people and never speak to them again. The tennis parent may inform the player of these types of scenarios and the necessity for cutting a man loose as they think this is the only way the sporting mission can be completed, as you can't take everyone with you to the top. But the brainwashing still needs to stand the test of time against the merciless modern-day media.

Things start crossing over into uncharted territory when the player begins receiving media attention, and the press probes at the belief systems that served the player well up to this point. The extreme philosophies and teachings have almost never been queried or interrogated, and the media makes a living from putting their own spin on a story and seeing a well-known athlete being destroyed. If the psyche of the athlete is sufficiently affected by the media, the athlete can start to question their own fabricated reality, which is not only disastrous for their tennis but also for their mental health.

Tennis parents try to protect their children as much as possible from the press. A good example is a video on YouTube in which a reporter probes at Venus Williams' self-belief. Before she answers, her father, Richard Williams, interrupts the interview and puts the journalist back in his place. Players can have rocky relationships with the media, as top athletes seem to ooze supreme confidence but are sometimes unskilled in handling the curve ball questions the press can throw at them. Typically, you see the players react extremely defensively in either an arrogant or ambiguous manner, which only incites the press to pick at the person more. These media sessions can bring about identity confusion in someone who is only accustomed to hearing and thinking in a particular way.

Potential champions are also chased by big businesses to be ambassadors for their brand, in return for a lucrative payday. A well-thought-out marketing ploy takes place to brand the athlete with an attitude and image closely aligning with the company's ethos. Unfortunately, tennis players don't get as much creative licence with their own branding as entertainers like Miley Cyrus and Justin Bieber do. It isn't an artistic pursuit and tennis traditionally has a distinguished heritage to live up to. Players get pigeonholed to uphold a regimented persona, on and off the court, and they are generally marketed as superior to the rest of society, while remaining just as flawed as any other person with whom they share the planet. Tennis rarely sees many bad boys, but if one is getting enough attention, companies will try to spin a story for the public, exploiting every angle. But ultimately there is behaviour protocol to abide by, and the player mustn't bring the game's or company's integrity into disrepute. This is how seemingly profitable sponsorship deals can lead athletes to a personal crisis point as they become exhausted from trying to maintain the inauthentic façade. Some players try living double lives in order to pay homage to the side of themselves abandoned because of the branding.

Public humiliation in people of places of privilege is one of society's favourite pastimes, so the media lie in wait for top players to damage their brand. Many people would look at someone like a Nick Kyrgios and say he doesn't deserve what he has, or that he has managed to fluke his way to the top—as if it's somehow dumb luck and not hard work. The public's thirst for pegging these guys down a few notches and bringing them back to reality is fierce. The public don't just want the traditional tragedy-to-triumph story, which is already hard enough to accomplish; they want you to repeat the process again and again, just to make sure it wasn't a fluke the first time around.

The only sustainable way to live is with authenticity. It's doable to be a fabricated version of yourself some of the time, but not all the time. I believe maintaining an alter ego for an indefinite amount of time eventually leads to burnout.

## Not everyone is treated in the same way

The media and public are fickle about who they let get away with what. Men have traditionally been able to push the boundaries further than women can, especially when it comes to being publicly outspoken and dabbling in the dark arts. To demonstrate this, let's compare the stories of a male and female player: both had extensive junior careers and were greenlighted as the next big thing to look out for on the tennis scene. They both had chaotic and unpredictable paths, but the media adopted different stances on them.

## Big boy with a giant appeal

The first one is the 6-foot-5 ruggedly handsome Russian, who looked just as good in sporting attire as he did in a tuxedo, Marat Safin. Athletes from Russia generally don't tend to get the endorsement deals American or English players attract—unless they are Anna Kournikova—so Safin broke the traditional trend when he became the pin-up boy for Adidas.

Safin was the talk of the town as a youngster and predicted to steamroll through slams with his clean ball striking and brute strength from either wing. He was unapologetically Russian and didn't try to change his character to become more likeable to the masses, which ended up making him even more popular. He had a wildly unpredictable personality, so you never knew if he was going to throw his racket like a discus or play some lights out tennis.

I think one of the biggest things that made Safin so entertaining was the psychological workout he gave the audiences when they tuned in to watch him play.

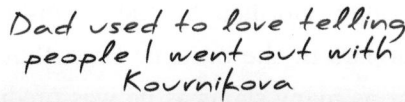

*Dad used to love telling people I went out with Kournikova*

Safin's limitations were generally self-imposed, and viewers were mystified to see this incredibly talented athlete being so fragile and sensitive at the same time. His best ball was better than almost anyone's, yet he would constantly go through patches where this type of tennis would totally disappear. Despite his unsportsmanlike conduct, Safin was always humble in defeat and never a boastful winner, just raising a casual fist to the sky. Because he wasn't trying to be anything he wasn't, Safin always seemed to see eye-to-eye with the media despite some of his questionable behaviour both on and off the court. Because he was authentic, he was able to laugh and joke about his own ridiculousness in press conferences, which was hugely refreshing in a sport where interviews are usually as boring as batshit.

The Russian's off-court shenanigans made him renowned as a party boy with an exquisite taste for busty young blondes. He randomly filled his player box with an array of high-class escorts that the TV cameras couldn't get enough of. He was continually doing the unthinkable, glorified by the tennis community and paid millions of dollars in the process. Even though Safin didn't win anywhere near as many slams as he was predicted to and his behaviour was continually called into question, he was let off the leash and saved by the public and media. Maybe it was because he owned all his so-called faults, so no one had anything on him. This was a rare case of a player who was able to live an authentic life. But I believe if the media and public were on his back more about his lifestyle choices and career expectations, he would have burned out as quickly as the next person I will write about.

## Turning a teen into a princess then publicly dethroning her

Jennifer Capriati was coached from the cradle by her old man, and at the age of 14 became the youngest ever player to reach the top 10 on the WTA rankings. The media and public went stir crazy with this teenage tennis prodigy, who was extremely marketable to corporate America. Capriati was young, cute, and athletic. Companies threw the kitchen sink at getting her to endorse their product, forking out millions of dollars in sponsorship money before she even played a professional match. Not bad cash for a Year 9 student in the early '90s.

Her public persona was moulded to be not too dissimilar to the childhood actors on the Disney Channel, casting her as innocent and sweet while always saying the right thing to all the right people. She immediately won the hearts of the public with her adorable, childlike charm and enthusiasm. Everyone wanted a piece of

Capriati, so much so that the age rules to protect athletes like her from being burned out were changed, to allow the phenomenon to compete in professional tournaments earlier than she should have. Very quickly she became a commodity and at the age of 15, not only was she financially supporting her family, but she was also expected to line the pockets of the companies she'd signed endorsement deals with, by performing and behaving in a fan-friendly way.

It quickly became a job and instead of playing for herself and getting enjoyment out of the game, she became a hostage to her own branding and enormous expectations. As she grew older, but still only in her late teens, Capriati started to push back against her father's will and the sweet, innocent public image created for her. The young American's attitude changed, and she became more of a rebellious teenager, symbolising her dissatisfaction with emo fashion while becoming visibly more arrogant in press conferences.

Still, the people in her camp did not pay attention to the warning signs of imminent burnout and continued to flog a dead horse. They scheduled her to do exhibition matches to profit off her current marketability, despite Capriati claiming in off-court interviews that she would prefer to be a normal teenager hanging out with friends. Clearly, they were becoming totally preoccupied with Capriati's public image and her results, and no one was paying attention to the young superstar's mental health and wellbeing.

Finally, enough was enough and she started to behave in a way I can relate to wholeheartedly. At 17 she was caught stealing a $35 ring from a shopping mall and the public tried to vilify her for it, as if she was hardened criminal. Can you imagine if everyone under 18 years old was on the news for stealing something under $50? It's not newsworthy at all, but the media sensationalise minor stories to feed the public's insatiable appetite for seeing celebrities make mistakes. That's what Capriati was now. She wasn't just a tennis player; she had transcended the sport and become a public figure. And unfortunately, when you're in the spotlight, there's a target on your back. Is it fair to hold a child in the public eye accountable to a higher standard than most?

She thought she was signing up to be a tennis player and was not necessarily aware of the additional expectations on top of that. The lack of authenticity outside the game led Capriati to make friends with people who didn't know who she was. That way she found the freedom to be herself without needing to live up to her fabricated identity. Then, during a weekend bender, police were called to her motel room after a noise complaint, drugs were found, and the media came for her head.

This is very common in the music and entertainment business but frowned upon in the sporting industry. The media circus made a huge deal of it, putting her mugshot on newspapers and Tv shows. They said she was a lost cause when really, she just wanted some sort of normality.

## Arranged friendships and evolving into who you are paid to be

Ethan was my loud and abrasive cousin and a breath of fresh air in a family full of finger pointers. The world was a stage to Ethan. He was lively and audacious; a natural entertainer who made family gatherings feel like an event you didn't want to miss. While the rest of the family were preoccupied with the latest episode of Bold and the Beautiful, Ethan would rope the kids into choreographing a Broadway musical to present to the adults after dinner, just to show off how fabulous his directing skills were. To someone like me who had been intentionally deprived of exploring different parts of my personality, experiencing Ethan was entering a personal revolution. He was an all-round sports nut, who took me under his wing and introduced me to a new world I'd been purposely sheltered from because of its potential to divert me from my specific mission. 'Tennisboy' was the cringeworthy nickname my family branded me with, and I already hated it with a passion. But Ethan looked passed all the facetiousness and found a way to treat me like a normal human being.

Dad kept a keen eye on all my relationships with other people. But because he disliked air-filler conversations with my extended family, I was free to socialise without being monitored like a scientific lab rat. Besides, Dad had to work after hours to make up for all the time he spent with me on the court during the day. From the outset, it was vital for him to create the foundations of who I was supposed to be. Dad wasn't interested in a democracy, but rather a healthy dictatorship with an impenetrable cocoon. After the words 'I want to be a tennis player' came out of my mouth, rubber hit the road and I was bombarded with a systematic indoctrination that wired my inner machinery in an extremist fashion.

Max didn't want me wandering off getting lost among the regular riff raff of normal life, so when he caught wind of the influence Ethan had over me, he saw it as a threat to what he was trying to create. In his eyes Ethan was a distraction who was going to mess up the whole process; he wasn't part of the script and didn't fit into his fantasy. But instead of immediately bulldozing Ethan out, Max thought of a better idea: he tried to make him his ally and use his influence over me to further his objectives. But when Ethan refused to play ball with his conspiratorial demands, the relationship was severed.

Not long after that, a new friend was introduced to me in what felt like the friend equivalent of an arranged marriage. My Dad carefully handpicked an older tennis player called Richard, who he thought was suitable to be my new best friend. Richard was a sporting desperado, so overawed by my freakish tennis ability that he was willing to do whatever my Dad wanted done. This way, Max could play the puppeteer and control even more facets of my already regulated life.

That was until another candidate came into the equation who Dad thought would be a better fit for me going forwards. Langman was a better player and easier to manipulate than Richard, who was starting to question Max's philosophies and his involvement in the strange arrangement. Max and Langman were two of a kind, and they used each other for their own motives. Langman used Max to get more insight into the tennis world, and Max used Langman, a younger dude dressed as my friend, by getting him to reinforce his important messages. Dad's voice didn't need to be the only one, but his message had to be the only message, and if you didn't get on board, you were out. These pieces of the puzzle were extremely important to Max in the consolidation of my tennis development.

Imagine growing up in an environment where someone is always in your ear telling you who to be. With the tennis parent, it starts off by conditioning their kid when they're barely out the crib, by telling them exactly who they are and what they are going to be. In the blink of an eye, sponsors come on board with specific guidelines for their sponsee to follow to maintain the company's branding and public appeal. All the while, outside influences such as friends, foes and the media are constantly hounding you with questions, trying to figure out who you really are. But you don't really know because you're just being the person these people have told you to be all along.

The public and press are unaware that even though some players look strong and confident on the court, they can be delicate and unstable off it and their sense of identity is shaky at best. I think the reason some players are so easily conned into being whoever companies want them to be, is because they have been conditioned to be malleable, instead of forming their own authentic identities. It's easier to be who you want me to be, if I don't know who I am. The players who seem to avoid burnout are those who remain somewhat true to themselves and are self-assured enough to know that as well as being tennis players, there is more to life than just the sport.

## Welcoming the day the deal turns sour

I believe if you ask professional players if they would have their own children follow in their footsteps, the most common answer would be 'no'. This is because of their firsthand experience of the front line and the psychological scars to prove it. But a lot of the people on the periphery of professional tennis—coaches, agents, trainers, commentators, parents, and diehard fans—would jump at the opportunity for their offspring to join the tour. Many of them seem unable to comprehend that for most sporting prodigies, tennis isn't a game anymore, it's a high-stakes, manual labour job.

Some parents try to guilt trip their kids into believing that playing tennis is some sort of privilege for which they should be eternally grateful. So not only have those players been subjected to years of arduous demands, but they're also now guilted into gracing their tormentors with appreciation for the opportunity to be enslaved. A coach who has been put through this ring of fire themselves has a lot more understanding of the need to keep things light and fun for players, when the time calls for it. The best coaches I have worked with had an ability to make training fun and enjoyable while still being extremely intense and beneficial at the same time. A yin and yang balance of two opposing elements is key for survival.

In the same way, I believe most burnout is caused through poor management by tennis parents and coaches who don't understand how important it is for their kids to have fun. There isn't a kid in the known universe who wants the seriousness a fixated tennis parent can bring to an already difficult sport. Tennis has an exponential progression, where the game can transition from a hobby into a profession far too prematurely, and the enjoyment a kid once experienced from the sport quickly evaporates. So where, and how, an aspiring athlete gets their kicks becomes a complex concern.

The most common mistake made by parents and coaches is to try to isolate fun, as something to be enjoyed only outside the sporting world. While this philosophy might make sense in theory, it tends to exacerbate young players' FOMO, which is already sky high from a lifetime of missing out on people, places, and pleasures. It's especially hard for young players these days, as we are living in a time where it's never been easier to watch what you're missing out on, just by tuning into social media. Seeing this unrealistic world where everyone seems to be happy and having fun tortures the player, and their FOMO intensifies. We're in an era of instant gratification where everyone is just a few swipes and likes away from mind-altering pleasure, so kids aren't interested in making the long buck and thinking about the end game. Going to bed at 8.30pm next to your half-naked snoring father, so you can wake up early for morning training, doesn't sound so appealing anymore. Making fun its own separate entity tends to only intensify the player's desires for a normal life once they get a taste for it.

The tennis community has a bad tendency of vilifying young players who act like normal adolescents. While I totally understand how partying excessively can ruin your career, I feel this unnecessary stigma makes the deal for players even less appealing, inevitably pushing them away from the sport. Athletes initially think they are signing up to play the sport they love, with the potential of making millions of dollars, while being idolised by the public. But this can quickly shift to the reality of a monotonous job, in which they must grind for every penny, while being held to ridiculously high standards of behaviour while chained full-time to an overbearing parent. Sounds terrible? Yeah, because it is fucking terrible!

## Please don't talk about losing while I'm eating

I could just about touch every wall in the hotel room that Max, Langman and I were cosied up in after a first-round qualifying loss at the All-England club. I couldn't even say that I played a singles match on the luscious lawns at Wimbledon, as l lost in the qualifiers, which was somewhere on the outskirts of London. So much for what I'd romanticised about as a 4-year-old kid, when l used to practise my championship victory dive on the living room floor so frequently that my knees were constantly riddled with carpet burn.

It was the first time we three stooges had travelled together; Dad had persuaded my best mate and hitting partner, Langman, to come along and assist him in shoving his own opinion down my throat in a new and different kind of way—by using a third party.

Langman didn't take much persuading, as he would've run through a barbed wire fence in the nude just to get a taste of the tour. Max's lackey wasn't overawed by the situation as he came in guns blazing, like the sporting equivalent of a poor man's Gordon Ramsay.

The reason for the persuasion was Max and l hadn't been seeing eye to eye since we started trudging the tumultuous trail of the junior tennis circuit. Living in each other's pockets for such a long time took a tremendous toll on our already fractured relationship. When the first and last thing you see every day is the face of a person you despise, it makes it difficult to shut your eyes in peace. Even Max, a person who knew no surrender, clearly understood we needed something to change. So, Dad went for a long shot and asked the inexperienced apprentice, Langman, to be his right-hand man in the mission impossible job of trying to get me to listen. And Max's protégé had been waiting for the call-up.

My European swing started off in shambles, l was winless for my first three tournaments of the clay court season, a surface l was as comfortable on as ice. The subsequent critiquing of these poor performances by my tone-deaf entourage meant l wasn't a happy camper. Despite fumbling around on the clay like a baby giraffe on roller-skates, l still somehow managed to qualify for the French open and unexpectedly beat a top ten junior in the first round, while Langman and Max practically vibrated in the players box like a couple of kids in a candy store. After the win, Langman and I peacocked it around Roland Garros for a few hours, soaking up the rare moment of victory. But when we got back to the hotel, we were blasted by mastermind Max for not coming back sooner to scheme with him for the next day's scalp. This incident put a massive dampener on the happiest day of my life, and I woke up the next morning on the wrong side of the bed. Later that morning, Langman saw French superstar Mary Pierce jogging near our practice court and tried to connect with her by booting his Aussie rules football to her from across the courts. But he shanked the kick, the ball interrupted multiple courts of practice, and each player colourfully reacted to Langman's buffoonery. I finally smiled for the first time in the day, while Dad shook his head with an air of disdain for his coaching sidekick. The session went from bad to worse, Max becoming overly fixated on the warmup, which was purely meant to be, fun, light and easy. I just needed to get a feel for the ball by tickling a few around, as all the hard work had already been done. But instead of that, Dad ranted and raved at me like a lunatic, forty-five minutes before I was due to play my 2nd round French open match against American Sam Querrery. I stormed off from the emotional encounter to the player cafeteria and ordered the worst thing on the menu, then wandered out to court and semi tanked in another lacklustre performance.

Defeats unquestionably provide a window of opportunity for information to be absorbed by the athlete at a deeper level, but the coach's corner must be tactful with how they go about the briefing, as the player is just as likely to refute the analysis if it's handled inappropriately, even if the information is on-point. Because Dad and Langman were two sporting sociopaths both fanatically obsessed with tennis, match reports turned into open-ended discussions, which ultimately did more damage than good.

As we moved away from the picturesque complex of Roland Garros to the outskirts of the Italian countryside, the three of us stayed in a budget hotel room with just two single beds, trying to see how far we could stretch the remaining 20k of my endorsement money. The frugal lifestyle meant no separation from one another, and that meant it was tennis from breakfast to bedtime. I could clearly feel the responsibility of other people's lives riding on my shoulders, as Max and Langman weren't even eating meals as they saved their pennies to keep the sinking ship afloat. Weird looking veins started popping out of Dad's gaunt face from stress and lack of nutrition. He and Langman would duck out for lunch every day at the nearest fruit farm, to pick berries on a private property. Apparently, the riper fruit was up high in the summer branches, so Langman would get Max on his shoulders to reach for the forbidden fruit, swiping at it with a racket, while trying to avoid being spotted by the local oncoming traffic. It gets a bit hard to eat a rib eye with a clear conscience, when you know your team are out scrounging the local vineyards for loose grapes. Their desperation to the cause was putting my lack of desire for the sport to shame.

As the trip went on, the dynamic between the team of stooges disintegrated and we became three separate individuals all unable to see it from each other's perspectives. Langman was prepared to do whatever it took to climb the sporting ladder, but once he realised that this was as far as the climb went, he wasn't prepared to continue reinforcing Max's message. Dad felt betrayed by Langman and went berserk on him one day when he didn't agree with a technical aspect of the serve that Max was teaching. I must admit, it was nice not being the one who was getting a mouthful for a change, but I was worried for Langman's safety even though he was a sizeable specimen who could've knocked my old man spark out.

But the lovers' tiff between Dad and my best mate didn't deter Langman from behaving in his usual manner, as his default settings was that of a pure larrikin. As per usual, he woke up the next morning and stuck his head out the 9th floor hotel room window and yelled at the top of his lungs down to a busy street, 'I'm going to jummmppppppp.' Langman's poorly timed attempts at weird and dark humour were differently received by Max and me. As much as Dad loved Langman and found his antics hilarious, he also felt Langman was just an immature kid who couldn't toe the line. Max equated seriousness with success and wanted me working with someone more professional. But the situation was already intense enough, and I found Langman's obscene comedy to be the fringe show I needed to give my tennis career a ticking heartbeat. As we rode the trains from one non-English speaking country to the next, the bickering back and forth between Max, Langman and I would have made for great reality TV. But not even Langman with his endless supply of humour could put a funny spin on this tragedy, and the only comforting thought was that Wimbledon wasn't far away.

A lethal concoction of ego, fantasy and defiance ambushed me at the All-England Club, as I devoted myself to a tennis death wish style of play. My childhood years of imitating Sampras and Becker in the backyard with a spatula and balloon caught up with me, as I stubbornly decided to serve volley on first and second serves despite the courts playing slower than the red European clay. Undeterred by the surface being a net rusher's nightmare, I kept hustling forwards in true Aussie spirit, looking to take balls in the front part of the court. But one by one, passing shots kept whizzing past my ears for stone cold winners.

Langman and Max couldn't believe what their eyes were witnessing, and subtly pleaded with me from the coach's box to abort my aggressive game plan and retreat to the trenches of the baseline. Who would've thought that after weeks of bitching back and forth like a married couple, these two would finally agree on something? But they were a day late and a dollar short, as I perversely enjoyed watching the pair of them pull their hair out from the sidelines, while I continued my suicide mission of kamikaze-ing toward my own demise. The icing on the cake was not hearing a single word of tennis talk uttered in our hotel room later that night. Finally, I'd silenced the critics.

The next morning, I got out of the room as quickly as possible to let the cheer squad grieve in peace. A few of the first-round losers were going to a nightclub in SoHo, and I was in the mood to soothe my self-pity in the city. Twenty quid was all I had, and it was barely enough to cover the door charge. But that didn't matter, because just being at the nightclub was intoxicating enough. I immediately fell in love with the nightlife, free to act as irresponsibly as I wanted without a running commentary reporting on my every move.

Alcohol seemed to have the ability to turn a lifelong nemesis into a temporary friend, and all the players at the club banded together as if they were family. Never in a million years did I expect to see this type of interwovenness between such individual creatures. The experience in essence seemed spiritual, and I wanted to stay there forever. It was a night I wouldn't soon forget. The next morning, I was court-martialled by both Max and Langman as I lay hungover in the community area of the hotel. The dynamic duo combined forces, taking turns tearing shreds off me with everything they had, while the regular folk walked by pretending not to hear. Selfish, undisciplined, spoilt, lazy, and disrespectful were just a few takeaways from the hour-long roasting where both parties played the role of bad cop. These were all indisputable accusations, so I silently gave no contest and hung my head in shame.

Until, that was, I heard a comment that kept hitting my ear wrong. 'You're missing out on the opportunity of a lifetime.' Opportunity? What opportunity? We clearly had differing opinions on what an opportunity was. The tennis life was still being sold to me as this wonderful, privileged existence I had to be forever indebted to. But from my angle, the 'opportunity' felt more like a 25-to-life jail sentence, where the real opportunists got to feed their common obsession on the back of a troubled sporting slave. I was completely toast and had been for some time, so it felt fitting that I staged my revenge fantasy at the most prestigious tournament in the world.

## DAMAGE RECEIPT

| Fuck-Up (Cause) | Aftermath (Effect) |
|---|---|
| Excessive tennis talk outside of matches and training. | Turned off the sport |
| Extremely unbalanced lifestyle | Disinterested, tanking, rebelling |
| No fun or enjoyment from tennis | Desperately desiring to experience fun and freedom |

### THANK YOU!

Athletes generally play tennis to begin with because they enjoy the sport. If they get to the point where they no longer get satisfaction from it, then why would they want to continue? Without an outlet for fun, young players run the risk of self-implosion while their coaches and parents often guilt trip them into feeling ungrateful for the opportunity. Unfortunately, a lot of athletes tend to take the bait and feel a severe sense of shame for not enjoying, what I consider to be, a niche type of torture. For parents and coaches to ignorantly portray elite tennis like it's a day at the beach is a rude joke to the many players who have had to endure the severe pangs of this problematic lifestyle.

```
     IT'S TIME TO PAY YOUR BILL.
  WE HOPE YOU HAD A PLEASANT EXPERIENCE!

  Subtotal:      Early retirement
  Tip:           Healthy doses of fun
  Total Costs:   Burnout
                 An inability to play and keep things
                 light
                 Regret
```

## The psychology behind injury (when you're not there to win)

Most people think burnout comes from extreme amounts of physicality in the form of too much tennis and lots of injuries. However, not only is that rare, but it's also easier for someone to play through physical pain than it is to play through psychological suffering. When the time comes and the player cannot cope with the rigorous demands of the stressful job, they generally use a physical excuse as the reason to pull out, as it is a more accepted reason to stop play. Some players can be in such psychological and emotional distress that they can manifest physical injuries to stop them from competing, and others can create injuries as a safety blanket to excuse poor results and lessen scrutiny from the public and the tennis community. A player would rather be seen as Mr. Unlucky than Mr. Not Good Enough, so come Grand Slam time, you see a lot of players with visible tape on show, and chronic yet undetectable injuries surfacing left right and centre.

The tennis community as well as the public and media can be fickle when it comes to players' mental health issues. Because of the perks and massive pay-days those athletes receive, mental torment is seen as a fair trade-off and just part of the job by spectators. Even though attitudes are slowly changing, the public is way more accepting of injury and illness than mental health issues; but just because you can pull the wool over the eyes of society, don't think you'll go fooling anyone in the locker room. The tennis community will entertain your farce to your face, but the second you're out of earshot, they will sledge and slander your name as if it's a sport of its own.

This type of behaviour is so normal in tennis that no one really thinks about why someone would go to such extremes to make up a fake injury when they have trained and sacrificed their whole life for the opportunity at hand. Would someone really come all that way to let a dicky shoulder stop them from achieving their dreams when it's been reported people who have been bitten by sharks have swum back to shore with their limbs missing? I'm not saying that players don't experience real pain; but in my opinion, when the player isn't fully there to win, the pain is often a manifestation of psychological stress. The dicky shoulder can be the mind's way of relieving itself from high-pressure situations without the player knowing it.

Sometimes, the justifiable reason for losing creates freedom for the mind of the player and the injury can work as an advantage, making the athlete far more relaxed. Weirdly enough, the best way for some players to get the most out of themselves is to be injured. For others it's completely debilitating and prevents them from reaching their potential whether the injury is psychological or physical.

## Is a lie really a lie if you believe it's the truth?

In Joplin, Missouri, in the south of USA, I wandered the streets in the stormy rain, a broken and beaten boy after a painful 7/6 in the third exit. These types of matches always take a good minute to emotionally recover from, but I was greeted by Dad immediately after the loss in the most inexcusable and publicly humiliating fashion I could imagine. Having people witness you being ridiculed by your dad is one of the most embarrassing things you can endure, and I just wanted to get out of the tennis complex as quickly as possible. I made it inside the clubhouse and pressed the button for the elevator, but Dad pushed me down the stairs like a rag doll. 'You fucking lazy ####,' he muttered while pacing down the steep staircase like a lunatic.

I waited outside for the courtesy bus to arrive, my father still in my face. As he was spewing some of the most profoundly inappropriate things you could imagine, bits of spit sprayed across my face. The minivan pulled up to player services and I went to put my bag in the back when divine intervention struck. I watched Mad Max hop in the van and at the last second something told me not to board, so I sprinted off down the road with my racket bag strapped to my back. For the next few hours, I walked the streets aimlessly, trying to figure out how to get myself out of the predicament I was in. I was ready to quit.

I spent the next eight or so hours kicking a stone in the pouring rain, contemplating what was the right course of action to get me out of this mess, and nearly got arrested for wandering through a private caryard. My intellect hadn't caught up with my soul, so I didn't feel I had the vocabulary to articulate everything I needed to say in a confrontational debate with my father. I needed to keep it short and sweet. To help calm my nerves before walking back into the haunting hotel room I was sharing with my old man, I bummed a cigarette off a homeless guy in the parking lot of the Steak and Shake.

Staying with each other on the road meant issues and arguments were always 'to be continued' as space wasn't ever able to play its part in the healing process. I walked back in saturated to see Dad sitting on the edge of his bed, rocking back and forth in the pitch dark like Jack Nicholson in The Shining. It was clear he had been thinking about the match, while I had been thinking about my life. He straight away confiscated my phone and asked who I had been calling, to which I replied, 'I can't do this anymore and I want to go home.'

The power outage caused by the relentless storm made the confrontation eerie, as I could only ever tell where Dad was in the room when the lightning struck. Max ruthlessly questioned my motives for wanting to go home, snidely saying, 'You don't miss your mother or your sister, so what's the real reason why you want to go home?' It wasn't a real question, just more of an insinuation that I was selfish and weak for wanting to abort the mission. But I wasn't getting into a back-and-forth with him, and I just kept repeating myself like a broken record. I slept with one eye open that night, as I had a strong feeling something bad might occur.

The next morning, I had an emotional hangover as if I'd had a night on the piss, and all I could hear was the piercing sound of silence lingering in the room. I hadn't woken up and had a sudden change of heart, but I could see Dad trying to brush it off like a heat-of-the-moment thing. My statement hadn't been a declaration of empty words. I genuinely meant what I said, but the very thought of Todd not playing tennis wasn't a rational concept in my father's mind; and to be honest, I found it hard to swallow myself. But deep down in the innermost part of myself, I knew I was completely done. I didn't have the stamina or support to state my case a second time, so the show continued, and we flew to the next city for the next tournament.

I was determined to get out once and for all, and since giving an honest reason wasn't good enough to stop the sporting saga, I resorted to faking an injury in the first round of qualifying, so I had a 'legitimate' reason to stop playing. Pretending to be hurt was easy but living with the decision proved to be difficult. The doctor gave his recommendation for six weeks' rest which meant I was getting what I wanted, and we were going home. Thank God for the medical professionals who will buy anything you throw at them.

Lies take upkeep to be maintained, and if you're selling the story well enough you can generally persuade yourself as well. By the time I got home from America, I had myself convinced I was carrying a real injury, and I sought medical treatment from a physiotherapist while still somewhere knowing the whole thing was a hoax. To be fair, I didn't really know what to do, because I had this lingering feeling people didn't believe me, which propelled me to strengthen the performance even more. Instead of seeking out much-needed help for my psychological and emotional issues, I went about consolidating the lie to convince the critics and naysayers.

Mental health was not seen as a valid reason to stop playing a game. But an injury would simply be queried before eventually being given the benefit of the doubt. I was looking for psychological relief in the form of a physical injury, while trying to remain optimistic about hopefully not being branded with the sporting stigma of being soft. My plan half worked, and half backfired, as it gave me temporary relief from the brutal nature of the sport; but the root of the issue was left untreated, which made me start to believe my own bullshit. I made sure my limp was at a realistic level, somewhere nicely in between a war veteran and an old fossil with gout. When you're wholeheartedly committing to a lie, it's quite easy to confuse falsehoods with reality, and soon I was hobbling all over town in my day-to-day life. But then the weirdest thing happened. The back injury I'd been faking genuinely started to hurt. Now I didn't know what to think or believe. Did I have a back injury or not? It was as if my mind was so unwavering on portraying the physical injury to get out of this stressful situation, I'd somehow manifested it into reality.

All this confusion added extra perplexity to my already overdue and outstanding mental health issues, which had gone untreated for so long that they finally found temporary relief in alcohol.

This bizarre performance was just a warm-up for a long line of bogus injuries and illnesses that I claimed to have instead of telling the truth. I didn't want to be known around town as the guy with mental problems any more than I already was, so I allegedly had just about every broken bone, flu and virus under the sun, as well as multiple recurring dead grandparents, cousins, and aunts. This deceitful character trait seemed to be my only way of surviving in the real world, but it perpetuated my long litany of issues, taking me further and further away from the truth. And the truth was that I was seriously suffering from psychological issues.

## DAMAGE RECEIPT

| Fuck-Up (Cause) | Aftermath (Effect) |
| --- | --- |
| Poor timing | Unnecessarily compounded situations |
| No free space to talk openly and honestly about feelings and emotions | Mental illness |
| Publicly humiliating a child for the tennis world to see | Constant state of shame |

### THANK YOU!

I was vaguely aware I was using the back injury as a crutch for my underlying mental health issues, but I believe that other players, in different situations, can physically manifest an injury without being aware of the psychological cause. It may be the athlete doesn't want to know or that they simply don't have the insight to be able to articulate their suffering. The fact psychological issues can manifest in physical ways is becoming more known among medical and psychological professions. My hope is that this field of knowledge grows and spreads more among sporting communities, because for now, there is a severe lack of it, particularly in tennis. What options do players currently have if they find themselves struggling? Their justifiable perception is mental health issues will not be accepted as a legitimate reason to not take to court, and therefore they are coerced into presenting with a physical injury or illness to obtain any relief from distress.

I wonder how often the distortion of truth used to cover up psychological pain may be keeping players unwell and prone to injury. Athletes should be asking themselves the serious question: 'Could I get better from examining the truth rather than hiring multiple different coaches, physios, doctors, and sports psychologists?' And 'better' could mean a reduction in frequency of injuries, a higher quality of their tennis game, or a different perspective on the difficult job they are doing. While doctors and physios certainly serve a purpose in tennis, I strongly believe the game needs a more holistic approach to health and wellbeing. The solution is a lot simpler than people realise, yet extremely difficult for a lot of players. It requires one to look inwards without bias, and not let society's ideals distort one's reality, or define the ways that are acceptable to suffer.

```
IT'S TIME TO PAY YOUR BILL.
WE HOPE YOU HAD A PLEASANT EXPERIENCE!

Subtotal:      Shame
Tip:           Private health insurance
Total Costs:   Undiagnosed mental illness
               Delusion
               An underlying sense of cowardice
```

## The academy that taught Max his final lesson

Everything turned full circle. Langman went from being the lackey to being the boss, and now Max and I needed him more than he needed us. You've got to be quite the risk taker to go into business with an alcoholic and a man facing bankruptcy. Langman has always done things unconventionally and given second chances to people who probably didn't deserve them; but no one was more undeserving of another chance than my father Max, who really was like the cat with nine lives. It didn't matter which way we tried to incorporate Max into the Langman and Ley Elite Tennis Academy, it always ended in disaster and disbelief. You would have thought Dad would have been able to play ball and do as we asked, considering the government was coming after him, but I guess it's true what they say—a leopard can't change its spots.

What started out with Langman doodling our business logo on a hotel serviette, turned into a thriving enterprise almost overnight. While most of the other able coaches around town got fed up with the BS that came with elite coaching, Langman seemed to be the last of a dying breed and was more passionate than ever to put out pro players. Even though I felt I had known Langman my whole life, working alongside him was quite an experience, and I came to expect the unexpected.

His coaching showmanship and the amount of time he spent on the court put my working week to shame. Langman's lessons were like a Broadway performance where his charismatic personality and knowledge of the game blended nicely, sweeping players and parents off their feet. Even though we were in business together, I could still feel our childhood rivalry bubbling, as I racked my brain with ways to compete against the larger-than-life Langman. After years of me brutalising him on the practice court, it was time for him to get sweet revenge by showing me who was boss in the coaching domain. Validation from tennis parents now seemed to be the currency of our existence, and I found it difficult not to be jealous of someone who could attract that kind of attention.

If there was any competition, it didn't take long for Langman to unofficially win by unanimous decision, which saw him continually refer to me as 'Number Two'. As much as this disturbed me, I knew Langman deserved all the accolades he got, and that I was better off with him than against him. Besides, my introverted personality seemed to complement his boisterous bravado, and the academy was going off like a frog in a sock.

Prior to working side by side with Langman, I'd been selective about how many 'elite' kids I took on, as this line of work almost always comes with demanding parents who could send me over the edge. But the word 'elite' was now promoted as our business description, and those extremists were now our regular customers. Suddenly, my place of work was infested with overbearing parents. Each of whom thought their child was going to be the next Kokkinakis.

As much as Langman's reputation and character were bringing in the business, his antics also incited the fanatical parents to greater extremes. Some defenceless children were copping the brunt of a fatal brew which I was ultimately profiting off while bringing my own brand of dysfunction to the party. The ferociously chaotic environment required some boundaries be put in place, but order and administration were foreign concepts to us uncivilised barbarians as Langman and I had come from a primitive existence where fighting to the death was an everyday occurrence. So, at first glance, everything seemed normal, until I started seeing semblances of my younger self mirrored in the players. Suddenly it dawned on me that I'd inadvertently created the type of hostile environment I'd once been so desperate to escape from.

As my professional life was starting to take shape, my excessive sprees of savage drinking were still causing complete disarray in my personal life. Being unable to put the bottle down meant I couldn't properly process the agonising defeat of my failed tennis career. But my alcoholism was a bittersweet affair, as drinking miraculously salvaged my fractured relationship with my old man, as we both toasted to the sport that had us triple match point down without a racket. Finally, Dad and I felt like father and son, as we shared a similar maladjustment to society which anointed us together as the ultimate outcasts. Max never failed to bring it to my attention on these benders about his lack of work, and how the tax man was coming after him. Hearing about his plight while I was under the influence filled me with an acute sense of responsibility. I offered Max a job at my tennis club without thinking to consult my business partner, Langman. When the haze had finally ascended, I realised I had jumped the gun, by not discussing the matter over with Langman. Not only that, but I held serious reservations towards my problematic father kowtowing to any sort of rules or regulations. Caught between a rock and a hard place, I begrudgingly proposed the idea of Dad working at the academy to his old protégé, Langman. Both of us doubted Max's capabilities at adhering to our rather loose set of standards, as we had tried to incorporate him into the program before, to no avail. But seeing we both had a soft spot for the enigmatic old bastard, we thought we'd give it one last go, for old times' sake.

Given that Langman was going out on a limb even working with me, I laid down the law to my old man, practically begging him to behave. I felt our reconciliation and alcoholic comradery would perhaps make Max take a knee and follow some orderly direction—especially since he was considering applying for bankruptcy. But before a ball was to be hit, we needed to give Max a makeover, to make him easier on the eye to our loyal client base of die-hard tennis parents. Langman and I rounded up a bag full of Thanasi's Nike hand-me-downs for Dad to wear so he didn't look like a pyjama-clad roadside busker; but on the very first day of work, Dad didn't wear a single piece of clothing we had given him. He was kitted head-to-toe in raggedy old duds that made him look like a homeless squatter.

*the ultimate outcasts*

When you're running group trainings, the most important things to get right are that: the session has a natural flow to it; you don't get too preoccupied with one individual; and you don't bang on about technique, as the kids are doing the squad for volume. But with Max's meticulous method of training, it was obvious he wasn't suited to doing group coaching, as he didn't have the time and freedom to hone in on what he wanted to sharpen with the players. Langman and I would constantly see him getting lost in helping one kid, while the other players remained unsupported for the five minutes that it took. In Dad's previous coaching experience, he'd never had to work to a strict timeframe, so he could get lost in hearing the sound of his own voice—and they didn't call him Maxy Talker for nothing.

We crossed group trainings off Max's roster and got him facilitating individual lessons, by providing extra sessions for the kids who were already being coached by Langman and I. However, teaching technique to players who already receive technical support from the private coach is known as malpractice. It confuses the player and undoes the work of the private coach, but Dad couldn't seem to grasp this basic concept. It should have been an easy fix, but approaching Max was an extremely difficult task that no one wanted to take on. He wanted to be the guy giving the ideas, and not necessarily the guy receiving the feedback. Instead of listening and taking on information, he'd debate about what he thought we should be doing instead.

Seeing that no one was interested in debating 'the figure 8 forehand' with a fanatical blowhard, we let Dad run his own clientele from the academy and work with whoever was game enough to hire him. Ironically, a lot of tennis parents very much appreciated Max's fanaticism in this context, and Dad slowly but surely started to gain a cult following of students. But now he was undercharging his clients and going overtime for as much as an hour, which caused issues with the other coaches.

Next, we tried to get him working at the private school where we coached, but Max couldn't seem to grasp the concept that these kids were just coming out recreationally and weren't trying to become global superstars. Running short of ideas, we allocated Max as our fitness coach and firmly stated to him there was to be no hitting with the clients. But in a matter of weeks, Langman caught Dad red-handed, wheeling a trolley of tennis balls out onto the court for a session with a girl he trained.

All out of options. we thought about paying Max not to come to the club at all, until finally I was left with the awkward job of sacking my old man. Even though I was the one who gave him the ass, Max's dismissal added fuel to his anti-Langman fire. He seemed unable to accept the fact that Langman was now the guru to whom people went for answers, and not him. Langman did all he could to help the guy who'd helped him, but Max wasn't able to see it that way.

## Mourning what was never there

A bad ending to a great week can leave a sour taste in an athlete's mouth. Tennis continually finds a way of robbing players of the joy that should come with rewarding victories, and athletes can't rest on their laurels because they know they're only ever as good as their next result. The nature of the business doesn't advocate for savouring the moment and smelling the roses along the way because there's always more to come, and there's always more to do. This indoctrinated method of thinking and unsympathetic way of life can become a sickness for highly successful individuals, and many players walk around severely dissatisfied.

The number one question the media wants to ask, coaches start to strategise for, and players hate to hear is: 'What's next?' Even when the tennis days are over, players are very often still burdened by the ingrained focus of 'more' and 'what's next?'. Which makes life mentally exhausting, even in retirement. I believe this is a key reason that a lot of players become disillusioned by the game, and therefore, no longer intrinsically motivated by tennis.

What happens to the players who have come too far to turn around and now find themselves stuck in circumstances they hate? The only thing I have ever seen work for players in this sporting midlife crisis (that happens way more than people think), is to challenge the 'why', and change the reward system. However, a lot of players seem unwilling to admit their goal may be more Instagram followers rather than tennis trophies.

There are no rules saying tennis can't be the vehicle athletes use to get the things they truly want. But if these desires are kept undisclosed, to keep up the appearance of an undying love for a game that's caused the player so much dissatisfaction, tennis tends to leave the athlete's life in tatters. If you're lucky enough to be smashed to pieces, real hope can be just around the corner, but liberation only lies ahead if the individual is brave enough to look at the ugly truth. Once the hiding, justifying, pretending, deflecting, avoiding, and running away are surrendered, a player can more honestly appraise their sporting circumstance and the invisible threads that have ruled their entire existence.

Seeing this way of life for what it is, can give a player much needed clarity. Ultimately, the idea of how it's 'supposed to look' needs to die, to make room for the way it 'actually is' to live. Only then can a complete cognitive reorganisation occur for the athlete, who finally gets to decide their own destiny and to choose why they genuinely play the sport of tennis. Essentially, the athlete will have reclaimed their power and unsubscribed from one of the game's many toxic ideologies.

## Trophy coaches

Everyone should have been riding high at the end of the European season. After a few new pieces of plaque were added to Julia's naked mantlepiece, it finally looked as if the self-proclaimed 'clock watcher' was going to have a decent crack at the calendar year. Prior to that midyear swing, no one had high hopes for anything out of the ordinary, despite the media's annual hype job of putting her on a pedestal which she'd acquired from being related to one of the nation's most revered players. The support crew always borrowed some of that hysteria for good measure, but there was a deepening cynicism as the hard-luck story continued to be our players narrative of choice. Whenever I probed Julia on her yearly goals, her answer was always the same. 'I just want to be fit and healthy,' she would reply, as if tennis was nothing more than a cardio session. So, I found it difficult to see Julia reaching her full potential, considering she shared the same goals as my sixty-five-year-old mother.

If a coach doesn't hide their desperation to do the job, they become a player's dogsbody. Standing for nothing comes at a cost and anyone else who joins the team is forced to adopt the same standards and swallow shit in a similar fashion. I only learnt this a few months into the gig when drawing up the new contract, and I wanted to make provisions for reasonable notice periods and travel accommodation specifications. The longer I was around, the more I saw the coaching staff conceding to Julia's every request, to ensure they didn't lose the pseudo rockstar life they were flaunting to their followers on Instagram.

Instead of getting Julia to face her real problems, we were busy at work fixing the imaginary ones and consolidating the false narrative, which always gave her an exit ramp and softer fall. The coaching panel was so shamelessly subservient that Julia could keep creating imaginary issue after imaginary issue without anyone calling bullshit on it. So, we went racing around trying to fix her dicky knee, then it was getting x-rays for the wonky shoulder, and next it was getting bags of ice for the bruised heel. But very few of these injuries were ever really substantiated by medical evidence.

You can't change what you don't acknowledge, and with the coaching staff's tongues already purchased, the chance of this talented girl reaching her full potential looked bleak. From my angle, Julia was so cushioned in a comfortable existence that it wasn't possible for her to experience enough pain to evoke true transformation. She'd been privileged to a life her results didn't necessarily warrant her to, which gave Julia a taste of making it without having to soul-search and put in more of the right type of work. She'd been around the traps for a while and was clearly disenchanted by how much more she'd have to give to upgrade her lifestyle. However, she didn't seem genuinely interested in making the sacrifices needed because the spoils and C-grade status were already at her disposal.

By all means, overindulge in all the hedonistic pleasures you want, I thought, considering the slavery she'd endured throughout her childhood years. That was her prerogative, but it made our jobs irrelevant, as it's not viable to get someone to improve when they are secretly hiding the fact they are completely content with where they are at. Instead of owning this train of thought, Julia became more preoccupied with setting up the next injury while giving off the appearance she was doing everything possible to try and improve.

So why were we there? And why was she still paying us when she knew she wasn't utilising our expertise? I couldn't understand. At the start, I thought she was just wrapped up in her own godliness and secretly wanted help but was too proud to take it from people she felt knew less than her. But as time went on, I began to see that we were like the gym membership of a yo-yo dieter. In that, if she cancelled us, it would be an admission of giving up. So, much like the overweight gym goer will keep a gym membership for years without ever earnestly attending, we were similarly destined to be coaches for show only. She kept paying us for appearance's sake, so she wouldn't have to concede to her innermost self that she wasn't really serious at all.

Julia didn't want to go down the infamous route a lot of burned-out tennis players had taken by denouncing the sport, while flaunting luxuries in the public's face. She wanted to do her own version of the same thing, by extracting as much sympathy from the public as possible, while never truly contemplating swimming where the water was deeper. Like the time she supposedly pulled up ginger from a WTA tournament in Florida and needed a week to heal her body and train for the upcoming events.

We were 95km away from some of the best academies in the world that had everything we needed; but instead of going there, she decided we would go do a 'training week' in the partying capital of Las Vegas, staying at a famous actor's multimillion-dollar holiday house. Julia held all the cards, and it seemed like she was doing us a favour by letting us come aboard for the luxurious five-star Contiki tour. We didn't hold the authority to do the jobs we were paid to do, and it felt like we were fated to pretend just so we could feel successful by association, and travel around the world without our other halves.

All I had to do was maintain my lackey status and continually repeat 'yes sir, no sir, three bags full sir', and I could've kept racking up those frequent flyer points and binge-eating my way through those delicious buffet breakfasts. But I audaciously asked for the unthinkable, and requested my own room instead of shacking up with a fitness trainer as if we were teenagers on school camp. The request was seen as an outrageous slap in the face, considering Julia was already forking out for us to all go on a round-the-world holiday. It was evidence she didn't consider coaching to be a real job requiring someone to have their own room. In her eyes, albeit secretly, it was a Contiki tour, and I should've just been grateful for the paid holiday. To me, that summarised Julia's attitude towards the profession in a nutshell.

## Hovering at the edge of the pit of despair

No one wants a contest when it comes to comparing problems, and people are reluctant to divulge the troubles happening between their ears, so society seems happy to chalk it all up as 'mental health'. It's a very vague yet complex subject, so I am going to do my best to articulate my experience with an extremely confusing condition of the mind, body, and soul.

My father's bloodline was riddled for centuries with a susceptibility to chronic alcoholism, which they all flippantly alluded to as 'the gift'. After I stopped playing tennis, it didn't take long for me to end up on the bones of my ass with this inherited present. The level of my sickness was unrecognisable to doctors and psychologists at first, as the tennis experience had turned me into a trained performer who didn't drop the charade once the racket was out of my hand. Finally, these quacks had a long enough look at me to realise I had just about every mental health condition under the sun. It was unanimously declared that I was indeed one sick cookie, however my drinking went relatively undetected, despite these professionals hearing about my frequent binges. My alcoholism took a massive sigh of relief when these specialists stated they wanted to focus more on my mental health, because lord knows, I couldn't seem to put the plug in the jug. As these professionals spewed out their evaluations, they didn't align with my own perception of myself in the slightest, and it made me feel terribly insecure about how little insight I truly had into my own misery.

I clung to materialistic and superficial reasons to confirm that I indeed wasn't what they were saying I was. I thought my sporting reputation, pointy shoes, and the fact I had a car proved I wasn't mentally ill; however, these luxuries had nothing to do with the matter at hand, and they stopped me from properly looking inwards at my obvious psychological instabilities. Besides, there were way more people around the world who were worse off than me. In my mind, the life I had lived had been relatively normal and even quite boring.

Looking back, it's hard to tell whether I purposely brainwashed myself into thinking I had a great family and upbringing, or whether I was so warped from living in a world full of psychotics and neurotics that I couldn't even compute what the term 'normal' was. When you coupled that level of unconsciousness with the fact I had a genetic predisposition to addiction, a bizarre twist of delusion and absurdity was all I had come to know. At times, I felt I had lived such an uneventful life that I was compelled to stretch the truth when talking to psychologists, so it seemed as if the punishment I inflicted upon myself fitted the crime. Whiskey and wine took my distortion to new heights, and quite frankly, I didn't know what to believe anymore.

Near death experiences and frequent bouts of drug- and alcohol-induced psychosis persuaded me to try to steady the ship. I set the bar as low as I possibly could: shower, brush my teeth, get out of bed, piss in the toilet and not in a stubby can. But finding a way to complete this bucket list was an impossible task. Watching the rest of the world flourish while I was comatose on the couch in complete darkness with agoraphobia became a weekly occurrence. Just hearing someone say my name was enough to frighten the living daylights out of me, so my phone was permanently on flight mode, I never answered the door, and I wouldn't even think of opening the mail. As I became more acquainted with the dark and heavy cloak alcoholism ensconced upon my shoulders, I embodied a Tom Waits and Johnny Cash persona to work with my dysfunction, instead of going against it.

Trying to make my misery look mysterious and cool was one of the scariest mistakes I made. It was as if the exaggerated part of myself put its cowboy hat on and kicked the real me out of a moving car to get behind the wheel. I had absolutely no connection to myself whatsoever and got completely lost in my own show. My method of dealing with the sheer lunacy was to laugh it off, as everything felt like a tragic joke. In the midst of all this mess and madness, you would think I'd put a pin in seeing the expensive psychologists and wholistic healers. But my incessant need for a minute's attention was fulfilled by seeing their reactions to the sideshow of my life.

Despite being in therapy, I was getting worse, a lot worse. Because I couldn't stop boozing and the psychologists couldn't tell I was a raging alcoholic, we were always forced to focus on putting out the fires my drinking created, instead of getting to the root of the issue. This thing I was dealing with was clearly multifaceted, as I had a mind that couldn't handle reality and a body which couldn't tolerate alcohol. I was beginning to see that these two separate issues were directly related but needed to be treated in the correct order. If my thinking problem was put ahead of my drinking problem, I wasn't ever going to get out of this excruciating maelstrom. Trying to tackle the trauma ahead of my drinking was like going to a physiotherapist when you've got a broken leg. Even though I believe that my alcoholism was a symptom of heredity and childhood trauma, the roller-coaster ride of living life as a practising drunk was almost as traumatic as the initial trauma itself, if not more so.

Pain tends to be my greatest motivator, and over the next few years I thankfully fried myself enough to become humble and dare I say teachable. While I was still desperate to continue drinking, I was equally desperate for the problems of my drinking to stop. I was prescribed Naltrexone, which is medication to help you stop using alcohol, and I thought that would be enough to do the trick. While not having to nurse a terminal hangover for the first few days was mightily refreshing, what came next was a cruel form of torture.

The pink cloud completely disappeared and living sober felt like the harshest drug of all. In the wake of my drinking, I went back to feeling like a scared and helpless kid again, mortally petrified of being in his own skin. All my childhood neurosis came back in the blink of an eye, and I didn't have anything to numb it while my mind was obsessing over alcohol more than ever, since I wasn't able to get it. I couldn't be part of the old world I used to live in, and I definitely wasn't part of the real world, so it felt like I was further away than ever, which was enough to have me at the jumping-off point. Going through the adversity I'd faced as a juvenile was difficult enough, let alone having the past flicker back in snapshot form every time I stopped at a red light.

My life was hanging in the balance, and though the professionals seemed to think I should be okay because I was off the sauce, in fact, I was crazier than ever. I mentioned AA, but it was disregarded and seen as a waste of time, so I was left to my own devices to wean myself off this chemical dependence. The opposite of addiction is connection, and since I didn't want to tell anyone about what I was doing because of the stigma surrounding alcoholism, I felt completely alienated and disconnected from the whole of humanity. I was starting to understand why I drank like I did.

I had a 24-hour, 7-day-a-week problem and the professionals were advocating for one appointment a month for 50 minutes, and a tablet of Naltrexone for insurance to stop my compulsive drinking. It was clearly an inadequate program for the king of crisis, so I went back to self-medicating and living with the consequences that came with my drinking for a few more years, and the penalties became even more severe.

The drinking culture in Australia is so rife that people are more accepting of binge drinkers who consume alcohol to their detriment, than people trying to better their lives in abstinence-based programs. While the self-help section seems to be the most popular genre at the bookstore. Even my doctors couldn't imagine a life in which a person would have to go without wine. Thankfully, when I was just the right amount of cooked and confused, I plummeted into a community centre full of ex-drunkards.

# Conclusion

When your arse hits the seat of a twelve-step program, there's a phrase that floats around to help the newcomers deal with the fact that they've wound up in society's sinbin. 'You're going to live a life beyond your wildest dreams,' is whispered around the room. And they were not kidding! Most people in meetings talk about what they've lost because of their boozing. House, health, family, and their trousers are some of the more common things that vanish because of someone's unshakable bond to a bottle of poison. And while I'd squandered some opportunities and forfeited a few others, for me, it seems to be more about what I had created from my drinking, rather than what had disappeared.

Early sobriety has been like waking up out of a lifelong coma. Getting the grand tour of my own existence feels nostalgically eerie, and nothing has been more unsettling than the dysfunctional dynamics between my disjointed family. In a twisted turn of events that even Satan himself couldn't have organised, I've wound up back at the start, living in the old family home some decades later with the very man who orchestrated my hellacious fate. Except now, the shoe is on the other foot, as Dad's brain eats itself by the second while he refuses to accept the fact he's suffering from a terminal illness. His dementia poses me with the ultimate test of character: how do you treat someone who has mistreated you in the past?

Not even baring my and tearing shreds off my own parents' behaviour have been able to destroy a deep-seated belief of mine, that things could have turned out differently if I'd voiced my frustration and unhappiness when I was a child. Clinging to this notion has made me accountable for my own suffering, while giving my parents the benefit of the doubt. Yes, I was mismanaged, abused, spoilt, neglected, worshipped, entitled, deprived, pampered—all the above—but I didn't have to suffer in silence. I could've asked for help, and maybe that would have stopped the chain of events that eventually unfolded. However, the way in which my family has handled my father's health has made me realise I had no other option but to be run over in a way that made me feel like a piece of highway roadkill.

Winding up in such a cruel predicament has made me question who's pulling the strings in this life? Sometimes I feel like I'm just entertainment for the spiritual world upstairs who watch me while eating their Starbursts and popcorn. Or maybe my situation is just a demonstration of what happens to a person when they don't take matters into their own hands. Did I have a choice in any of this, or has my destiny been predetermined by something greater than I can conceptualise? Categorically, people tend to philosophise about all sorts of things when they hit bottom, to make their stay in hell just a tad more comfortable. And maybe I am too, because I'm starting to think it's not by sheer coincidence that I've spiralled back here with Dad, who now talks in unfinished thoughts and dries the dishes by waving them around in the air.

Having lived my life in one long-winded blur with brief patches of consciousness, getting a gauge on my reality has been troublesome at times. That's why writing this book and going on its fact-finding crusade was of the upmost importance to me. It meant I could get myself up to speed with what I've been doing this whole time. Hindsight is a hell of a drug, and despite theorising the living shit out of my existence, I still somehow felt as if my story didn't belong to me. I wanted a cathartic purging of poison and pain but found myself feeling more like a journalist reporting on someone else's life.

But that all changed when Dad, living in a cesspool of squalor and inching towards homelessness, was served an eviction notice. The difficult man with his difficult disease fell right into my lap, and most of my family evaporated into thin air. Their actions spoke loud and clear, 'Not my circus, not my monkeys'. Everyone who was in close quarters with my father back in the day got burned, and I was unquestionably the closest person to the fire. Yet because of Dad's lifelong obsession with tennis, I was being seen as an accessory, held responsible for something that I felt innocent of creating. I couldn't control what happened after I came out of the womb. I wanted a father but was allocated a coach. Juggling the aches and pangs of early sobriety while dealing with Dad's dementia, meant it was just a matter of time before one of us ended up being certified.

But before qualifying for the sanatorium, we homebrewed our own madness by both residing under the same roof. Max moved in with his two milk crates worth of trash and treasure, while I kept most of my wardrobe in the boot of my car, so I could hit the road when the time called for it. Once again, the first and last thing I see every day is my father's face. Just hearing his undone shoelaces drag along the hallway floorboards is enough to make me want to seek refuge under my bed. I had experienced this same scenario twenty years earlier, absorbing the torture like a prisoner of war who'd taken a vow of silence for a government that betrayed him anyway.

This time, I decided to do what I should have done years before, and I voiced my grievances to my family. Taking off my imaginary superhero cape wasn't an easy strip, as I'd prided myself on being a rescuer of the less fortunate for my entire life. However, I couldn't save my face and my ass at the same time, and I needed to be present for my newborn son who'd just been diagnosed with bleeding on the brain. I could see Dad was a complicated and complex issue, after all, he'd affected everyone differently during his sporting death march.

But my trauma was once again active, Dad was now hitching rides with me to the courts to watch me coach young juniors, still passing on his wisdom to the other sporting extremists that looked up to him and were now like his new apprentices.

The toxic cycle was fast evolving and spreading like wildfire. So, I once again reluctantly turned to the people I thought you were supposed to turn to in a time of crisis. But this time I called the cavalry with a mayday warning, to make my family fully aware of the crisis I was experiencing with my father. This time, there was no mistaking the fact I was in dire straits. The way in which everyone dealt with my pleas for help shattered any false hope I'd clung onto, in thinking my life could have turned out differently if I'd waved the white flag earlier. I was now convinced this was fate. For whatever reason, it was my destiny to be slaughtered by the sport of tennis, while everyone turned their heads in silence to avoid any sense of culpability. In the end, living under the same roof as my father felt fitting in a warped kind of way, and my life seemed to make sense when I looked at it in reverse.

They say a man only comes alive when his father dies, and even though Dad's still wandering around the city streets and rocking up at the courts quite frequently, his rapid decline is waking me up to a reality that was in front of my face the whole time. The situation has ignited a fire within me to treat the rest of my life like the encore of my existence. At the end of the day, it doesn't matter that I was put on the toilet seat backwards, because it's now my job to turn my ass around. This rude awakening has worked out to be one of my biggest blessings. For that reason, I wouldn't change any of it at all. But now, there's everything left to be changed, starting with where I lay my head.

# Epilogue

WHILE THERE HAVE been a wide range of opinions, beliefs and wild anecdotes expressed throughout this book, the stories surrounding my family are real and the ramifications from the tennis experience continue. But if there's any upside to being broken and smashed into thousands of pieces it's that I have a chance of being reassembled into something new, and I look to take full advantage of this bizarre opportunity by never returning to the me of old. Refashioning myself into something else has required me to find humour within this this thirty-year and running tragedy, while winging a makeshift existence from the rubble that remains. For the moment, I'm still a monkey in the sporting circus, except now I try to use my position in the show to caution others to enter at their own risk. And as for my father Max, he now resides in a dementia ward where he holds regular art exhibitions for the hospital staff and continues to give me coaching advice when I have the stomach to visit him.

Max's final masterpiece

*Thanks for reading*

Keep up to date with all things Unsportsmanlike Publishing at toddley.com.au